B&T 12/20/91 44.95

Accident Prevention for Hotels, Motels, and Restaurants

Robert L. Kohr C.S.P., C.P.P.

Kohr & Associates

VNR VAN NOSTRAND REINHOLD
New York

To my Wife Shelley and our Children for all
Their Support and Love

This book does not purport to cover every hazard, nor to offer every possible solution for the ones that are discussed. However, every effort has been made to cover the most significant issues facing this industry. Many of the ideas came from the experience gained by those organizations that employed the author, but every design exercise requires professional judgment to be applied to the circumstances and activities that may be unique or peculiar to a particular setting. Every designer and facility owner should obtain the professional Loss Control services needed to meet their legal, moral, and ethical responsibilities to their invitees, licensees, and clients according to what has become known to the courts as "reasonable care."

Copyright © 1991 by Van Nostrand Reinhold

Library of Congress Catalog Card Number 90-49783
ISBN 0-442-23955-6

Printed in the United States of America

Van Nostrand Reinhold
115 Fifth Avenue
New York, New York 10003

Chapman and Hall
2–6 Boundary Row
London SE1 8HN, England

Thomas Nelson Australia
102 Dodds Street
South Melbourne 3205
Victoria, Australia

Nelson Canada
1120 Birchmount Road
Scarborough, Ontario MIK 5G4, Canada

16 15 14 13 12 11 10 9 8 7 6 5 4 3 2 1

Library of Congress Cataloging-in-Publication Data
Kohr, Robert L.
    Accident prevention for hotels, motels, and restaurants / by
Robert L. Kohr.
        p.   cm.
    ISBN 0-442-23955-6
    1. Hospitality industry—Accidents—Prevention.   I. Title.
TX911.3.S24K64   1991
647.94'0684—dc20   90-49783
                                                                                    CIP

Contents

Preface

After many years of working in the field of safety and security, primarily in the lodging and restaurant industry, it became apparent to me that there wasn't a book which addressed the needs of this type of business. It seemed that whenever there was an attempt to research a method, product or program, it was always set up for some other industry, usually manufacturing.

My hope is to save readers the many hours of reinventing the wheel so that they can concentrate on keeping their guests and employees happy and safe. However, there is never an easy answer or a simple shortcut alternative to hard work and dedication toward a goal.

There is much to be learned and applied by simply asking the person on the frontline, "What are your problems? How can we do this better?" This book is divided into two major parts. The first is titled "Responding to Accident Prevention." Within this part are the "how to's" for the owner, operator and Loss Control Practitioner. Some of the concepts put forth in Part I have traditionally been seen as the responsibility of a loss control staff person. According to the American Hotel and Motel Association, 72 percent of the lodging industry have 150 rooms or fewer at their facilities. I have tried to make this book a "how to" book, so even these traditional loss control staff responsibilities can be translated into an owner/operator's and/or a line manager's responsibilities.

For a small property you don't need a full time loss control expert to make safety and quality work for you. However, don't lose sight of the fact that a little shot in the arm once in a while from an outside consultant can help your effort, give a tremendous boost to the program, and save you some dollars. This book is also intended to provide the designer with some basic information on the human side of the Loss Control Triad.

The Loss Control Triad is comprised of three distinct legs, which form a triangle. The legs are people, equipment, and environment. All three legs together support the effort needed to meet the company's financial objectives. Without even one of the legs the triangle will collapse and the company will struggle. Loss Control is a tool of risk management to reduce the chances that one or all of the legs will collapse.

As the first part of the book deals with people and equipment, the second part deals with the environment. It is titled "Designing for Safety and Security." As the title implies, this part is intended to make the design world aware of opportunities in providing a safer environment for people who work in or visit a space. It is also set up to provide practical information to owners and operators on how to improve their existing environments.

The concepts and ideas expressed in both parts of the book are a compilation of the proven efforts of many safety, security, and design professionals and operators within and outside Marriott whom I have met and worked with and to whom I would like to express my sincere gratitude.

In addition, my sincere appreciation goes to the people in the trenches who have implemented the ideas contained in this book and made them a success story.

Part I

Responding to Accident Prevention

CHAPTER 1

Setting the Tone

The challenge of every manager is to maximize profits. There are many things managers can do; however, safety and security receive very little attention from most managers in the service sector. Why is this the case, especially today, when everyone complains about the liability crisis? On one side are the plaintiff's attorneys, on the other the insurance companies. Many feel that the latter are out to make up their losses at the operators' expense. But if we stop and look inward, is not some of the problem in ourselves? Do we not expect to be compensated for everything that goes wrong?

Recently, a fast-food chain was experiencing a downturn in profits and began cuts in their workforce. At about the same time, in one particular state, there was a lot of publicity given to the fact that a precedent had been set in workers' compensation benefits in that the law now covered stress. What would you do if you were a manager, overworked, underpaid, working double shifts, and your company was talking about layoffs? File a compensatable stress claim and then go onto unemployment benefit when you are laid off.

A TV advertisement shows a sports star pitching for a law firm—"If you've been injured on the job or injured due to someone else's negligence, don't take the law into your own hands. Call _____ They're on your team. Call 800—free help."

As an owner, operator, or manager you can no longer afford to sit back and say "This won't happen to me." Everyone knows that as soon as you think that, in this business, anything can and will happen.

This chapter is titled "Setting the Tone" for a reason. In today's world, management cannot afford not to be committed to accident prevention. Maximizing sales at the front of the house does little good if the profit edge is lost through mismanagement of overhead in the back of the house. A large part of that overhead is preventable loss. Preventable loss is managed through Risk Management and a good part of Risk Management is Accident Prevention and Loss Control.

WHAT IS THE "HOT BUTTON"?

For any program to be successful, it must have commitment. Until it has everyone's commitment, there will be hesitancy and ineffectiveness. There is one simple truth: The moment one person is committed, providence can move too. Involvement follows commitment. What is the magic button to push? Let me answer a question with a question: How are managers rated on performance? What is the criterion? Is not the performance based primarily on profits? This has been a failing point for many safety professionals. Modern risk managers must equate their concepts to the economics of business and speak in the language of business.

According to Veron Gross, an authority on the systematic approach to risk, there are basically two unfortunate assumptions:

1. Executives often assume that losses due to unmanaged risk can be prevented by an insurance policy.
2. Traditional risk managers assume that losses due to unmanaged risk can be prevented by an objective monitor, i.e. insurance inspector or internal safety/security group. (Gross, 1987, p. 88)

It is obvious in the first assumption that losses due to low morale, degradation of the public's image of your company, and adverse publicity are not covered. Regarding the second, the use of traditional audit and inspection programs is helpful to a degree, but they do not prevent a loss from occurring.

Gross continues this discussion and pinpoints the essence of a sound loss control effort in the following statement:

> Losses due to uncontrollable risk can be prevented—but only by those who control the scene in which these losses occur!

Modern safety and security practitioners must develop their risk strategy around three business concepts, like the three legs of a stool: cost, performance, and schedule (Gross, 1987). No matter which management philosophy is in vogue, the bottom line will always be the driving force. Fortunately, there is a new concept afoot, that in order to improve one's competitive edge, one must turn from short-term squeezing of pennies, to the long-term commitment to *quality*. Quality and safety go hand in hand—they are a natural marriage.

A Food and Beverage Director was only at his hotel for one year but made vast improvements in service and customer counts. What happened?

> We came off the year before I arrived $400,000 below budget, morale was low, accidents seemed to happen every day. Our attention was focused on the short-term profit margin and not taking care of our customers or employees. We set up a quality assurance committee and I am the chairperson. Everyone was skeptical at first, but we tried, we listened and we acted on the employee feedback. There were small successes at first but the results are just beginning to come around. Our counts are up, morale is better, and we haven't had an accident in months.

What was the single most important factor?

> Execution, follow-through is critical, listening and acting on what is suggested. Rewarding those who participate is very important to any program's success. It's nothing new, educate the employee and new managers, set the objective and hold them accountable. If we can get quality into the total organization, with the results so far, think of the competitive edge we would have.

I am a firm believer that we should conserve our human resources or there will not be anyone around to flip the burgers and make the beds. The smart manager of the future who has vision will be like the Food and Beverage Director and take the long-term approach and include accident prevention and quality as a part of his operation to conserve their human resources, satisfy their customers and protect the bottom line.

If a manager's performance is equated with the bottom line, then if we charge back to that bottom line all or a percentage of the losses that came from that department or property, what impact will that have on that manager? Imagine losing five percent of your bonus because of workers' compensation and liability losses! It works! That person's attention is now marrying accident prevention with day-to-day operations.

You may say to yourself, "No way will they go for this. Where's the positive incentive? It's too complicated. We're not self-insured . . . ." The question is are *you* committed? Whether your company is self-insured or not makes no difference. The positive incentive can be added very easily; it is like Retrospective Rating, which simply means, from an insurance viewpoint, that the insurance premiums are based on a minimum and a maximum dollar amount that is tied to the loss rate. If the experience is good, then the minimum is charged, the expense is under budget, and thus your bonus is higher. The accounting process is simple because most companies are computerized and simple spreadsheets can track charges and progress.

Another button that can be pushed is the assignment of a percentage of the manager's raise toward performance in achieving accident prevention objectives (see Chapter 8, "Measuring Results"). It is a simple fact that money talks. Every great endeavour or successful program begins with commitment, and accident prevention is no different. Find and push that "hot button"!

SHOWING COMMITMENT—THE POLICY STATEMENT

Every effective program needs a statement of policy. Once there is commitment, the formal policy statement lets everyone know that top management backs the program. It also provides the program direction and sets the goals. No matter how big or how small an operation, a policy statement is needed. An accident prevention policy statement is rather simple to draft. There is no need to reinvent the wheel, there are plenty of examples available.

The policy statement can be a sentence or a page. The hard part will be getting consensus on the program's objectives. There is one sure way to accomplish this task, i.e. put together a task force of the people who are going to have to live with the rules. There is no better way to gain commitment from people than by their having a piece of themselves on the platter. If management drop the policy on the employees and do not involve them in any of the decisions, then they will not sense ownership of the programs. Their commitment will be minimal and some will even resist.

What is in an accident prevention policy? Every accident prevention policy statement should include:

1. Management's intent to provide a safe place for guests and employees.
2. Scope of the program's activities.

3. Everyone's responsibilities.
4. Accountability.
5. Authority levels.
6. Standards to be met.
7. Safety professional's role (if applicable).

Accident prevention is a line management function. It must be integrated into the operation as a normal everyday activity or it is doomed to failure.

Once the motivational button has been identified and management expectations have been added in the form of a policy, a celebration should take place. Everyone's involvement and participation should be rewarded. Have the staff make a pledge and publicize the event.

Like any other product in the marketplace, accident prevention must be marketed to the entire organization. Pull the team together and develop a marketing plan. Plan a big celebration to announce the new Accident Prevention Program. Next comes the hard part—keeping the interest alive, that is, execution.

APPROPRIATE SIZE OF THE PROGRAM

The program should be only as big as needed! The very first thing to be undertaken is an analysis of the business for loss exposures. Another term for this process is completing a risk assessment. This sounds bigger than it really is. First, let us define some terms. A *loss exposure* is any potential event that could result in property, human, and/or financial degradation for the business. A *risk* is the probability that the event will occur. Thus, a *risk assessment* is the identification of all possible loss exposures and determination of the likelihood of how often they may occur.

For the small business, management should be able to carry out a risk assessment of their own. However, I recommend hiring an outside consultant in order to obtain a fresh look and assist management in the process. The cost is not exorbitant. The average charge per hour for a safety consultant is $84 according to figures from the American Society for Safety Engineers, Consultants Division, in the Winter 1989 *Division News*. Whether or not a consultant is used will not affect what must be accomplished. The steps to completing a risk assessment of your business are as follows.

1. Speak to the insurance provider and obtain a claims run for the preceding three years. The carrier also has a Loss Control Department which can help in the evaluation of accident types and trends.
2. List demographic features such as type of workforce, trainability, turnover, cultural differences, motivations, and customer type.
3. Evaluate internal and external environmental factors that may contribute to a loss.
4. Lastly, ask the employees.

Remember that the objective is to identify all possible risks, establish their severity and the probability that each event will occur, and rank them into a workable action plan. After the analysis is completed, it should be quite apparent where effort needs to be concentrated. Additionally, a business is required to comply with certain state and federal regulations. These include OSHA 1910 General Industry Standards and state workers' compensation laws. The insurance carrier, local OSHA office, American Hotel and Motel Association, National Restaurant Association, and the safety consultant can assist in ensuring compliance with the law.

Now the program can be outlined. The policy has been drafted; the employees are committed to assist in developing the accident prevention program. The next step is building the framework.

The essential framework of an accident prevention program includes:

- Policy Statement and Safety Rules.
- Structure for Accident Prevention—Quality Safety Committees.
- Risk Identification and Control.
- Training and Motivation.
- Managing by Walking Around (MBWA).
- Medical Intervention.
- Claims Management.

Table 1-1 is a guide to what elements should be included in the accident prevention framework for various sizes of businesses. Details of each element of the accident prevention framework are covered in subsequent chapters.

TABLE 1-1. Appropriate size of the program.

| | | | | | | Type of facility | | | |
Programs and activities	Fast food restaurants	Other restaurants	Budget hotel	Extended stay hotel	All-suite hotel	Full-service hotel (downtown)	Full-service hotel (suburban)	Convention hotel	Resort hotel
Policy and rules	C	C	C	C	C	C	C	C	C
Hot button	U/C	U/C	U/C	U/C	U/C	U/C	U/C	U/C	U/C
Behavioral analysis	C	C	C	C	C	C	C	C	C
Ergonomics	C	C	C	C	C	C	C	U	C
Task safety analysis	U	U	U	U	U	U	U	U	U
Quality Safety Board	U	U			U	U	U	U	U
Quality Safety Committee	U	U	U	U	U	U	U	U	U
MBWA	U	U	U	U	U	U	U	U	U
Formal inspections	U/C	U/C	U/C	U/C	U/C	U/C	U/C	U/C	U/C
Accident prevention tour	U	U	U	U	U	U	U	U	U
Slip, trip and fall	U	U	U	U	U	U	U	U	U
Central first aid	U	U	U	U	U	U	U	U	U
Medical unit						C[a]	C[a]	C	C
"We Care" and modified duty	U/C	U/C	U/C	U/C	U/C	U/C	U/C	U/C	U/C
New loss control concept	C	C	C	C	C	U	U	U	U
Designing for safety and security	C	C	C	C	C	C	C	C	C

U = unit or property level sponsored and controlled.
C = corporate sponsored and/or outside resources utilized.
[a] 600 or more rooms.

But we still have not answered the question of how big the program should be. To answer this question let us start at the top. If the total annual cost of all casualty loss exceeds $1.5 million, a full-time safety professional should be on your staff (Culbertson, 1981, p. 17):

> The total cost of casualty losses is simply the workers' compensation and general liability insurance premium if first dollar coverage is purchased. If partially or fully self-insured, all costs must be collected. The costs to be accounted for are:
>
> 1. Total incurred losses, i.e. paid plus reserves for future payments to be made;
> 2. Increased costs from prior years' accidents which are still open;
> 3. Claims adjustment expense, including legal costs;
> 4. The excess insurance premium;
> 5. Administrative expense, which includes the loss prevention expense of your insurance carrier or outside service companies.

Mr. Culbertson's tenets still hold true. A full-time competent safety manager will cost around $50,000 a year. The median income as determined by a survey conducted by the American Society of Safety Engineers and published in June 1985 was $37,500. Considering inflation, that 1985 median figure is probably closer to the $50,000 salary figure.

Obviously the advantages of employing a full-time professional include:

- Completing risk assessments and evaluations.
- Matching the program to the operation.
- Developing and conducting training programs.
- Monitoring the program's effectiveness and providing direction.
- Reviewing loss reports and evaluating corrective action.
- Intervening in the claims management process.
- Engaging in the planning, design and development of new systems or products to ensure consideration of all potential hazards.
- Incorporating safety and health into all purchasing and contracting.
- Measuring loss reduction and determining cost benefit.

Simply put, the job of a safety or loss control practitioner is to manage the risk.

The list can go on and on. So the question arises: "What kind of return on investment can I expect if I hire a full-time safety manager?" This is easy to compute; just add the salary, benefits, support staff, travel and other controllables to get the total annual budget. If the individual is any good, he or she should be able to reduce losses in the first year by at least 10 percent without blinking an eye. Considering the $1.5 million bench mark: hiring a safety manager should net at least 30–60 percent return on investment, which is not bad for the first year.

"Fine, but I'm a small to medium sized owner/operator with a couple of small 100-room motels, one 450-room hotel and a couple of free-standing restaurants. I can't afford a full-time safety manager, what do I do?" More than likely at the hotel there is a security staff and a manager or supervisor. Why not approach the manager/supervisor and ask whether they would be interested in upgrading their function and increasing their status. I am prepared to bet that the answer will be "Yes". I call this the New Loss Prevention Concept, which in essence consists of the marriage between safety and security management. This concept will be discussed in depth in Chapter 4. Suffice it to say that the person in this newly created position, with a little training and support, can provide the organization with many of the same services as a full-time safety practitioner but also maintain his or her current management role at the hotel. Another option would be to use the services of an outside consultant on a full-time or part-time retainer or supplement the hotel's Loss Prevention Manager. The one thing I would recommend against is to assign the function to an already burdened Operations or Human Resources Manager, because at the first sign of trouble or job pressure, safety will take a back seat and the situation will be back to the beginning. However, it should not be forgotten that losses are prevented and controlled at the front line.

Small owner/operators with one or a few facilities and no access to the Loss Prevention Concept should go back to basics. They should follow the basic framework for setting up the accident program, get their employees involved, and manage by walking around (MBWA) (Table 1-1). As stated earlier, use all your resources and get some help from a professional safety consultant; it represents a few dollars well spent.

HOW TO MANAGE THE ACCIDENT PREVENTION MANAGER

This subject was touched on briefly in discussing the advantages of and need for an Accident Prevention Manager on staff. But what are the manager's job duties? What should be looked for in qualifications? Who can one contact as a resource? How is the person managed after they are on board? Let us look at each question as a separate issue.

Job Duties

There are four fundamental job duties:

1. Identifying and evaluating loss-producing conditions and practices and analyzing their frequency and severity.
2. Developing accident prevention procedures and programs.
3. Communicating effectively accident prevention information to all levels of management.
4. Measuring and evaluating the effectiveness of the accident prevention system and modifying it to achieve maximum results.

Under each of these duties is a list of activities to accomplish each function. A good resource for specifics is the National Safety Council.

There are myriad names that can be given to the position, such as Director of Safety or Accident Prevention, but what is more important is that it be a management level position and that it receives the recognition, support, and commitment of top management.

Qualifications

Experience is a must. Generally the individual should have 4 to 5 years' experience in safety management and at least 2 years' in the hospitality and restaurant industry. Additionally, they should possess a minimum of a bachelor's degree in safety, science, engineering, or business management. They should have their CSP (Certified Safety Professional) designation. This designation is important, because it is a recognition of professional excellence through examination by the American Society of Safety Engineers (ASSE).

Resources

- Outside safety consultant.
- Local or national chapter of ASSE.
- American Hotel and Motel Association.
- National Restaurant Association.
- National Safety Council.

Managing the Manager

Accident prevention affects the bottom line. One of the primary duties of the Safety Manager is to measure the program's effectiveness. As a result, this person should be managed in the same way as any other profit center in the organization. But remember, this is a specialist who must exert influence over every aspect of the business even though there is no direct line authority.

The Safety Manager must be able to communicate effectively on all levels. It is important to be certain that he or she is providing the line managers with the service that they need, not what he or she thinks they need.

> Assure that your safety manager understands the contradictory pressures of your position. Do not let him become a safety purist with no concern for budget limitations, space, timetables, marketing, conflicts, etc. (Culbertson, 1981, p. 34)

Direct the safety effort by setting measurable objectives, by planning, organizing, and executing to achieve them: build a three-legged stool.

Where should the Safety Manager fit in the organization? No-one ever agrees exactly on where to position this function. Dan Peterson, a leading safety consultant, does offer some guidance:

> We can however, offer some criteria in assessing the right place for safety in your organization.
>
> 1. Report to a boss with influence.
> 2. Report to a boss who wants safety.
> 3. Have a channel to the top.
> 4. Perhaps, install safety under the executive in charge of the major activity. (Peterson, 1971, p. 35)

To that list, I would add one more, high visibility. In my opinion, the accident prevention function should be located in the upper echelon of the organization. Here the manager can feel the pulse of the organization and exert influence over every aspect of the business. Remember that the primary function is to control risk. However, the Safety Manager should retain a staff role, and in the process manage, assist, council, and facilitate line management in achieving accident prevention goals and reducing risk.

WHEN TO START

If you subscribe to the eight attributes of successful businesses as outlined in Tom Peters and Bob Waterman's (1982) book *In Search of Excellence*, the answer is to have "a bias for action, for getting on with it." Now is the time to get rolling. For each day's delay, more money is lost from the bottom line and the farther you are away from improving productivity and maintaining a competitive edge.

CHAPTER 2

Structure for Accident Prevention

In the January–February 1988 *Harvard Business Review*, Peter Drucker authored an article entitled "The Coming of the New Organization." The article focused on how businesses are changing to become knowledge-based, composed primarily of specialists who react immediately to the feedback of customers, colleagues, and headquarters. He stated:

> The traditional sequence of research, development, manufacturing, and marketing is being replaced by synchrony: specialists from all these functions work together as a team, from the inception of research to a product's establishment in the market.

To paraphrase Mr. Drucker, task forces of specialists will be established to tackle all forms of business challenges.

Chapter 1 discussed the need to establish a task force of line managers, hourly employees, and other appropriate personnel in order to achieve three objectives for accident prevention: (1) getting commitment, (2) drafting a policy, and (3) implementing a program. Now we need to look at how to organize the accident prevention program effectively. We will accomplish this by reviewing (1) the best organizational structures, (2) individual responsibilities, and (3) the role of committees. First we need to define some fundamentals and basic terms of accident prevention.

FUNDAMENTALS OF ACCIDENT PREVENTION

There are several basic tenets inherent in all aspects of accident prevention management:

1. All accidents are preventable.

15

2. Injuries are a result of many causal factors, including the management system, unsafe behavior, and unsafe conditions.
3. Accident prevention should be managed as though it were a profit center.
4. Circumstances that produce injuries can be predicted and controlled.
5. Line management is the key ingredient for effectiveness.
6. Accountability must be assigned on every level.
7. Accident prevention must be integrated into the operation, not added on.
8. Quality and accident prevention are synonymous.

BASIC ACCIDENT PREVENTION TERMS

Accident can be defined as any unintended occurrence that disrupts the normal sequence of events.

Incident can be defined as an accident in which no injury has occurred—a "near miss."

Unsafe act is defined as a departure from normal practice or procedure; 80 percent of all accidents are a result of unsafe acts.

Unsafe condition is any physical condition that if left unattended is likely to cause an incident or an accident; 20 percent of all accidents are the result of an unsafe condition.

Hazard is any condition that has the potential to cause injury and/or loss of property.

BASIC ACCIDENT PREVENTION FRAMEWORK

Accident prevention is a state of mind. It must be put on a personalized basis. The line manager is the key but his or her boss is the one who turns the key. When management takes hold of the key, the doors will open and the results will be outstanding. But if management does not assume full responsibility for accident prevention, then it has given up some of its resources for effective management (DeReamer, 1958).

Today's new management direction toward quality assurance in order to improve one's competitive edge starts by working from the bottom up. Involving employees in all phases of service and product improvement is exactly what accident prevention programs have been based on for years.

Consider this classic example of how quality, safety, and production are interwoven, related recently by a hotel general manager: over the years many sheets had been discarded because of rips and tears. Each year the loss was assumed to be a normal cost of doing business because the department's operating statement percentages were well within corporate guidelines. Additionally, medical costs were incurred due to occasional back strain experienced by the employee responsible for sorting laundry from the chute.

Upon investigation of the accident, the supervisor attributed accidents to poor lifting and pulling by the employee and reminded the employee to be careful. But no-one ever asked the employee what was happening; as a result, an opportunity to save the $27 per sheet and an average back injury cost of $6,000 slipped by until this general manager implemented a quality assurance process. When the employee responsible for sorting was asked how the laundry could be improved, his reply was: "If you smooth out or remove that burr in the metal inside the chute, the sheets won't get hung up and I won't have to pull so hard to free the sheets and they won't tear"! Simple; yet so obvious that we lose sight of the key to success. If line management is the key and top management is the hand that turns the key, then the door of opportunity is the hourly employee.

Organizing for Action

Volumes have been written on how to organize accident prevention programs effectively. The key is to devise the best possible organization that fits the particular operation. Let us start at the top with the corporate structure and then work through the various possible and most effective unit organizations.

Corporate with a Full-Time Safety Professional

Chapter 1 discussed "How to manage the safety manager" and listed some basic criteria for determining who in the organization the safety manager should report to. Now is the time to take a definitive stand. Figure 2-1 represents the situation in which the safety manager's effectiveness is maximized—he or she reports directly to the president of the company. The obvious advantages include (1) an ability to interact with all disciplines

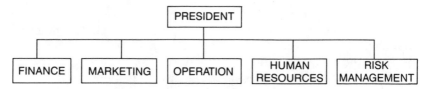

Figure 2-1. Organizing for accident prevention: a preferred positioning for the Risk Management and Loss Control functions.

and cross division boundaries, (2) involvement in all relevant corporate decisions, and (3) commitment from the top.

On the other hand, the reporting relationship does not necessarily connote a successful program. So long as there is commitment and the person reported to is a competent and respected manager within the organization, the safety personnel can be effective, but they may encounter obstacles that can hamper their performance.

Figure 2-2 represents such an option and should be considered the number two choice. This may be a better solution because of the size of the company—$2 billion plus in sales and a president who is too inundated to devote day-to-day attention. Within this option is the option of reporting to the financial officer or the operations vice-president. Either is satisfactory; refer to Chapter 1 and the criteria for the best selection.

To answer the incidental question "What about Human Resources?", I simply do not feel that human resources is the desirable location.

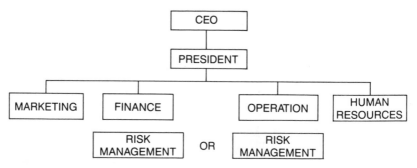

Figure 2-2. Organizing for accident prevention: an alternative approach.

Corporate without a Full-Time Safety Professional

No organizational chart is needed for this case. Chapter 1 suggested that the use of an outside safety consultant may be the way to go. However, someone in the organization must coordinate the consultant's efforts and approve the direction. That individual should probably be the financial officer, because he or she is already accountable for monitoring and guiding the financial health of the organization. Accident prevention represents an economic gain or loss. But, as with anything added on, safety will take a back seat to other job pressures. The one advantage of its being a financial responsibility is that *lack of action* will not last long as the costs rise.

If you are a small operator, you are obviously where the buck stops. Getting your hourly employees involved in the program can have the same level of success as for the big boys. You may have an even greater impact because you are "hands-on," with little or no bureaucracy.

Full-Service Hotel—Unit Level

The classic organizational chart in Figure 2-3 is still one of the best ways to manage the property accident prevention program. As with the corporate set up, the top person is the individual who turns the key; that individual is the general manager, and his or her level of commitment is critical to the success of the program. The general manager is the chairperson for the Quality Safety Board (QSB). The QSB is responsible for setting policy, objectives and overall program direction. It is the "decision maker." Reporting to the QSB chairperson are the hotel executive committe managers, security manager, and most importantly the chairperson from the Quality Safety Committee (QSC).

The Quality Safety Committee is made up of a cross-section of employees (Figure 2-4), a sort of task force or "synchrony." The primary responsibility is to identify and eliminate loss-producing events that would hamper the quality of the operation or cause harm to people or property.

As at the corporate level, there is a need for an individual to be responsible for facilitating the accident prevention program at the unit level. The criteria for selection are the same as for the corporate safety person. However, the individual usually never performs just the safety function, except in very large hotels

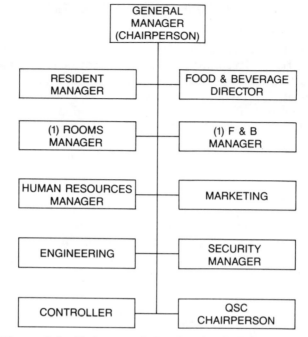

Figure 2-3. Make-up of the Quality Safety Board.

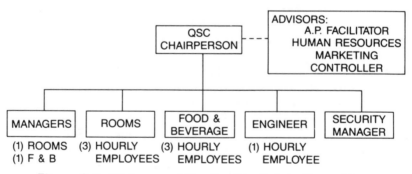

Figure 2-4. Make-up of the Quality Safety Committee.

or complex resorts. In most hotels the function is usually assigned to the human resources manager. This does not imply that a food and beverage director could not administer the function. In fact it may not be a bad idea, because many of a hotel's accidents are in the food and beverage area.

The area of management from which the person is drawn is least important to the end result. The individual and whether they have the support of the general manager is the critical component. Chapter 4 discusses how the security manager can assume an expanded role in accident prevention and have a very effective marriage of the two functions.

There is one other very important entity that will only briefly be touched upon: the Fire Emergency Team. The primary function of this team is to react in the event of fire, bomb threats and natural disasters.

As the maintenance inspections of fire protection equipment and systems are usually the responsibility of engineering, overall responsibility for this special team should belong to the hotel engineering manager. If the property has a security manager, that individual should be second in command. The two hotel safety committees should support the Fire Emergency Team through the accident prevention tour program discussed in Chapter 3 and by creating an awareness of fire safety issues among the entire staff.

Fire safety training of new employees and managers is a critical program because of the potentially catastrophic consequences of fire and also because of the tremendously bad press a hotel receives when there is even a small fire with slight property damage.

An effective Fire Emergency Team can significantly reduce damage exposure and minimize business interruption. But, as we have seen on TV and in the newspapers, the matter is often "put on the back burner," with tragic results.

It is worth noting that the process we are considering can also work as a quality assurance process, as a means to increase sales, or to tackle any other problem or opportunity that arises. The name of the game is to get people involved by allowing them to participate in the process. You will be more successful if you have their commitment.

Budget Hotels and Motels—Unit Level

Smaller size is not predictive of fewer accidents. In fact the exposure can be greater, especially where guest security is concerned, than with other, larger hotels. The buck stops at the owner/operator or property manager, and in the case of absenteeism, they have to pull the shift. Detailed paper programs don't solve the problem. What should be done?

Stick to basics, set up and push the Quality Safety Committee program. Make it a part of every employee meeting. Manage by walking around (MBWA) the property, keep close to the customers and the employees. Train, train, and train some more. Use all the outside resources possible. Get the QSC to maximize its role as a total multifaceted property program.

Utilize shift managers to develop and facilitate the other aspects of the accident prevention program and the Fire Emergency Team. It will be excellent training to help them mature their management abilities. At the managers' meeting, set time to discuss accident prevention and fire safety issues. It takes very little time when the program is integrated into the operation.

If there is an evening or "graveyard" security person, their job description can be rewritten to add some responsibility for fire and accident prevention. They can be sent to outside local classes in safety, crime prevention, and fire. This will make their job more challenging and help to reduce turnover in this all-important position. And there is no reason why this cannot be done with the maintenance engineer, especially in the area of fire safety.

As discussed in Chapter 1, retaining an outside safety consultant may be of critical benefit, especially in getting the program going. There can be added value in having them do a periodic health check, just to see how things are going or to do some specific training. The cost for a follow-up visit is nominal compared to the potential "shot-in-the-arm" effect. There is no need to be bashful: the insurance carrier has loss control services—so use these services.

Restaurants—All Types

Quality and safety are synonymous—this cannot be stressed enough. For a restaurant owner or manager, the impressions on the guests created by the employees is paramount to the business's success. As is the case with a small hotel, the available resources are limited. Therefore, it is paramount to the operation's overall success to establish a Quality Safety Committee. The committee's role becomes even more diverse and begins to include human resources issues. The committee can be asked to draft a plan to solve some of the operational issues as well as accident prevention issues. The two are naturally integrated. The QSC can be an extension of the regular employee meetings. At these meetings everyone can share their thoughts and ideas with the one significant benefit that management can have their commitment almost immediately to any new ideas.

Individual Responsibilities for Accident Prevention

The General Manager

Chairperson, Quality Safety Board (QSB). A general manager of any facility must be empowered with the full responsibility for executing and enforcing the accident prevention program. Listed below are some general responsibilities that should be a part of their job description.

- Integrate accident prevention into the operation by:
  1. Educating and motivating all employees in safe work methods.
  2. Providing a safe and hazard-free environment for the employees and guests.
  3. Holding all employees accountable for all accident prevention procedures.
- Budget sufficient funds to carry out the accident prevention programs.
- Actively participate in and support the Quality Safety Board and Quality Safety Committee.
- Insure that all employee and guest accidents receive immediate medical attention and are investigated and reported to the claims adjusting group.
- Hold individual managers accountable for their accident prevention efforts via their performance reviews.
- Inspect the property on a daily basis for the purpose of identifying unsafe work practices, recognizing safe work behavior, and removing accident prevention hazards (MBWA, managing by walking around).
- In the event of a federal or state safety or health inspection, notify corporate staff.
- Manage the Accident Prevention Facilitator/Manager.

Accident Prevention Facilitator

Member of QSB and advisor to the QSC. This is a very important position in the overall structure of the accident prevention program. The need has already been stressed for the right individual for this position and the importance of this selection cannot be overstated. Perhaps the committee should help decide on who should fill this position. This is an excellent way to begin the quality process by bringing it up from the bottom. Traditionally in hotels the responsibility has been with Human Resources but very successful programs also have the function assigned to another manager. Chapter 4 looks in depth at integrating this function into the security area but this may not work in specific cases. Ask the committees!

The Accident Prevention Facilitator coordinates the accident prevention program for a facility. This includes serving on both the Quality Safety Board and Quality Safety Committee, program development, claims management, first-aid, safety orientations, record keeping, and follow-up accident investigations. Some of the responsibilities listed below could be transferred to other management positions or shared as a joint responsibility should there be a need. The following are the primary responsibilities for this position:

- Provide guidance and assistance to the Quality Safety Board and Quality Safety Committee.
- Manage the accident prevention budget.
- Maintain resources of accident prevention materials and training aids for use by department managers and committees.
- Establish and monitor all accident prevention and fire safety training of all employees and maintain records of that training.
- Maintain and administer the hazard communication program (right to know).
- Advise and assist human resources in effective employee pre-screening for injury potential and matching the right employee to the right job.
- Assist the committees in various promotional campaigns to improve accident prevention awareness.
- Review basic accident prevention and fire safety policies at new employee orientation.

- Monitor the total program's effectiveness through tracking behavior, incident and accident frequency, trend analysis, and costs.

- Maintain all required federal and state employee injury records and inspections.

- Maintain an adequate first-aid and cardio-pulmonary resuscitation (CPR) program to include equipment and trained property personnel.

- Monitor all workers' compensation and guest liability claims. Act as the property liaison with claims adjusting group.

- Insure that all accidents and incidents are thoroughly investigated by the manager responsible for the area or employee.

- Conduct follow-up investigations to insure that corrective action has taken place.

- Coordinate all "We Care" and modified duty programs.

- Assist the Fire Emergency Team Leader in training team members and property staff in all emergency policies.

- Accompany federal, state and local officials and safety professionals on property inspections.

Quality Safety Committee Chairperson

Member of the QSB and Chairperson of the QSC. This individual is extremely important to the overall program effort. To be effective they must have the complete support of the general manager. The ideal individual should be selected by his or her peers and possess leadership skills and a drive to succeed. It may sound too good to be true; however, this is the perfect opportunity to groom a deserving individual for management. Their primary functions would be to:

- Lead the efforts of the Quality Safety Committee in developing new ways of improving the accident prevention effort.
- Keep the committee on track with its mission.
- Actively promote safety awareness amongst all employees.
- Act as the representative of hourly employees on the Quality Safety Board.

Department and Line Managers

Member of the QSB and QSC. Line managers are the key to every successful business endeavor. The same is true with accident prevention, because accident prevention is a line management responsibility and is an integral part of the operation. Line managers must be held accountable for safe work behavior and a safe work environment. The following are their primary responsibilities:

- Observe, monitor and enforce safe work behavior by rewarding those responding to safe habits and coaching and counseling those who do not adhere to safe procedures.
- Identify, correct and report unsafe conditions.
- Conduct accident prevention orientation to the job hazards. Insure the employee has signed off on each applicable Task Safety Analysis before they undertake that task.
- Insure that the employee has been properly indoctrinated to the hazard communication program.
- Conduct ongoing safety training at every employee meeting.
- Identify the physical requirements of the position to assist human resources in matching the correct employee for the job.
- Support departmental QSC members, by taking an active role in recognizing their efforts at team meetings and encouraging all employees to join in the team effort.
- Participate on the QSB and QSC if elected by the employees to do so.
- Become first-aid and CPR qualified and maintain department first-aid stations.
- Investigate all employee and guest accidents and incidents. Report all actions directly to the Accident Prevention Facilitator and follow up on all corrective actions.
- Insist on good housekeeping practices.
- Contact employees who are off work due to illness or injury through the "We Care" program. Cooperate and assist in implementing the modified duty program.
- Actively participate in the Accident Prevention Tour program.
- Effectively evaluate all subordinates on their performance reviews for support of accident prevention objectives.

Resident Manager and the Food and Beverage Director

Members of the QSB. These two managers have a very important role in the total program. They are jointly responsible for 90 percent of the employees of a hotel and 90 percent of the employee accidents fall within their remit. Their primary functions are:

- Follow up, support, and enforce the accident prevention policies and programs in their respective areas.
- Hold accountable all departmental managers at their performance reviews for meeting accident prevention objectives.
- Know, understand, and participate in the Quality Safety Board. Support and actively promote the Quality Safety Committee.
- Assist in implementation of the "We Care" and modified duty programs for all injured employees.
- Insure that all employee and guest accidents receive immediate medical attention and are investigated and reported to the claims adjusting group.
- Become first-aid and CPR qualified.
- Inspect the property on a daily basis for the purpose of identifying unsafe work practices, recognizing safe work behavior, and removing accident prevention hazards.
- (Food and Beverages specifically) Insure that all managers are certified in food sanitation, Heimlich maneuver, and serving alcohol responsibly.
- (Resident Manager specifically) Insure that a driver education and screening program is in effect for van drivers.
- Insure that all employees are trained in fire safety procedures.

Other Executive Committee Members

Members of the QSB and advisors to the QSC. This group of managers includes the Director of Marketing, Controller, and Human Resources Manager, unless they are the Accident Prevention Facilitator. Their responsibilities are the same as already listed for the Food and Beverage Director and Resident Manager except they also have a few other unique special duties because of their jobs.

The Director of Marketing is responsible for assisting the Quality Safety Committee in developing and implementing all awards and promotional programs.

The Controller is responsible for tracking and reporting on all accident prevention costs including insurance, injury costs, property damage, and program expenses.

The Human Resources Manager is responsible for maintaining records, pre-screening, and advising both committees on human resource issues that may be impacted by accident prevention programs.

Director of Engineering

Member of the QSB and team leader of the Fire Emergency Team. Because of this manager's intimate knowledge of the physical plant, the Director of Engineering has the lead responsibility in maintaining an overall safe property. If there are budget cuts, this is one area that should be looked at *last.* As engineering is responsible for plant maintenance, it follows that the following are the primary functions:

- Administer the Accident Prevention Work Order program.
- Develop and keep current evacuation plans for guests and employees.
- Maintain an up-to-date Fire Emergency Team Plan and conduct monthly drills.
- Complete all life safety inspections.
- Establish written emergency plans for fire, power failure, water and gas ruptures, and natural disasters.
- Accompany federal, state, and local officials on property inspections.
- Have a working knowledge of federal, state, and local codes and regulations.
- Follow up, support, and enforce the accident prevention policies and programs in the engineering areas.

Director of Security

Member of the QSB, QSC, and Fire Emergency Team. The Director of Security also plays a very important role in the accident prevention and fire safety programs. As this individual has a staff of people who are trained to respond to any security-related incident, it is only natural that they have a strong role in responding to emergencies and assisting in accident prevention through their patrol activities. The Director of Security has the following responsibilities:

- Assist the Director of Engineering in developing and carrying out all emergency programs.
- Develop and coordinate a bomb threat plan.
- Assist in training new employees in fire safety procedures.
- Insure that staff are fully trained in first-aid and CPR.
- Accompany federal, state, and local officials on property inspections.
- Have a working knowledge of federal, state, and local codes and regulations.
- Follow up, support, and enforce the accident prevention policies and programs in the security areas.
- Assist in training new managers in fire safety, accident prevention, and security procedures.
- Have security staff routinely check for unsafe conditions and correct or report them to appropriate personnel.

The Hourly Employee—the Door of Opportunity

It is critical to get the hourly employees' attention. Without their support and commitment, you are out of business. If it were possible to do so, hourly employees should be listed on the balance sheet as an asset to the company. Far too often, the opposite occurs and they are forgotten. Remember the earlier analogy: top management turns the key, line management is the key, and the hourly employee is the door of opportunity.

Quality begins from the bottom up. By involving hourly employees in the total property process, management can begin to direct their behavior toward working more safely and improving profits. The following are the fundamental responsibilities that must be instilled in each employee:

- Observe all accident prevention policies and rules.
- Follow all prescribed safe work practices.
- Report any unsafe condition or equipment.
- Practice good housekeeping and sanitation procedures.
- Utilize all personal protective equipment.

- Promptly report all injuries to the supervisor.
- Dress properly.
- Operate equipment with all guards and safety devices in place.
- Keep work area, aisles, walkways, and stairs free of obstructions.
- Know the chemicals in use and use them only as directed.
- Do not use or be under the influence of alcohol and/or illegal drugs.
- Do not engage in horseplay.
- Comply with all federal, state, and local laws and regulations.

These responsibilities are *everyone's* responsibility.

Committees and Their Roles

What makes a successful committee?

- Duties and responsibilities clearly defined.
- Members carefully chosen by their peers.
- Chairperson selected by the committee.
- Procedures in place for prompt action.
- Rewards and recognition.
- Response by management, whether positive or negative to every committee recommendation.

Committees can fail miserably if any of these are not observed. Also, the committee should be viewed as a team evaluating not only accident prevention but the entire gamut of quality assurance. In other words, there must be a total concept of applying and learning basic techniques to identify problems within their areas, analyze them, and present solutions to top management. Getting employees involved gains their commitment; without it customers will not be taken care of and injuries will increase.

The two committees discussed are essential to the unit-level accident prevention program. In smaller facilities only one committee is necessary. Each committee has a unique but inter-related role. Let us review each one in a little more detail.

Quality Safety Board

The role of the Quality Safety Board can be defined in terms of chairperson, that being the property General Manager. In its role as decision maker, the Quality Safety Board takes on the following responsibilities:

- Review recommendations and program suggestions from the Quality Safety Committee. Take immediate steps to respond to their ideas and develop implementation strategies for all approved concepts.
- Order corrective maintenance on equipment and facilities as a result of all inspections and tour programs.
- Review all claims and program costs.
- Review and analyze behavior analysis reports, incident reports, and claims for the purpose of identifying and ranking risks and developing corrective actions.
- Establish a process to insure ongoing middle management emphasis on accident prevention.
- Establish training needs and priorities.
- Coordinate property-wide procedures for recognizing safe behavior and reinforcing accident prevention policies.
- Review all accident and incident reports and contact appropriate parties to verify corrective follow-up.

Membership on the board includes the following persons (Figure 2-3):

General Manager, Chairperson
Food and Beverage Director
Resident Manager
QSC Chairperson
Director of Engineering
Director of Security
Human Resources Director
Director of Marketing
Controller
Line Manager

The Line Manager should be selected by his or her peers and be on the committee for one year.

Quality Safety Committee

As the name implies, this is the most important committee of all. No matter what the size of the business, this team is essential. Quality comes from the bottom up and when there is pride and ownership there is commitment. The Quality Safety Committee is responsible for the following:

- Develop an awareness among all employees of the value of accident prevention.
- Conduct property Accident Prevention Tours.
- Study problems and ideas uncovered by their peers, through accident and incident analysis and from other sources.
- Develop incentive and award promotion programs.
- Develop and promote interdepartmental team efforts to meet accident prevention objectives and foster some healthy competition.
- Educate committee members and employees at large on on-the-job and off-the-job safety.
- Brainstorm new and innovative programs and concepts to improve overall safety and quality of the operation.

This last responsibility is the quintessential ingredient to foster the creative juices. This is what will motivate the committee to get involved and take a proactive approach rather than indulge in a bitch session. However, guidance is needed to help the committee gel, and that is the role of the advisors.

The committee's make-up is of all types and levels of employee. All members are elected by their peers in their respective departments. As a result, they make reports at department meetings on the committee's progress. The membership should include (Figure 2-4):

An elected person from each department. If this is too big a group, which it probably will be, it can be changed to one person per major area or, for a small operation, it could be everyone at the employee meeting.
A line manager from Food and Beverages and one from Rooms.
Security Director.
Advisors.

The chairperson of the committee should be nominated and elected by the committee. The committee should rotate membership once a year but this is not an essential. Some may really enjoy the work and wish to stick with it; by all means let them.

Fire Emergency Team

The Fire Emergency Team is a specially trained group of employees whose primary functions are:

- Extinguish small fires after notifying the fire department (*only if properly trained*).
- Provide orderly communications to the fire department, employees, and guests, and assist in evacuation and damage control.
- Promote fire safety awareness among all employees.

Management should select this team from among interested employees. The Director of Engineering is team leader and the Director of Security is assistant team leader. The team should include all security and engineering personnel, the executive committee, night audit manager, and a few other employees to round out the team on evening and graveyard shifts.

Making Committees Work

Here are a few tips on making committees work:

- Pay the employee while attending meetings and activities.
- Offer an incentive increase for participation on any committee, especially for hourly employees.
- Consider performance bonuses to members based on achievement of specific objectives.
- Recognize their efforts often, in company publications and all employee meetings.
- Make active involvement a prerequisite to entering management or future promotions.

Whatever you do, do not set up committees for the sake of doing it, because you will be wasting everyone's time and will actually demotivate your team.

A FINAL WORD

Accident prevention must be internalized. It must become a group norm, an individual value that is a part of the company's culture.

Committees, programs, internal and external safety consultants, and all the fancy terms cannot replace *commitment* and *involvement*. When we commit to change our behavior, others around us will be touched by that commitment and if it is channeled in the right direction, they too will join us.

CHAPTER 3

Proactive Approach to Accident Prevention

In 1989, the National Safety Council reported the injury incidence rates shown in Table 3-1. As can be seen, hotels, motels and restaurants have more work-related injuries than the mining industry. This is not to say that the hopsitality industry is more hazardous. Obviously mining has a much higher severity exposure and death rate. However, in terms of the bottom line costs, they are related. According to the National Safety Council's *Accident Facts* 1989 edition, the average cost per disabling injury was $16,800 while the average cost of goods that had to be produced to offset this cost was $410 for each and every worker. The problem is not a small one. Medical costs rise at a significantly higher rate than inflation, which means that if the frequency rate over prior years can be maintained, costs will still rise by as much as 15–20% annually. What is to be done? It is necessary to throw

TABLE 3-1. Incident rates for various industries.

| Industry | Incident rates | | |
	Total cases	Medical only cases	Lost time cases
Hotels and motels	10.6	5.9	4.7
Restaurants	8.3	5	3.2
Mining	8.5	3.6	4.9
Manufacturing	11.9	6.7	5.3

Note: Incident rate $= \dfrac{\text{number of injuries} \times 200\,000}{\text{total manhours worked}}$

away preconceived ideas and take a proactive approach to accident prevention.

The functions of accident prevention can be broken down into two major areas. Figure 3-1 illustrates these areas as Pre-Loss, and Post-Loss.

Pre-Loss

All accident causes and risks must be identified in order to develop programs to control and eliminate potential injury-producing events. Pre-Loss activities are proactive in nature. Unfortunately we generally learn the hard way, taking the attitude that "It won't happen to me."

This is the point where having a safety professional is a big bonus. They are trained to research and gather the data, to ferret out the root causes of accidents. If that resource is unavailable, then Figure 3-2 offers the methods used to identify the real

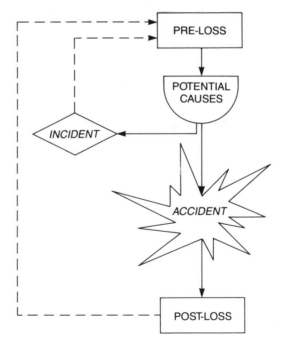

Figure 3-1. The relationship between pre-loss, incidents, accidents, and post-loss.

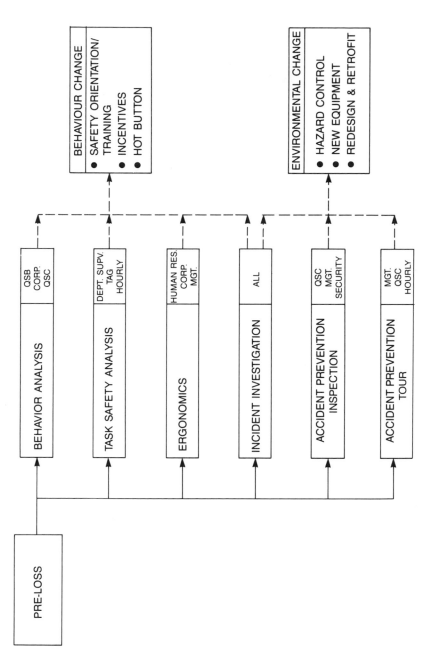

Figure 3-2. The activities and programs that occur prior to an incident or accident.

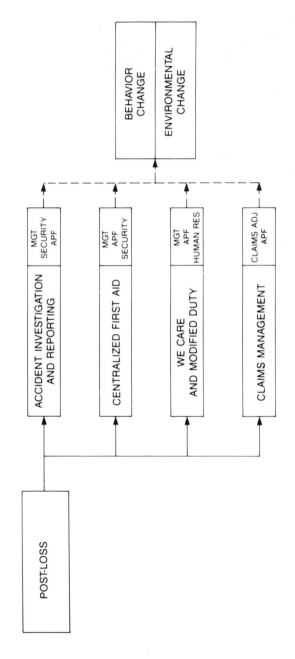

Figure 3-3. Programs that occur after an accident.

problems and who should be responsible. Each of these will be discussed later under the heading "Identifying Causes of Accidents."

Post-Loss

As the name implies, Post-Loss activities minimize accident losses. These activities are reactive in nature. Here prevention is too late. The accident has occurred and injury and/or property damage has resulted. However, we can still learn from these unfortunate scenarios to fine tune our programs. Figure 3-3 shows the various programs involved in Post-Loss control. These programs will be covered in Chapters 4, 5 and 6. Let us take a look at the Pre-Loss scenario and how we go about identifying potential accident causes.

PRE-LOSS

Identifying Causes of Accidents

Behavioral Analysis

The focus of behavior analysis is behavior. The aim is to define unsafe behavior and to uncover those factors that tend to support unsafe behavior. Even though management through its policies states that safe performance from employees is required, the employees will not necessarily respond. Employees will decide individually for themselves whether or not they will come to work, how hard they will work, and how safely they will work. Behavior analysis is the study of those factors that influence that decision. Some of the factors that influence behavior are:

- Peer group attitudes.
- Employee selection and placement criteria.
- Orientation and training.
- Management's system—participative versus authoritarian.
- Personality and motives.
- Skills, knowledge and abilities.

Where should you begin? There are two methods which should be followed: (1) direct observation and (2) employee meetings.

To conduct direct observation it is necessary first to define what is to be observed. Take each position and develop a list of safe and unsafe behaviors; in other words, list the risks. As an example, Figure 3-4 shows a possible list for a restaurant server. From this data, it is possible to calculate a response rate that is equal to the frequency divided by the time interval and plot it on a

SAFE WORK ANALYSIS
FREQUENCY RECORD
(RESTAURANT SERVER)

DATE: *LOCATION:*
TIME INTERVAL: *RECORDED BY:*

BEHAVIOR	NUMBER OF OBSERVATIONS	
	SAFE	UNSAFE
1. Knees are bent when lifting		
2. Tray is carried correctly		
3. Tray load is four settings or less		
4. Approved footwear worn		
5. Ice scoop used for icing glasses		
6. Tray stands or carts used for serving/breakdown		
7. Spills cleaned-up		
8. Work station kept clean		
9. Hands washed		
10. Ash trays checked for lighted materials		
FREQUENCY		
TIME IN MINUTES		
RESPONSE RATE		

Note: Frequency = Total Observations
      Response Rate = Frequency/Time

Figure 3-4. A sample Safe Work Analysis Record form, which is used by a trained observer to record worker behavior.

simple graph to demonstrate how well the restaurant servers are performing their duties safely.

Another approach to obtaining or refining this list is to discuss incidents which are accidents without injury at the next employee meeting. The challenge will be to uncover the behavior of all parties rather than environmental factors. Once the behavior lists have been completed, observe and record the *frequency* (how many times it occurs), *response rate* (frequency per unit of time) and *duration* (the total amount of time the behavior occurs). Next, track progress on a graph that plots the response rate of servers over time—Figure 3-5.

Two objectives have been achieved: (1) definition of what behaviors must be changed and those that need reinforcement and (2) establishment of a benchmark to measure future success of the accident prevention program (Geller, Lehman and Kalsher, 1989).

Employee meetings have tremendous potential not only for defining behavior but for modifying it. Discussing prior incidents

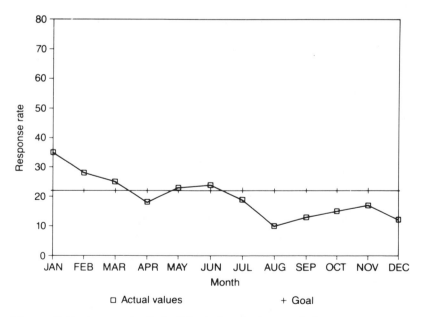

Figure 3-5. A sample Safe Work Analysis graph for a restaurant over the course of a year. The horizontal line depicts the company goal, while the irregular line is a record of each month's frequencies as calculated using the Safe Work Analysis Record of Figure 3-4.

and response rates with the employees and recognizing their achievements unwittingly germinates the seeds of commitment by showing management concern for the employees' safety and health. Sometimes observation of behavior is not feasible. Employee meetings can be used to obtain opinions directly or through the use of questionnaires. Employee meetings can also be used to develop safe work practices for a specific task, which eventually can be translated into a Task Safety Analysis, which is a highly effective training tool. The classic *safety committee* has thereby been created.

Accident prevention must become a value:

> People do not like to feel controlled. One's commitment to a safety policy will increase with the individual's perception that their compliance with the policy is voluntary (Geller, Lehman & Kalsher, 1989, p. 66).

Task Safety Analysis

A Task Safety Analysis (TSA) is a process that uncovers potential accident hazards and risks. When properly developed, it becomes a training tool, which guides an individual step by step through a specific *job task*. As a TSA is created, safer and better task procedures are developed for that job. While developing a TSA, supervisors learn more about the tasks they are supervising. Once developed, it becomes a training tool for the supervisor or "tag" person in instructing the new employee. A "tag" person is an experienced employee assigned to oversee the new employee's training.

The function of a Task Safety Analysis is to integrate safety into production, to personalize it for the employee. It will help ensure that the training takes place and that the correct procedures are followed (National Safety Council, 1988).

Step 1. Identify which tasks need a TSA. Rather than trying to list all the possible tasks that should have a TSA developed, consider a general criterion. A job task should have a TSA whenever it has the potential to cause (1) severe injury and/or (2) a high frequency of accidents. A few examples include:

- Using buffalo chopper.
- Using a meat slicer.
- Using a powder-actuated driver.
- Cleaning a guest room bath.

Step 2. Use a form similar to Figure 3-6. At the top is space for the task name, date, and job positions that the TSA applies to. List the sequence of basic steps needed to complete the task in column 1. This is the point where getting an experienced employee or discussing the task at an employee meeting can pay big dividends. Column 2 gives the proper way of completing the step and any need for special protective equipment and/or proper tools. The last column is very important. This is where the potential hazards are identified that could cause an injury and key points to remember are listed.

Step 3. Hand out the Task Safety Analysis at an employee meeting and demonstrate the task in order to get feedback on clarity and accuracy. Do not overdo it; select a few specific TSAs that seem to be targeted at the more prevalent potential accident causes. Concentrate on these few at the beginning and add new ones as the concept is accepted. Once it is tailored by the employees, a little ownership is developed and the job standards can then be enforced easily. Figure 3-7 is a simple completed TSA on using a grinder.

Step 4. "Roll-out" the program. As discussed previously, the benefits of a Task Safety Analysis are gained during and after its development. One of its greatest uses is for new employee orientation. New employees are easily motivated to do a good job. This enthusiasm can be used to begin to incorporate safe work methods into production.

To orient the new employee, an experienced worker called a "tag" is used to walk the new person through each step of the Task Safety Analysis for that particular task. This will accomplish two goals: (1) it will begin assimilation of the employee into the peer group and (2) it will teach new employees the correct procedure before they develop bad habits. In this capacity, the TSA becomes an "action" and not a paperwork activity for the supervisor. Once the employee has been instructed, they are required to sign the form and it is placed in their personnel file. The TSA now becomes a useful document for coaching and counseling and for accident investigation.

For the senior employee, the Task Safety Analysis can be used at employee meetings to reinforce safety awareness and regain commitment. An interesting way to accomplish this is have the employee do a demonstration. Alternatively, the local

TASK SAFETY ANALYSIS

Page:

Task Description:
Date Completed:
Job Position(s):

TASK STEPS	HOW TO COMPLETE STEP	POTENTIAL HAZARDS/KEY POINTS

_____   _____
TAG/Supervisor Signature   *Date*

_____   _____
Employee Signature   *Date*

Figure 3-6. Sample Task Safety Analysis form.

TASK SAFETY ANALYSIS

Task Description: Using a Grinder
Date Completed: xx-xx-xx
Job Position(s): Maintenance

TASK STEPS	HOW TO COMPLETE STEP	POTENTIAL HAZARDS/KEY POINTS
1. Check the condition of the grinder.	1. Visually inspect the electrical power cord, housing, pedestal stand, guards, grinding and brush wheel for damage and/or defects.	1. Laceration, contusion, and/or burn injury caused by the failure of the cord, housing and/or wheels. DO NOT OPERATE—report to supervisor and place lockout on equipment.
2. Perform the grinding operation.	2a. Put on eye protection.	2a. Eye injury caused by flying debris.
	2b. Grasp electrical plug and insert into wall socket.	2b. Electric shock and burns.
	2c. Position the wheel's upper guard and lower guide assembly, relative to the size of the object being ground.	2c. Failure to use guards could result in hand injuries, and ricochets causing injury to others. Be sure to place lower guide at midpoint of wheel.
	2d. Place the power switch in the "On" position.	2d. Be sure wheels are clear.
	2e. Firmly grasp the item being worked on with both hands.	2e. Hand injuries could result. Do not operate with jewelry and/or loose clothes.
	2f. Place the item on the appropriate wheel's lower guide assembly.	2f. Prevent kick back.
	2g. Press the item against the wheel to perform the grinding or brushing.	2g. Hold firmly or ricochet and/or hand injuries may result.
	2h. Maintain a firm grasp and control of the item while it is against the wheel.	2h. Hand injury could result.
	2i. Remove the item and inspect.	
	2j. Place the grinder's power switch in the "Off" position.	2j. Never leave power equipment unattended while "On".
	2k. Grasp the electrical plug and pull it from the wall socket.	2k. Electric shock and burns.

TAG/Supervisor Signature   _Date_   _Employee Signature_   _Date_

Figure 3-7. Completed sample Task Safety Analysis for use of a grinder.

manufacturer's representative can be invited to come in and demonstrate the equipment. A good example is to have the fire extinguisher supplier come to a housekeeping meeting and set up controlled fires in the parking lot to teach employees proper use of the extinguisher. This is fun and quite educational.

From a behavior analysis standpoint, a Task Safety Analysis is an excellent way to monitor and record behavior to see which habits are retained versus those that are modified. Some additional benefits include (1) documentation of required training to comply with the OSHA Hazard Communication Standard and (2) defense support for possible negligent retention law suits. Whatever happens, the TSA should not become a piece of paper that is handed to the employee and with the instruction "just sign it."

Accident Prevention Inspections

Inspections are a classic way of uncovering causes and preventing accidents. There are many types of inspections. Some are formal and in writing while others are informal checks. Inspections are usually:

- Continuous and ongoing inspections by managers and supervisors; in other words, MBWA.
- Planned at some required interval, such as for vehicles, machinery, and general safety.
- Required by outside agencies and usually conducted by that agency.

Additionally, inspections assist in defense efforts by diffusing a plaintiff's allegations that management failed to meet constructive notice, which simply means maintaining the area free from physical hazards through an effective inspection program.

The first step is to do an inventory of what needs to be inspected, which should include:

1. Environmental conditions—lighting, ventilation.
2. All equipment (preventative maintenance lists).
3. Fire protection equipment.
4. General housekeeping.
5. Walkways and stairs.
6. Electrical equipment.

7. Elevators and escalators.

8. Storage areas.

9. Roadways, sidewalks, and parking areas.

10. Warning and signaling devices.

11. First-aid supplies.

12. Chemicals and other hazardous materials.

13. Guest rooms.

14. Public areas—restaurants, rest rooms, lobbies, vending areas, ballrooms, meeting rooms.

15. Health clubs and pools.

16. Vehicles, especially courtesy vans.

Wherever possible, the accident prevention inspections items should be included in already established inspection programs. For instance, the night manager or "manager on duty" report should include a tour of the facility to check for any safety, fire, and security hazards. The room-ready check by the housekeeping supervisor should include checking the bath floor and tub areas for hazards, insuring that other entrances are secured, and even checking the bed frame for burrs. One of the most important inspections is the preventative maintenance rooms inspection performed by the engineering staff. Here all the furnishings, hot-water temperature, wall-mounted fixtures, electrical outlets and fixtures, door locks, closures, and emergency notification materials should be checked and logged by the engineer.

There are also specialty checklists, which should be a requirement for any hotelier and restaurateur. The first is the sweep log. Sweep logs serve one purpose, to record the fact an area was checked on a regular basis for safety hazards such as wet floors, lighting, and cleanliness. It is an important document in showing you have inspected the areas to prove that constructive notice has been met, a critical element in slip and fall liability defense (see Chapter 12).

Another is the sprinkler valve and alarm system test inspection, which verifies that control valves are in the open and locked position and all alarm systems and the emergency generator are functioning properly. One more example is the vehicle safety inspection checklist, completed by the hotel van drivers when they begin their shifts and before operating the vehicle. This inspection insures that all safety equipment is operating, including lights, brakes, first-aid kit, safety belts, and the fire extinguisher.

A New Approach—Accident Prevention Tour

Probably the most important inspection of all is the one that can be conducted by the Quality Safety Committee (QSC) and/or management staff. It is called the Accident Prevention Tour (APT). This is more than just an inspection program, it is actually a process that involves the employees in improving the quality, safety, and security of your facility.

We must first recognize the fact that the Accident Prevention Tour concept grows out of the need to provide safety and security for guests and employees. We must also recognize the fact that the APT must be tailored to meet the unique needs of each type of facility.

A resort property has unique areas that are different from those of an airport hotel or a free-standing restaurant. However, the concept of managers and hourly employees becoming the "eyes and ears" of the facility holds a tremendous appeal in making a significant impact on the success of the Quality Safety Committee and the total accident prevention program.

There are four factors to consider when implementing the Accident Prevention Tour:

• *Frequency of the tour.* How often the tour is conducted depends on the size of the facility, the type of facility, and the availability of staff. A novel idea is to recognize it as being supplementary to or in lieu of a security staff. If this is an endeavor exclusive to the QSC, then once a month prior to their meeting should suffice. However, an adaptation would be to involve managers as well as hourlies, assign individuals to conduct the tours on each shift, and include security items to be checked. This will help to supplement the program if there is no security staff used for ongoing security effort.

• *Tour structure.* In order for the tour to be most effective, it should be structured to complement the way in which it will be conducted. For example, for a small hotel, tour by area (e.g., front desk, lobby, meeting rooms, restaurant, guest rooms, back of house, and parking); for larger hotels, tour by floors; for a restaurant I would suggest touring by area (i.e. seating area, buffet, rest rooms, entry, parking, kitchen, and storage areas). Another alternative is to create mini-tours within areas. This is an excellent approach for very large hotels and gets department members involved in their own areas.

- *Tour checklist.* The checklist is a critical document for guiding the person conducting the tour and recording the conditions observed. It should ensure that it is designed with clearly identified spaces for (1) check marks and comments, (2) items to be checked and (3) arrival time in each area visited (see Chapter 13 for an electronic approach).

- *Tour responsibility.* A manager or higher level person should make the Quality Safety Committee responsible for administering the Accident Prevention Tour program. One of the first steps after the three above will be to train those who will conduct the tours and develop tour schedules. Some examples of schedules and assignments would be:

- Assuming there is a security staff, adding APT elements to their basic patrol.
- Incorporation into the night manager's tour routine.
- QSC members completing a tour as a team or individually during their shift.
- Composing a staff of specially trained "APT Officers," who can be relied upon to conduct the tours.

Obviously such assignments will depend upon whether or not this is daily activity or performed, say, once a month.

No matter what inspection program exists, the key to success is follow-up. Corrective action must be taken immediately for any safety hazards or repairs that are noted during the inspections. The following are some steps to ensure timely follow-up.

1. Immediately handle those problems that can be corrected easily (e.g., put up wet floor signs, lock doors, close down area or equipment).
2. Report those hazards or repairs that require maintenance or engineering personnel via a work request.
3. Where problems cannot immediately be remedied, follow up to ensure that all corrective actions are taken promptly.

An excellent method of ensuring that engineering personnel give such problems a high priority is to follow an Accident Prevention Work Order (APWO) program. The Accident Prevention Work Order form should be safety green or orange in color and be a four-part form with automatic carbons. The form is completed by the person conducting the tour, with the top copy sent to engineering, second page to the Quality Safety Committee, third page to the general manager, and the last page for the originator. It should also be noted on the tour report that an APWO was completed. The color of the form draws attention to it and aids in distinguishing this work order from routine work orders. It also carries the highest repair priority.

An adjunct to the Accident Prevention Work Order is to set up a Safety "Hot Line". The purpose of the Hot Line is to report unsafe conditions that need immediate attention. Also, it can be used by employees who are intimidated by paper or who cannot communicate in writing.

Records retention is the last aspect and one of the most important for future litigation. Inspections can be a double-edged sword. On the one hand, they can demonstrate the duty of care to provide a facility free of safety hazards. On the other hand, if you fail to correct the deficiencies they can show your negligence in not providing for the guests' safety. But the good definitely outweighs the risk, because inspections show our "good faith," which is an important aspect in an effective defense strategy. Records of all types of inspections and tours should be maintained for at least three years unless a claim has been filed or the case is in suit, in which case they should be maintained until the case is closed. Some records will need to be kept longer as they may be subject to state or federal laws, regulations, and codes.

Ergonomics: "The Human Equation"

Ergonomics or work flow analysis can be defined as maximizing the quality and efficiency of the operator through improving the design relationship between man, machine, and the environment.

Ergonomics or designing the workplace to fit the person is a hot issue with OSHA these days. OSHA has targeted the meat packing and automotive industries for repetitive motion injuries like carpal tunnel syndrome. However, before long the same standards of ergonomic design will be required of all industries. The effect of this on hotels, motels, and restaurants is quite obvious. Consider those positions where employees are subject to sprains and strains over a long period of time. Some of those positions are (1) PBX operator, (2) reservations, (3) housekeeper, (4) line cook, and (5) kitchen prep. All of these positions have various hazards that can cause repetitive motion injuries. For instance, the PBX operator and reservations clerk are exposed to VDT hazards, while the housekeeper is exposed to back strains.

Part 2 of this book covers design criteria that incorporate many safety engineering principles to meet the concepts of ergonomics. However, there are other issues to consider when putting together a program on ergonomics (materials handling), and they include:

- Physical and mental condition of the workers.
- Work methods and motivations.
- Training and knowledge.
- Job demands.

Why should we be interested in ergonomics? Because materials handling accidents account for 40–50 percent of the total costs of accidents for a typical hotel, motel or restaurant. This breaks down to:

- Weight a factor (lifting, pushing, pulling): 25–30%.
- Weight not a factor (cuts and burns): 10%.
- Struck by object: 10–15%.

Materials handling accidents are those accidents that result in back sprains and strains, carpal tunnel syndrome, cuts, burns, and other muscle maladies. These accidents are generally caused by:

- Mismatch between the worker and the job.
- Improper tools being used.
- Lack of or improper use of personal protective equipment.
- Unsafe operating procedures.
- Poor housekeeping and/or equipment in poor condition.
- Too much weight being handled.
- Lack of proper warm up and physical flexibility.
- Pre-existing conditions and cumulative trauma.

One thing to always keep in mind is that most musculoskeletal injuries are legitimate, whether or not there is sudden pain or a slow dull ache. However, there are those who attempt to get a free ride on the system because compensation benefits are far better than unemployment benefits. These individuals can be contained and weeded out through an aggressive injury-management program, which is discussed in Chapter 5.

The methods and programs already discussed support the concepts of ergonomics or human factors engineering. Behavior Analysis studied the work methods and attitudes that needed to be modified and reinforced. Task Safety Analysis uncovered procedural discrepancies in completing a specific task, while inspections helped evaluate and improve the physical environment. The only things missing for an effective materials handling program are job screening and placement; training; claims management; and professional ergonomics evaluations.

Job Screening and Placement

This is probably the most controversial area of any accident prevention program. The hospitality and restaurant industries are facing, in some areas, significant labor shortages and the situation is not going to get better. Many operators and human resources professionals say that we are in the "warm body" syndrome, defined as hiring anyone who is alive and breathing without regard to prior work experience or capability of performing the job. This situation can have a profound effect on the frequency and costs of accidents. But how are the effects to be minimized? First of all, do not give up; instead focus on the positions that incur the greatest likelihood for back injuries, because they represent the highest cost.

Housekeepers have the highest number of back injuries in the lodging industry, servers have the most in restaurants, and kitchen workers in both industries combined. This is not to say banquet houseman, engineering and even office workers are not exposed to back injuries, but it is necessary to focus effort to get the "biggest bang for the buck." An additional reason for isolating some key positions is to avoid Equal Employment Opportunity Commission (EEOC) implications. In other words, the jobs selected for materials handling screening must involve a significant amount of time involved in lifting, pushing, and pulling of materials.

Materials handling must be job based and properly validated. Screening for materials handling positions is no different from giving a typing test to a prospective secretarial candidate. It is legal and nondiscriminatory, according to Uniform Guidelines on Employee Selection Procedures (29 CFR1607). The primary purpose of the screening is to avoid buying someone else's compensation claim and to match the individual to the job. It is necessary because cumulative trauma is the single largest contributor to increased workers' compensation injury costs, and as our labor force continues to age this will become an even more significant exposure.

With the signing into law of the Americans with Disabilities Act (ADA), there are specific prohibitions to any form of pre-employment medical inquiry or medical examination. A pre-employment inquiry can be made only if it concerns the ability of the applicant to perform job-related functions. This new law does allow post-offer employment medical examinations, but they must be given to all employees, kept confidential, and the results cannot be used to discriminate against a qualified individual with a disability. Medical questions should be avoided during pre-employment interviews and on employment applications. With the enactment of this law it behoves the operator to ensure each and every job position has a clearly defined job description which delineates all the required abilities to complete that job.

How to screen? What to start?

1. A job review and validation must be undertaken for each job position in the facility to determine the degree of materials handling, strength requirements, and other physical consider-ations. Only those jobs that require a substantial amount of bending, stooping, and lifting should be identified as materials handling positions. All job descriptions for materials handling positions should include a statement similar to the following:

> *Repeated bending, stooping and lifting of weights up to and including (X) pounds will be required*

2. Job application form should include the following types of questions (subject to review by counsel for the locality):

- Have you ever filed a workers' compensation claim? If yes, please explain.
- Are you able to perform this job with these physical tasks? If not, please explain why.

The purpose of these questions is obvious. Workers who have experienced a back injury or knee surgery, or who have some other musculoskeletal difficulty, are considered a higher risk for re-injury. Once they have re-injured the area, you have bought the claim. With a good screener, and the right questions asked, you can weed out the applicants who have been hired in the past but never worked because of questionable injuries. Some believe that once a worker has been paid compensation for an on-the-job injury, the probability is better than 80% that they will repeat the process and make a claim when hired again (English, 1988). Again, keep in mind the ADA Title I provision which prohibits medical inquiry and check with local counsel to review the kind of questions that your screener can utilize.

3.   Each applicant for a materials handling position should be given a physical test, because studies conducted by a leading workers' compensation insurance company have shown a direct correlation between physical condition and susceptibility to musculoskeletal injuries. The interesting thing about the tests is that they do not discriminate. Someone smoking six packs a day and with a beer gut has passed and teenagers have failed. This does not invalidate the test; it tells us that the stomach muscles are stronger in one individual than another. It also relates to the flexibility of an individual. Physical tests should be given only to those applicants who desire a materials handling position and only if they have passed the medical screening. ADA Title I does allow for physical testing and drug testing as long as you stay away from medical issues. Before embarking on this form of screening, local counsel should be involved to determine whether there are any restrictions in the program to be overcome.

Review the job requirements for bending, stooping, and lifting with the applicant. Then ask the question: "Are you able to perform a job with these tasks?" If the answer is "No," do not have the applicant perform the physical test. However, you should ask the following questions.

Would you like to be considered for a non-materials handling position?

The reason for this question is to assure the person that it is for safety alone that they are not being screened for the materials handling position. If the answer to this question is also "No," then ask:

What do you think can be done to modify the materials handling position to accommodate you?

Document the suggestions and end the conversation. Now is the hard part. If you need the body and everything else is fine, you are the one that must weigh the risk! With enactment of the

Americans with Disabilities Act, accommodation has become the focus, to ensure all possible allowances are made in adapting the job to fit the disabled worker. There may be no option but to apply ergonomic design and adapt the workplace to fit the worker rather than screening the applicant out.

If the answer to the first question is "Yes," then the following three physical tests should be completed. These test the three primary job functions of bending, stooping, and lifting. The tests should be administered in privacy but with a screener of the appropriate sex or a witness present.

1. Instruct the applicant to stand, knees stiff, feet spread to shoulder width, then ask them to bend at the waist to come within six inches of the floor. While they are performing the task, ask them what degree of difficulty they are experiencing and mark it on the form.

2. Have the person perform one sit-up: with their hands folded across their waist, feet together, have them raise slowly to the full straight torso position. If they cannot complete one sit-up, then placing them in a materials handling position poses a high risk. Again ask them to rate the degree of difficulty.

3. In the classic knees bent position, have the applicant lift a (X) weight (X = 95th percentile of expected lift), preferably in a single container, although two boxes are satisfactory for women in skirts. Have them raise the box to waist height and then return the box to the floor in the same motion. Ask them to rate the level of difficulty. (*Note*: be sure to label the boxes with their appropriate weights.)

If the applicant can perform all three tests with relative ease, they are considered a low risk for a materials handling injury. However, there are a lot of factors involved in musculoskeletal injuries, such as dealing with behavior, environment, and training of the individual.

There is one other physical attribute which is a major contributor to low back pain, that is, flexibility. It may be appropriate to consider a fourth test, which measures flexibility of the hip, hamstrings, and lower back muscles. Good flexibility means that the joints of the body and the muscles are elastic and free from tightness and tension. Studies have shown that a lack of flexibility has a direct relationship to lower back problems. I would rather see flexibility introduced as an activity and training program rather than as a screening program, because if you are going to hire the warm body anyway, one way to prevent back injuries is through getting employees to "care for their backs."

Training

The back is like any other piece of equipment: take care of it and it will take care of your. Everyone has had back pain, but being aware of the state of one's back and how to improve flexibility and strength is the key to minimizing injury. Employees need to be taught how to care for their backs and to be offered time, training, and counseling to make it happen.

"Care for Your Back" is a special program of awareness, flexibility and strengthening of the back to help prevent back injuries. In a nutshell, it is a program that can be put together with the help of a professional physical therapist/exercise trainer and which should accomplish three key objectives:

- Warm-up.
- Stretching.
- Strengthening.

The program will require committing 10–15 minutes each day before the employees start work to complete a routine to get the body ready for materials handling. It is a highly effective and fun program.

However, the classic training on proper lifting and handling of materials must continue. The "bend your knees" concept is still valid and so is the newest lifting method, which states:

- Keep the object close to the body.
- Maintain footing and avoid quick movements.
- Lift in a way that is comfortable.
- Do not twist the body while lifting.

There are numerous publications that can be used for training purposes. Some excellent publications include *Your Back Is Always Working* (Kramer Communications; Dale City, Calif.); *You and Your Back* (Channing L. Bete Co.; South Deerfield, Mass.); and *Prevent-A-Backache Guide* (Positive Promotions; Brooklyn, N.Y.)

These booklets cover how to care and maintain your back in fit condition with easy-to-follow basics on backs relating to lifting correctly and flexibility. But materials handling is not just a matter of backs: what about knife cuts from shucking oysters or burns from chemicals and heat? All of these require proper training in procedures and provision of the necessary protective equipment and tools. Many of these tasks can be covered in a Task Safety Analysis. Chapter 8 will discuss a program, required by law, known as "Right To Know" or "Hazard Communication Standard." This program involves the education of workers in proper handling in the day-to-day use of chemicals.

Claims Management

Even with appropriate prevention programs, some injuries will occur. Aggressive treatment and management of the injuries is critical to reduce costs and to put employees at ease about their future. You must continue to monitor the injury and provide sound disability management. Vocational re-entry must be considered early and planned into the total program. Chapter 5 addresses how to manage these and other workers' compensation claims effectively.

Professional Ergonomics Evaluation

At times the need for a professional evaluation by a safety engineer trained in human factors may be a cost-justified exercise. A professional ergonomics evaluation is necessary whenever there is a significant increase in sprains/strains or cumulative trauma disorders for a particular task. The purpose of the review is to determine the causal relationship between the injuries and the work task. This is accomplished by evaluating the work methods; work station design; worker posture; tool usage; and materials moved including weight, distance, and frequency.

Once the evaluation is complete, the results are then compared with anthropometric information contained in the National Institute for Occupational Safety and Health (NIOSH) *Work Practices Guide for Manual Lifting* and other studies. A determination is then made of whether administrative, engineering, or some combination of controls need to be implemented. In some cases a simple change in the tool can relieve the stress and prevent cumulative trauma disorders like carpal tunnel syndrome. This type of injury is quite prevalent among food preparation workers and has received a lot of attention, including major fines against the meat-packing industry.

Carpal tunnel syndrome is caused by compression of a nerve that passes through the carpal tunnel, a channel in the wrist. It is often the result of adjacent inflamed tendons or tendon sheaths. There are variations including "trigger finger" syndrome and de Quervain's syndrome, all dealing with different areas of the hands and arms. These are costly injuries because standard treatment involves physical therapy, often surgery and rehabilitation techniques. It appears the primary causes are repetitive hand motions, awkward posture, and mechanical stresses.

In any event, a sound ergonomic evaluation can pay big dividends in the prevention of materials handling accidents and possible fines and legal action.

Small operators may feel they cannot afford this kind of outside consulting cost. The following section provides some advice on what can be done without having to employ a professional ergonomics evaluation.

Sensible Materials Handling Procedures

- Require all kitchen personnel using knives for all preparative work to wear a special woven glove designed to eliminate cuts. Use wire mesh for oyster shucking or the new mechanical machine openers. Additionally, insure that there are sufficient gloves to separate those used with poultry vs. other meats and vegetables. There are simple ways to keep the gloves sanitary and the manufacturers can help.

- Footwear can help prevent strains by providing sound footing for the worker. It is hard to say how many back injuries are related to slipping on floors. Many shoe manufacturers are making slip-resistant footwear (urethane/rubber soles) for kitchen and housekeeping personnel. Insure that they also provide comfort and durability. Banquet housemen, grounds and engineering staff should wear steel-toed footwear. Chapter 12 discusses in detail setting up a footwear program.

- All high traffic doors need a vision panel.

- Aisles should be marked for proper locations for Carter Hoffmans and queen maries.

- Dance floors, tables, platforms and chairs need to be in good repair, free of burrs and splinters. Housemen should wear gloves and work in teams of two.

- When housekeepers make beds, they should do them one side at a time, completing one side entirely before proceeding to the other side. Housekeepers should position their bodies close to the bed with their back rigid when pulling covers on and off.

- Many injuries have resulted when a housekeeper has tried to prevent a housekeeping cart from tipping over or tried to pick a cart up that has tipped over (see Figure 3.8).

- Do not stack materials on top of cart higher than a drinking glass.

- Empty waste and dirty linen bags regularly during the shift.

- Most tipovers are a result of too much weight, and the carpet buckling, tripping, and binding the cart wheels. Be sure carpets are installed correctly and minimize weight.

- Obtain newer carts that have been designed with wider wheel bases, lighter weight and lower handlebars for better maneuverability.

- When cleaning the shower/tub walls have the housekeepers use a long-handled sponge/brush rather than stand on the tub apron and try to wipe the walls down. Even better, use a tall person once or twice a week to wipe down hard-to-reach places.

Figure 3-8. New lightweight plastic linen carts help reduce worker fatigue and susceptibility to strains.

• Purchase goods in smaller and lighter weight packages, for example, buy 50-lb sacks instead of 100-lb sacks of flour.

• Store all items weighing more than 30 lb on shelves at between 30–54 inches above the floor.

• Minimize travel distances for moving materials without use of carts.

• Use two people to move portable bars.

• Use large air-filled wheels on bellman dollies.

• Break down all cases of goods into individual units for storage on shelves.

• Institute a pre-shift "Care For Your Back" program.

These are easy things to accomplish and they will prevent injuries. The employees could easily triple this list of ideas.

NEAR MISSES AND INCIDENT INVESTIGATIONS

When something happens but nobody is hurt or property is not damaged, it tends to be shrugged off. This misses a tremendous opportunity to evaluate people, methods, and systems. The well-known Heinrich law states that for every 330 potential injury-producing accidents, 300 occur with no injury, 29 with minor injuries, and 1 will result in a major injury.

Near misses and incidents must be investigated, discussed, and evaluated in the same manner as if they were accidents involving loss. The reason is simple: One of those near misses will be an accident in the near future and it could result in a major injury. Investigating incidents also provides a measure of how well the accident prevention program is doing. The form of the investigation can range from a discussion at the next employee meeting to an in-depth analysis, depending on the severity of the exposure.

Near misses should be tracked in the same way as accidents to determine the frequency and duration, in order to institute behavioral changes and other corrective actions. Incidents and near misses are simply the people, machines, and the environment telling management where they stand and where they need to go. They are the ultimate feedback.

NEW EMPLOYEE ORIENTATION AND ACCIDENT PREVENTION TRAINING

A direct result of identifying accident causes is the development and implementation of employee training. There are two types of employees: the new employee and the experienced employee. To begin, let us discuss new employee orientation and what should be covered from a loss control point of view.

A new employee orientation typically should be an overview of the company, their benefits, and general expectations. Additionally some of the loss control issues are:

- Fire emergencies and evacuation.
- Accident Prevention Policy and general safety rules.
- What to do in case of an accident or incident.
- Basic security measures.
- QSC and QCB responsibilities and functions.
- Heimlich maneuver.
- Sanitation issues.
- Hazard communications.
- CPR.

Once the employee is assigned to his or her job, the more specific job training takes place with the use of TSAs and other training tools. The orientation training must be documented by placing in their personnel file a copy of a document signed by the employee stating that they received this training.

As discussed for other areas, training of experienced workers can be accomplished at department meetings by using all sorts of resources. Films and videotaped programs are available from the National Safety Council, OSHA, American Hotel and Motel Association, or the National Restaurant Association to but name a few. Additionally manufacturers and distributors of equipment and chemicals are more than willing to attend a meeting to discuss how to handle or use their products properly. There is also a legal obligation to continually retrain employees in accident prevention. For instance, management is required to train employees in basic fire prevention on an annual basis. With the enactment of the Hazard Communication Standard, employees must be trained regularly on the use and hazards of chemicals in the workplace; it is simple training and makes good sense. It continues to reinforce expectations and the correct way of doing the job. As a famous, now deceased, restaurateur/hotelier once said (in paraphrase): "If you take care of your employees, they will take care of the customer and you will make money."

ACCIDENT PREVENTION TRIAD

As Figure 3-2 showed, there are many ways of identifying accident causes and ways of preventing those accidents. By putting all of the elements together we can form an Accident Prevention Triad. Figure 3-9 represents the three key legs of a successful accident prevention program; they are the individual, their behavior, and the environment where they work.

If synchronism is achieved, the legs will remain unbroken and constantly in balance. If any one of the legs changes in length or the angle changes between the legs, our triangle will be broken and an accident will result. By involving people in establishing the behavior and providing the correct environment we cannot only reduce accidents but improve quality and enhance profits.

Accident prevention is a dynamic process of observation, intervention, interaction, and evaluation. However, people must know what to do and have the desire to do it in order for change to occur.

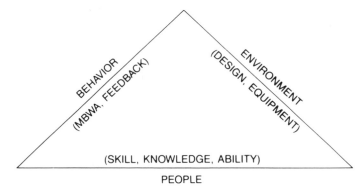

Figure 3-9. The Accident Prevention Triad.

CHAPTER 4

Impact of Security on Accident Prevention

Some years ago, I was involved in a new approach that reorganized the accident prevention efforts at a hotel. This was a classic bottom up approach. The executive committee, primarily the General Manager, was very dissatisfied with the results of his hotel's efforts to curtail and contain accident costs. At one of his executive committee meetings, he tossed his observations of the problem on the table. However, instead of directing the discussion, he introduced everyone to a brainstorming process.

After much discussion, it was clear that the problem was quite complex. However, one theme kept recurring—there was a lack of focus in the program. It lacked a mission and direction. Their first step was to develop a mission:

> To prevent and manage accidents by simple, effective, and efficient methods to control, in accordance with corporate and property guidelines: (1) injury and lost time frequency, (2) financial loss.

During the committee's deliberations, it became apparent that they had to identify someone to get the program off the back burner and move forward.

The original program was formed on the lines of a classic safety structure. Along with this classic structure was the classic failing, which was assigning the function to someone who did not have time or the inclination to push the program. The individual was the Human Resources Manager, but had it been with any other member on the executive committee it would still have failed for the same reasons. When the pressure was on they could not devote the time to manage the program. After a very short but thorough thought process, they achieved consensus on who the proper individual should be to carry the ball forward; that individual was the Security Manager.

But why should this be a good fit? Actually, it was rather simple and logical: Security had the resources available, the most critical being manpower. Also, many of the accident prevention functions were already being performed by the security officers, such as accident and fire inspections and first-aid. The fit seemed natural.

However, accident prevention is a major new responsibility that is integrated into a department already busy with its primary function of security; therefore, how can the employees be expected to rally around the mission? Other concerns also arose: Will corporate headquarters support this deviation from policy? How should the security manager and staff be got up to speed? How should the role be clarified? Where to begin?

I happened to be the corporate safety person for this hotel. One day I received a call from the General Manager about their new concept for accident prevention. He asked me to help them answer their concerns and other questions. Creative thinking should be supported, especially when the idea belongs to the operator. This was a tremendous opportunity to advance the cause of safety from the bottom-up approach. We worked as a team to develop an implementation strategy that included the following:

- Phase-in strategy.
- Role clarification.
- Action steps.
- Structure and responsibilities.
- Procedures for handling guest and employee accidents.
- Revised job descriptions.
- Inspections and floor maintenance program.
- Measurement criteria for success.

I told my boss at corporate headquarters that there was something exciting going on and that we should support the hotel's endeavor, because the concept had the potential for major impact in loss reduction. Everyone agreed that this should be set up as a pilot test program, with myself and the corporate Human Resources Director assigned to help the property implement the program. It took a full 2 years to implement every aspect of the program. However, the impact of this new direction showed immediate results within the first 3 months into the phase-in program.

The pilot program had the following results:

- Employee accident frequency: *down* to 11 vs. 75.
- Lost time frequency: *down* to 0 vs. 16.
- Costs of injuries: *down* 87%.
- Return on investment: 155%.

These were quite dramatic reductions; the General Manager was ecstatic over the results. The program gained the title "The New Loss Control Concept." This program has since been adopted throughout a large segment of that hotel chain, but only where the resources and the right individual was in the security manager position. The results, though they varied because of the liberal workers' compensation benefits of some states, were just as impressive. There was a small problem, which was ensuring qualified people were prepared to backfill these positions when a vacancy occurred. What follows is how to implement this program at your property.

PHASE-IN GUIDELINES

1: Preliminaries

Phase 1 can be broken down into three components: technical knowledge improvement; establishing a plan; and conducting a role clarification.

Technical Knowledge

The Security Manager should be provided with the proper tools. The Security Manager should attend classes to learn the intricacies of safety management. Classes attended should include:

1. A course in the fundamentals of safety management, for example, National Safety Council or American Society of Safety Engineers.
2. Local workers' compensation seminars.
3. Fire safety management course.
4. Management course on consulting skills.
5. Advanced first-aid or emergency medical services certification.

Specialized training should be completed with the corporate safety department on the following topics: accident prevention management; company safety policies; claims management; accident accounting programs.

The Security Manager should then become a member of the American Society of Safety Engineers and work toward achieving an Associate Safety Professional designation.

Once most of the training is complete, the Security Manager begins to transform into a Loss Control Manager.

Establishing the Plan

Now the Loss Control Manager is assigned to take on the mission, to develop a long-range plan including objectives and action steps, and lastly to gain the concurrence of the executive committee to implement the new program. The key areas that need to be addressed in the plan are:

Prevention of accidents (Chapters 1, 2, 3)
Management of employee accidents (Chapter 5)
Management of guest accidents (Chapter 6)

Considering the mission statement, the following is a sample plan by a Loss Control Manager.

Prevention of accidents

1. Institute an Accident Prevention Inspection program as a part of routine security patrol activity as well as formally on a monthly basis by the Loss Control Department.
2. Institute Accident Prevention Work Order Program—a copy to the Loss Control Manager for follow-up.
3. Loss Control Manager to facilitate and develop training programs for entire staff in accident prevention to include:

- New employee orientation.
- New manager orientation.
- First-aid, CPR and Heimlich training for all Loss Control Officers and pool personnel; Heimlich and CPR for all servers.
- Emergency medical services training for Loss Control Manager and Loss Control Supervisors.
- Accident investigation and claims management training.

- Assist department managers with specific departmental training plans.

4. Assist the committees in accident prevention awareness, promotional programs and administer the programs.
5. Assist the Quality Safety Committee chairperson in keeping the committee motivated and focused.
6. Implement a slip and fall prevention program.
7. Implement an ergonomics program for housekeeping, laundry, bellman, and housemen to minimize back injuries.
8. Implement a safe work behavior analysis program.
9. Develop a library of safety materials, literature and films.

Management of employee accidents

1. Security Department to be transformed into a Loss Control Department by:

   - Completing first-aid and CPR training of officers.
   - Completing EMS training of supervisors.
   - Developing a "cool down" approach to injury management (Chapter 5).
   - Training supervisors in basic claims management.
   - Officers completing supplementary accident investigations to management.
   - Administering all property first-aid through a centralized first-aid program.

2. Implement an aggressive claims management program to include:

   - "Cool down" facility (Chapter 10).
   - Injury treatment procedures—decision on need for outside medical care; joint decision between senior first-aider and employee's manager.
   - Completion of State documents by employee's manager and Loss Control Manager.
   - Accident investigation by employee's manager and follow-up by Loss Control Manager.
   - Coordination of all claims handling activity by Loss Control Manager.

- Administration in conjunction with department managers and Human Resources of the "We Care" and Modified Duty programs.

- Development of clinic referral program to control outside medical services and costs.

- Acting as liaison with claims adjusting group.

Management of guest accidents

1. Develop guest accident claims management program to include:

- Loss control to respond to every injury and investigate each accident.

- Establish arrangements for outside medical care.

- Instruct management on proper handling of guest accidents.

- Act as liaison with claims adjusting group.

Other general requirements

1. Update loss control staff job descriptions.
2. Upgrade pay scale of officers and supervisors upon completion of training.
3. After 6-month probationary period, upon successful implementation of the New Loss Control Concept, upgrade Loss Control Manager's salary.
4. Re-write all pertinent policies.
5. General Manager to inform staff of reorganization of the accident prevention program.

The only thing that is missing is a time frame for completing each action step and that's up to you.

Using our classic accident prevention structure discussed in Chapter 2, this new program and strategy is in reality a detailed approach to establishing a stronger Accident Prevention Facilitator by giving that person the resources of the Security and Human Resources departments, to more effectively administrate the accident prevention program for the hotel.

Clarifying Roles

In some facilities the responsibility for accident prevention is in the Human Resources area. Whether or not this is already the case or if a program is just being started, a role clarification needs to be completed.

During this process the Security Manager becomes an *ex officio* member of the executive committee (in some hotels this may already be the case). This is an important step, so that constant dialogue is maintained with the executive committee to keep the program in focus.

Figure 4-1 is a role clarification document that has been completed as an example. Note how the form is structured with the tasks on one side and the responsible position listed in the other column. In each box is a letter corresponding to the role that individual is to take relating to the task. For instance, the task is: Assist department managers in developing and implementing employee accident prevention training. The roles for each position are noted as: the Human Resources Manager *approves*, the Loss Control Manager *initiates and does*. The line managers also *do* the training while the human resources staff *do* the recordkeeping. This document specifies who is on first, second, and third bases, and who is the pitcher.

Once the role clarification has been completed and we have our plan approved, phase 2 begins.

2: Implementation of the Employee Injury Management Program

1. Complete first-aid and CPR training.
2. Implement the centralized first-aid program.
3. Put together all the components of a "cool down" and first-aid room.
4. Set up programs with the medical clinic, claims adjusters, and Human Resources Department.
5. Draft policies and procedures for the handling of employee and guest injuries and illnesses.

This part of the New Loss Control Concept has a profound effect on cutting the costs of medical treatment. It is also the means to gaining control of claims handling which is implemented in phase 4.

Task/Responsibilities	HRM	DL/C	MGR	HR	L/CO
1. Assist the QSB and QSC in promotional campaigns and other administrative activities including dissemination of training materials and other committee information.	AD, A	AD, I	C, AD	D	
2. Provide guidance to the committees by monitoring the effectiveness of all programs and reporting on the status of all activities.	AD	D	AD		
3. Assist the QSB in establishing recognition and incentive programs.	A	I, D	AD		
4. Conduct new employee loss control training to include work rules, policies, entitlements, security and fire prevention.	C	D	AD		
5. Monitor new employee training within each department to ensure all Task Safety Analysis and proper materials handling training have been completed.	C	A	I, D	AD	
6. Assist department managers in establishing a new and existing employee training program.	AD	A	D	AD	
7. Train all managers in all loss control activities and policies.	A	I, D	AD	AD	
8. Maintain a library of loss control materials for training and promotional activities.	AD	I	AD	D	
9. Insure all committee members are identified by a special name tag and all property personnel trained in CPR and/or first aid are also noted by a special name tag.	A	I	AD	D	
10. Provide the General Manager with sufficient data and agenda in order to effectively conduct Quality Safety Board meetings.		I, D			
11. Maintain a Loss Control Bulletin Board.	AD	I	AD	D	
12. Insure emergency ambulance, police and fire department numbers are posted in all departments and at all non-guest direct dial telephones.	AD	I, D	AD	AD	AD

Figure 4-1

Task/Responsibilities	HRM	DL/C	MGR	HR	L/CO
13. Insure the meeting minutes of all safety committees are processed.	AD	I		D	
14. Maintain an adequate number of trained CPR and first aiders.	C	I, D	AD	AD	D
15. Maintain first aid supplies for all areas. Establish an inventory system to control stock and insure that first aid logs are maintained.	C	I, A	D		D
16. Set up centralized first aid unit to include:					
a. All Loss Control Officers trained in at least a 40 hour first aid and 8 hour CPR course.	AD	I, A	A		D
b. Insure one qualified LCO on duty to run unit.	AD	I, A	A		D
c. Set up "cool down" procedure and room.	C	I, A	A		D
d. Provide immediate first aid treatment and/or arrange for emergency transport.	AD	I, A			D
e. Investigate all accidents and incidents.	AD	AD	I, D		D
f. Make decision on need for outside medical attention.	AD	A, C	C, A		D
17. Administer the We Care and Modified Duty programs for all injured employees.	C	C	I, D	AD	
18. Compile and maintain statistical data on accident frequency, cause and cost in order to identify trends and establish preventative programs.	AD	I, D	I, D	AD	
19. Where required assist management in obtaining food handlers' certificates.	AD	C	I, D	D	
20. Maintain all required federal, state employee injury records.	AD		I, D	AD	
21. Process reports and maintain records of all auto accidents.	AD		I, D	AD	
22. Administer all workers' compensation claims made against the property. Provide the claims adjuster with all documentation required for each case.	AD		I, D	AD	D
23. Insure Manager's Accident Investigation Report is completed.	AD	A	I, D	AD	D

Figure 4-1 continued.

Task/Responsibilities	HRM	DL/C	MGR	HR	L/CO
24. Assist the Chief of Fire Emergency Organization in establishing and maintaining a complete emergency response team.	AD	AD		D	
25. Assist in training all employees in fire prevention, fire extinguisher use and evacuation procedures.	AD	C	D		
26. Establish written security procedures for all types of emergencies, i.e. fire, power failure, water, gas rupture and natural disasters.	AD	I, D	AD	AD	AD
27. Develop and maintain written security procedures.	AD	I, D	AD	AD	AD
28. Formulate a bomb threat plan to include: training, search procedures, local bomb squad procedures.	AD	I, D	AD	AD	AD
29. Be familiar with state and local penal codes. Maintain coordination with local authorities on methods of arrest and elimination of undesirable people from the property.	AD	I, D	AD	AD	D
30. Accompany federal, state and local officials on inspections and maintain any required documents.	D	D	D		
31. Assist in formulation of replies to official inspections and act on behalf of the property at all hearings.	AD	D	A		
32. Loss Control Department to conduct a formal Loss Control inspection each month.	AD	I	AD		
33. Establish and monitor the Accident Prevention Work Order and Hot Line programs.	C	I, D	D		D
34. Each Department to complete a physical hazard inspection on a weekly basis and issue APWO as required.	AD	A	I, D		D

Figure 4-1 *continued.*

Task/Responsibilities	HRM	DL/C	MGR	HR	L/CO
35. Manage the guest accident management program.					
a. Treat for first aid.	AD	D	D		D
b. Arrange for outside medical treatment.	AD	AD	D		
c. Arrange for payment on initial medical treatment.	AD	C	A		
d. Write accident and supplemental reports and notify adjuster.	AD	C	I, D		D
e. Implement guest "We Care" program.	AD	C	D, A		
f. Maintain files.		D		D	
36. Implement and maintain driver screening program.	A	C	I	D	
37. Implement and maintain ergonomics program.	AD	I, D	AD, D	D	
38. Be a member of all safety committees.	D	D	D		
39. Implement slip, trip and fall prevention program.	AD	I, A	D		D
40. Implement Behavior Analysis program to track safe work habits.	AD	I, A	D	D	D

Figure 4-1. A sample completed. HRM = Human Resources Manager; DL/C = Director of Loss Control; MGR = manager; HR = Human Resources staff; L/CO = Loss Control Officer. A, approve; D, do; C, concur; I, initiate; AD, advise.

3: Implementation of Loss Control Roles and Responsibilities

Phase 3 is another action phase. The Loss Control Manager has completed his own personal training on basic safety management techniques and claims administration. At this point it is time for the Loss Control Manager to assume full responsibility for the handling of employee and guest claims and the role of Accident Prevention Facilitator.

Now is the time to revise the job descriptions for the Loss Control staff. The security responsibilities remain the same as before; however, the changes involve adding the new accident prevention responsibilities to each position as follows.

Loss Control Manager

- Member of the Quality Safety Board, an advisory member to the Quality Safety Committee, and an Assistant Chief of the Fire Emergency Team.
- As the Accident Prevention Facilitator, acts as a resource person to all the committees, executive committee and line managers.

General duties

1. Assist the property in promotional campaigns and other administrative activities, including dissemination of accident prevention materials, development of all accident prevention policies and related information.
2. Provide guidance to the Quality Safety Board and Quality Safety Committee.
3. Insure minutes of all committees are routed and discussed at all individual department meetings.
4. Conduct new manager and hourly employee accident prevention orientation.
5. Oversee TSA program to ensure proper employee departmental training.
6. Maintain accident prevention promotional resources.
7. Assist department managers in targeting and developing specific training needs and implement behavior analysis program.
8. Administer the Hazard Communications Standard program.
9. Establish and administer the claims management program.

10. Administer the ergonomics program.
11. Ensure all emergency numbers are posted in various locations.
12. Administer the behavior analysis program.
13. Maintain an accident prevention bulletin board.
14. Manage the budget for all accident prevention activities.

Recordkeeping and reporting

1. Monitor all workers' compensation and guest claims.
2. Monitor the "We Care" and modified duty programs for all employee accidents.
3. Insure a manager's accident investigation report and state first report of injury is completed on every incident and accident, with all accidents reported to the claims adjusting group.
4. Insure each modified duty job offered is in writing and all "We Care" contacts properly documented.
5. Insure every guest accident has been thoroughly investigated and properly reported to the claims adjusting group.
6. Maintain statistical data on accident frequency, causes and costs in order to identify trends and measure program effectiveness.
7. Maintain all Material Safety Data Sheets (MSDS) for current and prior chemical use.
8. Maintain OSHA recordkeeping mandates.

First-aid

1. Establish and monitor the centralized first-aid program.
2. Maintain an adequate number of first-aid, CPR, and Emergency Medical Services trained personnel.
3. Maintain adequate first-aid supplies and oxygen. Conduct periodic inventory of small satellite department first-aid kits.
4. Insure a first-aid log of all supplies used is maintained at each satellite station.

Inspections

1. Administer the Accident Prevention Tour program.
2. Conduct a formal accident prevention inspection of the entire property once a month.
3. Conduct a behavior analysis monitoring check-up.

4. Accompany federal, state, and local officials and safety professionals on inspections of the property.
5. Assist the General Manager and Engineering Manager in the formulation of replies to inspections as needed.
6. Maintain files of all accident prevention-related inspections.
7. Assist the engineering manager in fire safety inspections.

Fire emergency planning
1. Assist the engineering manager in establishing and maintaining a complete Fire Emergency Team.
2. Assist in training property staff in fire safety and evacuation procedures.

Loss Control Supervisor
- May be a member of the Quality Safety Committee and is a member of the Fire Emergency Team.
- In the absence of the Loss Control Manager, assumes all responsibilities associated with the accident prevention program.
- The primary function is to assist the Loss Control Manager in running the Loss Control Department.

General duties
1. Assist the Loss Control Manager in all loss control procedures.
2. Verify compliance with hotel accident prevention policies.
3. Observe and report any unsafe behavior or conditions.
4. Assist in the behavior analysis monitoring program.
5. Assist the training department in proper handling of security incidents to minimize potential injuries.
6. Maintain an Emergency Medical Services or Advanced First-Aid certification.

Reporting and recordkeeping
1. Insure all required reports are completed for employee incidents and injuries including:

> Manager's accident investigation report
> First report of injury
> Medical treatment authorization
> Refer to Loss Control Manager for modified duty and "We Care"

2. Insure all required reports regarding incidents involving guests are completed and forwarded to the claims adjuster.
3. Verify satellite first-aid logs are being maintained.

First-aid

1. Insure all officers are first-aid and CPR trained.
2. Maintain "cool down" first-aid room in ready condition.
3. Make decisions on treating and/or sending injured employees to the outside clinic.
4. Maintain all satellite first-aid kits.

Inspections

1. Insure all officers are conducting accident prevention inspections as a part of their normal patrol.
2. Conduct a daily accident prevention inspection on a rotational department basis.

Fire emergency planning

1. Know all fire emergency procedures and be able to assume the assistant chief's position.
2. Adhere to all fire safety policies and correct and/or report any violations.

Loss Control Officer

- To make continuous patrols of the property, insuring the safety and security of the assets, employees, and guests. A member of the Fire Emergency Team and possibly a member of the Quality Safety Committee.

General duties

1. Note any safety hazards and either correct or report to appropriate personnel.
2. Maintain first-aid and CPR certification.
3. Perform first-aid services as necessary.
4. Conduct accident prevention inspections as a part of routine patrol.
5. Complete all required incident reports for employee and guest accidents and incidents.
6. Assist hotel during disasters or emergencies as required.
7. Know and perform all duties according to the Fire Emergency Team policies.

When implementing this program it is necessary not to lose sight of the fact that other areas in the hotel also have responsibilities for accident prevention. Human Resources still has a very important role to play. Theirs is a support function that includes:

1. Maintaining employee records, for example, TSA.
2. Assisting managers in coaching and counselling for unsafe behavior.
3. Maintaing and displaying all required federal, state, and local posters and other materials.
4. Assisting the Loss Control Manager in administering the "We Care" and modified duty programs.
5. Providing support for QSB and QSC.
6. Pre-screening of materials handling positions.

Another critical role or opportunity for the Human Resources Manager is in working with the Quality Safety Committee. Here the Human Resources professional can address employee issues that deal with the quality of the work life. He or she can also help to guide the committee in group dynamics and problem-solving skills. The Quality Safety Committee is not just another safety committee, it should be an all-employee forum to (1) improve the quality of the operation, (2) prevent accidents, (3) reduce turnover, and (4) improve customer service, all of which will improve the bottom line and increase profits.

4: Prevention of Accidents

In all the other phases we concentrated on gaining technical knowledge and implementing the claims management effort. Phase 4 is the last piece of the puzzle, when the Loss Control Manager assumes the administration of the prevention aspects of the total Loss Control Program.

One of the first things the Loss Control Manager must do is assess all current efforts in accident prevention and complete a trend analysis. This can be accomplished through sitting down with each department head and conducting a self-audit or inventory of activities as well as a behavior analysis of each operation. From this joint analysis a plan should be developed that is tailored to that manager's needs. This would include:

1. Identifying training topics.
2. Supplying training materials.
3. Tracking the training efforts.
4. Identifying physical requirements for employees to fit the job, and implementing back injury prevention.
5. Setting up an inspection and accident prevention work order program.
6. Identifying QSC members and review roles.
7. Setting up TSA program on targeted job tasks.
8. Identifying and setting up appropriate hazard communication information.
9. Establishing behavior-monitoring program.
10. Reviewing all jobs for special needs such as hand, eye, and/or hearing protection.

This is probably the most challenging phase, because along with everything else that competes for that manager's time, asking them to integrate all of these programs will be tough. However, doing a joint analysis should target those aspects of an accident prevention program that will give the greatest return on the investment of time.

Once the analysis is complete for each department, the Loss Control Manager should assume all of the responsibilities of the Accident Prevention Facilitator plus those unique to the New Loss Control Concept. There is only one other phase left.

5: Measuring Results

This is where "the proof of the pudding is in the eating." It also provides the program insight into focusing and targeting the accident prevention efforts. This is a joint responsibility between the Loss Control Manager and the Controller.

Measuring the success of your program is critical to rewarding performance and knowing whether you are on track and making realistic gains or losing ground. It also acts as a motivator to push management's "hot button."

In conclusion, this program is not for everyone or for every facility. The good thing about the concept is that you can implement a portion of the program, such as the centralized first-aid, and achieve some remarkable results. Even for a small property with no security manager, many of the ideas and concepts can be easily translated into the owner's or line manager's responsibilities.

By causing a marriage between accident prevention and security you not only increase the value and professionalism of that department but cut your losses to boot. The key is the right manager in the role of Accident Prevention Facilitator, and support by the General Manager and commitment to the concept.

Get people involved; let them have a piece of the action. You will develop ownership and support for your goals among all of the employees.

CHAPTER 5

How to Cut Your Workers' Compensation Losses

Most people do not even know that they are covered by their employer for work-related injuries and illnesses. It is surprising how many managers do not realize that they are covered and what their entitlements are under the law. If a secretary is sent out to pick up something, even on her way home, and she is involved in an automobile accident, this is considered compensatable in many states. Even the owner is covered by the workers' compensation policy.

Workers' compensation laws were designed to provide a means of handling occupational disabilities. In earlier days, up to 1910, if someone was injured on the job, the only means of recouping the monetary loss was through suing the employer. In those days, compared with today, the pendulum swung in the opposite direction as regards litigation. The injured party had to follow the well-established common law principle that an employer was only responsible for death and injuries of employees resulting from the employer's negligence. This was costly for the employee and took considerable time.

In many instances, the injured person was unable to recover any damages. Then, in 1911, the first true workers' compensation law came into being in Wisconsin. It took until 1948 before every state had enacted some form of worker protection legislation. The sole purpose of having workers' compensation is to take care of the employee expeditiously; in return the employee gives up the right to suit against his employer.

Today, with the economic and public policy changes that have occurred, increases in benefits and scope have received mixed reactions. However, the basic concepts have not changed. Labor says that the benefits are insufficient while employers are critical of the system for covering injuries and illnesses they believe to be non-job-related. We are also seeing more and more involvement of attorneys and some third-party litigation, especially against manufacturers for defective products that may have caused an employee's injury.

OBJECTIVES OF THE LAW

Since its inception, the fundamental objectives of the workers' compensation law have not changed:

- Provide prompt care and medical benefits to the injured worker, with some income flow to the injured worker and his or her dependants.
- Provide a direct remedy for the restoration of earnings capacity and return to productive work.
- Relieve the burden from public and private charities.
- Eliminate payment of fees to attorneys and time-consuming trials and appeals for personal injury litigation.
- Encourage employers' interest in safety.
- Promote the study of the causes of accidents to reduce preventable human suffering (U.S. Chamber of Commerce, 1987).

The first two objectives are considered to be the most important. But, in reality, they tend to work against each other unless effective claims controls are in effect. These two objectives also describe, in general, the basic entitlements of each worker under the law.

Entitlements

Simply put, entitlements are those benefits that are provided for under the law. During 1988 over $40 billion was paid out in workers' compensation. Specifically, the benefits provided were:

- Cash benefits that replace loss of income during the disability.
- Medical benefits, which covers 100% of the medical costs and with no time limit.
- Rehabilitation benefits, which involve both medical and vocational rehabilitation.

Cash Benefits

There are four classifications of disability used to determine the amount and extent of income replacement:

1. *Temporary total* covers the period of time when the injured employee is totally disabled but will recover to return to their normal work. Benefits are paid as a percentage of their weekly income. In many states this is usually 2/3 of the average weekly wage, not to exceed some maximum value.

2. *Permanent total* is paid when the employee is unable ever to return to gainful employment. Benefits are determined as a percentage of wages similarly to temporary total disability.

3. *Temporary partial* assumes a physical condition that is temporary disability although the worker is capable of light duties.

4. *Permanent partial* is divided into two areas: scheduled and nonscheduled benefits. Scheduled benefits are applied to a specific loss or loss of use, for instance an amputated part of the body, and paid over a fixed period of time. Nonscheduled benefits are based on a wage-loss replacement percentage. The percentage applies to the difference between wages earned before and after the injury.

Another benefit involves a specific payment made to survivors for the work-related death of a worker. It is intended to furnish income replacement for the family. As is true with all of these benefits, they vary from state to state and it is vital to check the relevant state law.

In order to obtain disability benefits, most states require a waiting period. This serves the purpose of discouraging would-be malingerers. Generally, waiting periods last from 3 to 7 days. The disabled employee recovers the lost wages for the waiting period only after a period of time, for example, 10 days. Again, each state varies and it is necessary to consult state laws.

Medical Benefits

Every state requires employers to provide prompt, immediate medical care for every injured employee. There are no restrictions such as waiting times or degree of disability. Coverage is 100% of the entire costs including hospitalization, prescriptions, and specialists.

A major issue concerning medical benefits is the selection of the physician. Almost half the states give the employer the right to specify treating physicians. Among the rest, employees have the right to select the doctor. From a claims management perspective, it is obvious that the chances for abuse and the costs are higher whenever you give up control. When the company does not control the medical selection, it is very difficult to enact modified duty and other programs to contain claims costs.

Rehabilitation

Rehabilitation is applying medical and vocational assistance to make the injured worker as whole as possible. Fortunately, cases requiring rehabilitation are in the minority, but one should not be complacent because this type of injury does occur in hotels and restaurants. Even when these workers receive effective medical care, so that they can eventually return to gainful employment, their lives are changed permanently. The unfortunate reality is that some of these people never return to work because of their disability.

Rehabilitation is a continuation of care from the initial treatment of the injury. Sometimes it may involve only physical therapy or it could involve training and fitting of artificial appliances.

Vocational rehabilitation is giving the injured employee a new skill to allow him or her to be productive again. I know of cases where the person was sent to obtain a degree in order to obtain employment in a totally new field.

Many insurance companies have access to public and private rehabilitation centers and some even own them. These facilities are a means of total medical management for seriously injured workers.

Second Injury Fund

Many states have established second injury funds for the express purpose of keeping permanently disabled workers employable. The fund pays for any care needed should an aggravation of a preexisting condition occur on the job. In this way the new employer does not assume the liability for a prior disability. It is easier in some states than in others to collect from the fund. Employers should never give up on the idea of accessing the fund, because they are paying for it through a pooling of funds from all compensation plans. It amounts to a sort of a tax on their premiums.

THE LAW: WHAT IS COVERED AND WHAT IS NOT

In general the basic statute is intended to cover only those personal injuries caused by an accident that *arises out of or in the course of employment*. Most states have included occupational diseases in the basic statute. Psychological difficulties such as the situation in which employees claim stress as an illness are only covered in a very few states. However, the law does cover a psychological malady arising out of, say, an armed robbery or sexual assault on the job.

For the right of full coverage on the job, with a type of "no fault" provision, the worker gives up the right to sue the employer. This is called the *exclusive remedy* doctrine. However, workers' compensation benefits may not be the only remedy available to the employee. The injured worker may file a liability suit against another worker or the manufacturer of the equipment, or survivors may institute an action against a third party. Recently, even the exclusive remedy doctrine was usurped when suit was filed against an employer for committing an intentional tort* that resulted in the employee being injured. Additionally, in many states it is illegal to fire an employee for filing a compensation claim. The lesson is to know the state laws before a problem arises.

INCENTIVES FOR ACCIDENT PREVENTION

Our last two objectives deal with encouraging an employer to apply basic safety management techniques to reduce workers' compensation claims and promote the study of accident causes. Generally speaking, the only monetary incentive is being experienced-rated, retrospectively rated, or self-insured.

Experience rating is a technique used by insurance company underwriters. A range of premium costs is determined by the insurance company for general liability and property insurance. The range has a high end and a low end dollar value for each policy. Where required the range is filed and approved by the state insurance commission. Experience rating provides a degree

---

* See p. 110 for definition of this legal term.

of flexibility to the underwriter for debiting or crediting an insured company on their individual policy on the basis of that company's prior loss experience. For workers' compensation it works a little differently: The state regulates an *experience modification factor* that can be applied to the premium and is based on an individual company's loss experience. If you are *self-insured*, then you pay an initial cost up to your retention level and then insurance applies thereafter. Most small businesses are rated as a straight figure charged per $100 of payroll. Here the incentive is to avoid becoming an assigned risk, which costs additional premium dollars over the base cost.

Remember that the premium includes costs for loss control services from the insurance carrier. Take advantage of those services, invite their representative in to help establish a program or conduct a seminar on employee safety.

Given this basic law, how are costs minimized? Even if everything is done to keep people from getting hurt accidents do and will happen. As Figure 5-1 portrays, once an accident has

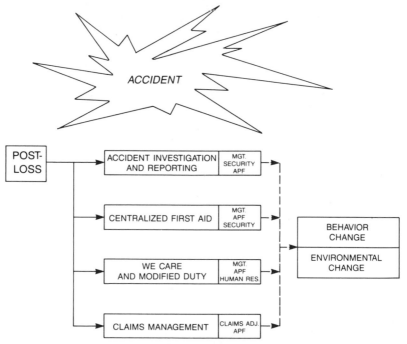

Figure 5-1. The activities and programs that need to be implemented after an accident has occurred.

occurred, we are at the no turning back point of *Post-Loss*. The emphasis now is towards working to minimize accident losses. There are two phases to control Post-Loss: (1) injury management and (2) disability management.

To cut costs, you must have control from the moment the accident occurs until the employee returns to work at their normal duties. If at any time that control is lost, claims costs will triple.

INJURY MANAGEMENT

Centralized First-Aid

This program in itself can significantly reduce workers' compensation costs and operational costs for first-aid supplies. Every facility in the organization should have this program no matter what size or number of employees.

Step 1. Identify and train sufficient staff so that each shift has at least one advanced first-aid or emergency medical first responder trained individual. OSHA mandates an employer to insure that there is an adequately trained person (or persons) available to render first-aid and also that adequate first-aid supplies are readily available for emergency use. For the small concern, it should be the owner/operator/manager. Otherwise it should be the manager/supervisor on duty; or with the New Loss Control Concept it should be the security staff. Also, some additional training is necessary on the proper paperwork that must be filled out regarding every injury including:

State form for first report of injury
Medical authorization for outside treatment
Manager's accident investigation report
Security incident report

Most of these reports are a manager's responsibility except the security report. However, the first-aid responder needs a first-hand knowledge to assist the manager, especially if the manager is new.

Step 2. Set up a first-aid room. This should be a dedicated space with a sink, hot and cold water, good lighting, a large well-stocked industrial first-aid kit, clean linens, and examination table (if space permits) and/or chairs. If there is enough space, there should be a separate room off the first-aid room to serve as a "cool down" room. In a small operation with no space available, the next best thing is the owner/manager's office. One other special item required is an emergency responder's kit for responding to emergency situations in which the employee should not move or be moved. This requires a judgment to be made and even someone with good first-aid training should always be conservative. To move a seriously injured person can be disastrous: keep them comfortable until emergency medical services arrive.

Step 3. The unit is ready to start operation. The designated First-Aid Responder is contacted immediately upon the first indication of any employee injury or illness. This person responds to the scene of the accident and takes charge until a higher level of medical response arrives, if applicable. Otherwise, the next step in the process is implemented.

"Cool Down" Process

I first used this process in my early safety days when my job was handling the safety program for a medium-sized general contractor. The contractor was a union contractor, so implementation of various claims management techniques proved difficult at first, but once the value and genuine concern for the workers' health and well being was demonstrated, there was no more resistance.

What is the "cool down" process and how does it relate to the contractor? I illustrate it through an example from my first-hand experience in using this process to control and manage the injury. A worker came into the job trailer with his hand bleeding and a little banged up. When people are injured they go into a shock because the body is putting up a natural defense. At one time there would have been little concern for the employee and he would have been told to go to the clinic without a second thought, or worse to "get back to work." This would not alleviate the concern or the shock and would be a waste of money. In such a situation the thing to do is administer first-aid and talk to the man to take his mind off the injury. Use the opportunity to begin gathering information for reports. The significant action involves two things: letting the worker rest for at least 15–20 minutes, and alleviating his concern by assuring him that if he felt worse over the course of the next 24 hours he would go to the best medical facility around. But the basic advice is let's wait and see. Over the course of the rest of the day and the next morning, his condition should be checked and he should be provided with a medical authorization before leaving the shift with advice along the lines: "This is just in case you have any problems tonight, and see me first thing in the morning." In this case the man was up to date on immunization shots; the injury was not serious enough to require sutures and if the swelling had persisted he could have been sent for evaluation immediately. The lesson is that many cases do not have to go to the clinic immediately and many not at all. A lot of injuries can be effectively handled on the property.

This is "cool down"; in a hotel, motel, or restaurant the process is no different. "Cool down" is the next step after first-aid is administered in an effective injury-management program. At this point, if nothing else is done, there is a guaranteed reduction in claims costs, especially for the self-insured. But this is only the beginning in effective claims management, especially in controlling the high-value claims.

Choosing Outside Medical Care Wisely

Even with a top-notch first-aid program some injuries will require the attention of a physician. Selection of a medical provider is a critical element of injury management, especially for the control of medical costs in potential high-value claims such as those involving back injuries.

As stated earlier, some states allow the employer to direct the employee only to their physicians. Take full advantage of this situation. Other states give the employee the right to select medical care. However, there is no law against recommending a medical facility to the employee. The next step is to find a provider.

The first thing is to contact the claims office in the local area. They will have a complete listing of conservative, reasonably priced, yet excellent medical practitioners. The list should include a general practitioner, an orthopedic specialist, a chiropractor, and a 24-hour clinic or emergency room.

In each of these cases, the Accident Prevention Facilitator, who is now acting as claims coordinator, should visit each physician and clinic to discuss overall injury and disability management programs and insure that the facilities are of top quality.

The workforce must be educated in proper notification of

injuries, procedures to be followed, and who provides the outside care. This "panel" of physicians should be posted throughout the facility.

Implementing the Decision on Care

The injured employee is cooling down. Out of earshot the First-Aid Responder and the employee's manager are discussing the preliminary "survey" of the extent of the injury. During this time the decision for outside medical attention is made. If the manager and the First-Aid Responder do not agree or are indecisive, outside medical attention should be sought. If it is decided that outside attention is not necessary at this time, then a second decision must be made about whether the employee returns to regular duties or modified duties, or goes home for the rest of the day and is fully compensated for that shift. Whichever decision is taken it must be explained to the employee and they must be told that they will be followed up regularly to see how things are going. At this point the manager should complete the state-required First Report of Injury and Manager's Accident Investigation form (Figure 5-2). Decide whether it is an "incident" or "accident"; this will alert the Accident Prevention Facilitator to the nature of the claim. The Reports must be turned into the Accident Prevention Facilitator within 24 hours of the accident. Also, the manager is to provide a brief description of any temporary modified duty that was instituted. A follow-up investigation will then be completed by the Accident Prevention Facilitator along with the manager and employee to insure that a sound prevention effort has been put in place. Should the Accident Prevention Facilitator be on duty at the time of the injury, he or she should be involved in each step of the process and assist the manager as needed. For a small operator all that is required is completion of the state workers' compensation first report of injury. OSHA accepts this report in lieu of completing its Form 100. However, a multi-site company should use the Manager's Accident Investigation Report form to supplement the state form. This extra piece of paperwork is designed to aid developing specific data for trend analysis as well as to force the manager to complete an investigation and develop corrective actions. Remember that OSHA requires that a Form 200 log and a Form 100 or an acceptable equivalent be maintained of all recordable injuries, but this is not a trend analysis. Whether you

MANAGER'S ACCIDENT INVESTIGATION REPORT

STATUS: [] Incident
            [] Accident

PROPERTY: DATE:
ADDRESS: DEPT.:

EMPLOYEE DATA

NAME:	SOC.SEC.:
HOME ADDRESS:	HIRE DATE:
TELEPHONE:	POSITION:
SEX:	TIME IN POSITION:

INCIDENT/ACCIDENT DATA

DATE OF INJURY:	LOCATION OCCURRED:
TIME OF DAY:	WITNESSES:
DESCRIBE WHAT HAPPENED:	

TREND ANALYSIS DATA

Slips and Falls

Surface Type (check one)	Location (check one)	Conditions (check applicable)
[] Quarry Tile	[] Level Surface (indoors)	[] Water
[] Seamless Epoxy	[] Stairs (indoors)	[] Food Debris
[] Unglazed Ceramic tile	[] Ramps (indoors)	[] Grease/Oil
[] Glazed Ceramic tile	[] Sidewalks	[] Uneven Surface
[] Smooth Concrete	[] Stairs (outdoors)	[] Ice/Snow
[] Rough Concrete	[] Ramps (outdoors)	[] Threshold
[] Vinyl Tile/Sheet Floor	[] Level Surface (outdoors)	[] Objects
[] Marble/Stone	[] Other (specify)_____	[] Other (specify)_____
[] Carpet		
[] Asphalt		
[] Dirt/Grass		
[] Wood		
[] Other (specify)_____		

Figure 5-2. Sample Manager's Accident Investigation Report form that has been designed to assist the intended analysis while focusing the manager on identifying preventative solutions.

```
                            Materials Handling
Type (check one)                          Equipment or Object (check one)
[] Weight a Factor (strains, sprains)     [] Knife
[] Weight not a Factor (cuts, puncture, bruise) [] Wheeled Cart
[] Struck by Object not Carried           [] Tables
[] Struck Against Object                  [] Dance Floor
                                          [] Platforms
                                          [] Other (specify)_____
```

PREVENTION ANALYSIS

```
Causes (check applicable)   Preventative Solution    Date        Who
[] Physical Hazard          1.
[] Unsafe Work Outcome      2.
[] Job Training             3.
                            4.
```

MEDICAL DATA

```
Treatment Status (check applicable)   Other
[] First Aid
[] In House Medical                   _____
[] Outside Physician/Clinic           Physician/Clinic/Hospital
[] No Lost Time                       _____
[] Lost Time (number of days ____)    Address
[] Fatal Injury
```

RESPONSIBILITY

```
_____
Supervisor                        Date


_____
Department Head/Executive         Date


_____
Accident Prevention Facilitator   Date
```

Figure 5-2 *continued.*

are a multi-site or single-site operation, you should track your accident experience and try to uncover trends for which corrective actions can be developed. In a headquarters with a few or many facilities, the Accident Prevention Facilitator could be a staff person to serve all sites or a specialized claims coordinator.

If outside medical attention appears necessary, the following steps should be taken.

1. Complete a Medical Authorization Form (Figure 5-3) and hand it to the employee before they leave the facility. Next instruct the employee to check in with the Accident Prevention Facilitator and/or their manager when they return, or to call should a problem arise. Additionally, they must return the bottom portion of the form before they will be allowed to start work.

2. If at all possible provide transportation to and from the medical provider. Be sure to contact the facility prior to sending the employee and reinforce the fact the center must call you with the diagnosis whenever lost time is anticipated or when modified duty must be implemented.

3. If modified duty is necessary, the Accident Prevention Facilitator and the manager get together to establish a modified duty job that will not aggravate the injury. If the employee desires to go home or the clinic instructs them to rest for the day, pay them for the remainder of the shift and let them go home. This single act pays more dividends than you can imagine. If the physician says bed rest for three days to a week, compensation will not be paid due to the waiting period. This can be explained to the employee and they can decide whether they would like to use their sick or vacation leave to help in compensating their brief time off. It is very important not to forget to call the employee each day to see how they are doing. If you find that you are facing an extended disability, where temporary total disability applies, your disability management program must swing into full gear.

4. The manager completes the First Report of Injury and Manager's Accident Investigation Form and turns the forms into the claims coordinator or Accident Prevention Facilitator.

In-House Medical Unit, "A Step Beyond"

In my work experience with a major hotel chain, I designed and developed one of the first on-site complete occupational health medical units in a hotel for that chain. This facility was unique;

MEDICAL AUTHORIZATION FORM

To Doctor _____

Address _____

Employee _____

Soc. Sec. _____

Date Injured _____

This form signed by the Employer is your authority to render treatment for the named employee in accordance with the provisions of and under the conditions described by the Workers' Compensation Act. Your bill for all services, in accordance with the Act, along with this form may be forward to:

Employer _____

Address _____

ATTENTION

The XYZ Company has a We Care Program that includes modified duty. We offer light work to our injured employees with no loss in wages based upon your restrictions. Job descriptions which accommodate the infirmity will be furnished upon request.

PLEASE DO NOT AUTHORIZE TIME OFF FROM WORK WITHOUT NOTIFYING THE EMPLOYER

Employer Contact _____

Telephone Number _____

----- ---------- ---------- ---------- ---------- ---------- ---------- ---------- ---------- ---------- -----

MEDICAL TREATMENT RELEASE

Employer _____

Employee _____

Date Injured _____

Your employee was treated by me for a work related injury on the above data and is hereby released:

○ For Normal Duties
○ For Modified Duty
With these restrictions: _____

_____

_____

_____

Effective Date _____

Physician Signature _____

EMPLOYEE MUST DELIVER THIS FORM TO THE MANAGER BEFORE RETURNING TO WORK

Figure 5-3. A sample Medical Authorization form that authorizes an employee to seek outside medical care as well as alerting management to modified duty requirements from the physician.

it was not the earlier situation in which there was a house physician at some hotels and resorts.

When I first put the program down on paper, it indicated a 70 percent return on investment. In actual practice the unit far surpassed that figure and provided so many side-benefits that facilities were opened across the country. Some of the side-benefits included:

- Reduced turnover and absenteeism.
- Creation of an employee benefit.
- Preventative health care, which in turn prevented injuries.
- Improved morale.
- Counseling and referral services.

The list can go on and on. With today's attention focused on reducing health care costs, one of the new control programs is "Wellness." How better to execute this type of program than through the medical unit.

How does one set up a unit and when is it justified? In Chapter 10 there is a basic design for an in-house medical unit. The very first one I designed and opened was located within a 1500-room hotel. The history of that facility demonstrates that a medical unit consisting of nurse's office, waiting area, treatment room, "cool down" or rest area, and a small bathroom can be cost-effective for 700 rooms or more or for a major resort complex. When there are several properties owned within a metropolitan area, this unit can provide various services to all units, thus spreading the cost. For the small operator and hotels of fewer than 700 rooms, the cost of an occupational medical unit on site is obviously not justified. However, some of the same concepts of a centralized first-aid, discussed under Injury Management, can be applied. In this situation the owner/operator is the Accident Prevention Facilitator, the Claims Coordinator, and the first-aider all rolled up into one person.

Once the unit has been designed into the property, it has to be got operational.

1. *Establish an operating budget.* Typical equipment start-up costs range from $5,000 to $7,000. This figure includes all medical supplies, examination table, scale, blood pressure tester, oxygen, lights, and a cot. It is wise not to purchase the equipment until a lead occupational health nurse has been hired, and that is the next step.

A study I conducted showed that 95 percent of the accidents in a typical hotel occur between the hours of 7:30 a.m. to around 10:00 p.m. This is common sense—the greatest potential for injury is around the busiest times of the day. On this basis, staffing of the unit should be set at two full-time and one part-time position to cover sick and vacation times. The unit should operate seven days a week, but it may be possible to cut back on hours on Sunday nights as this is usually a very slow time and very few accidents occur. The bare minimum staffing should be one full-time and one part-time to cover weekends and sick/vacation leave; however, I do not recommend this level of staffing as it cuts back on some very important services.

2. *Locate a qualified Occupational Health Nurse.* This will not be easy because of the overall shortage of nurses. However, an excellent resource is the local chapter of Occupational Health Nurses. This organization can refer qualified personnel skilled in treating occupational injuries and illnesses. When interviewing and selecting an appropriate individual, "bed side" manner is important as well as the toughness required not to put up with hypochondriacs. Another type of nurse to consider is the Physician's Assistant. These are qualified to perform sutures and a few other treatments traditionally only performed by a physician, but their salary is considerably higher than that of an Occupational Health Nurse.

3. *Retain a physician consultant.* This is important in order to minimize the malpractice exposure, by having a physician sign off all treatment procedures for the medical unit and be on call to the nurse for diagnostic and treatment counseling. The physician is usually the general practitioner to be used for all outside medical treatment beyond the scope of the in-house unit. A contract is negotiated between the hotel and the physician. The legal people should be involved. Additionally, you should obtain malpractice coverage for the medical unit.

4. *Draft all treatment procedures for all anticipated injuries and illnesses and have them approved by the consulting physician.* Invite the claims adjusting group to meet with the unit's staff and the Accident Prevention Facilitator. An important control aspect is to have the unit under the direct control of the Accident Prevention Facilitator.

Additional programs should be developed as the unit matures to cover:

"Wellness" programs
Back injury prevention
Smoking cessation
Drug and alcohol abuse counseling and referrals
Ergonomics pre-screening
Non-on-the-job illness treatment

One question that usually crops up is whether the unit should treat guest injuries or offer medical services if the guest is ill. This is the proverbial risk management "Catch 22." In my opinion, the in-house medical unit should not provide advertised services; however, if a guest is seriously ill or injured, the nurse should respond to the guest with Security until paramedics arrive. The reason is simple: If the guest sustains a major disability or death as a result of your negligence and your nurse could have prevented or lessened the severity of the injury but failed to respond, you are likely to be in trouble. In all situations, Security and management should handle the initial call, assess the need for intervention and in most cases have outside medical providers handle the guest problem. There are exceptions in the cases of health spas and resorts, where medical and nutritional guidance is provided as a part of the spa's overall program. Here, as in the first case, discuss the role of in-house medical personnel with legal and insurance representatives before making any decisions.

5. *Introduce the unit to all the employees and get to work.* As with any program, people must be aware that it exists, how it functions, and its impact on the individual. Bring together the Quality Safety Committee and Occupational Health Nurse to develop a program of employee awareness by making it a big event to show everyone that management is concerned with their health and welfare.

Claims Reporting

Every employee injury that involves outside medical treatment must be reported to the state and the claims adjuster. Failure to report to the state can result in fines, while late reporting to the claims adjuster can mean loss of control and higher costs. It has already been described how the manager is to fill out a First

Report of Injury and a Manager's Accident Investigation Report and mark them as an "Incident Only" for in-house first-aid cases and "Accident" for those requiring outside medical treatment. Even those marked "Incident Only" should be sent to the claims adjuster in case a claim does arise. This removes reliance on the manager to follow up at a later date. It is important to discuss incident reporting procedures with the claims adjusters so that they are not setting up erroneous files and charging additional fees.

All injuries requiring outside medical attention require the same reports as an incident except that it is necessary to indicate the treating physician or clinic. Documentation should be sent to the claims adjuster within 24 hours. You should not be afraid to call and verify whether the adjuster has received the reports— they work for you!

Coordinating the claims effort falls squarely on the shoulders of the owner/operator of a small operation. If the means exist to implement the New Loss Control Concept or an In-House Medical Unit, these would act as the claims coordinating function. However, in typical hotels this is usually a shared function between human resources staff and the Accident Prevention Facilitator.

Another excellent method is to have Centralized Accident Reporting. This approach is very successful with chains containing numerous restaurants and/or hotels and motels. Centralized Accident Reporting is an extension of the Accident Prevention Facilitator in so far as there is a full-fledged claims coordinator who is at the main business offices of the company. Their primary role is claims recording, monitoring, and reporting for all types of claims to the adjusting firm. It is a support function for management and the Accident Prevention Facilitator. This capability will enhance the disability management program and ensure proper record keeping (English, 1988). The primary advantages of Centralized Accident Reporting as stated by William English are (English, 1988, p. 61):

- Same-day phone reporting gets the supervisor of the injured worker into immediate first-person contact with the claims coordinator, who can then ask the right questions to document important details and coach the supervisor in what to say and do for the injured person.
- Medical treatment can be better monitored and controlled if the coordinator is kept informed in a timely manner. Once

the injured person goes to an emergency room or to the wrong doctor, it can be difficult to establish control.

- A much higher percentage of reports will be on time. Timely reporting to the relevant jurisdiction is a statutory requirement, and fines against the employer may be levied for infractions.
- All reports sent to the claims adjusters and to the state workers' compensation commission will be complete and much more accurate.
- All department and location codes will be specific and correct.
- Any required special investigations can be arranged on a timely basis.

Whichever program fits the specific operation, after completion of the Injury Management Phase the work has just begun, because the Disability Management Phase is now entered.

At this point, the employee is off work because of an on-the-job injury that has left him or her temporarily totally or partially disabled. The following are tried and proven programs that get the employee back to gainful employment and can save the company many dollars.

DISABILITY MANAGEMENT

Successful disability management goes hand in hand with successful injury management. If control is lost on the medical side it is very difficult to get back on track and control the disability aspects of an employee injury.

During 1988 it is estimated that $40 billion was paid in workers' compensation. Their are many reasons for this high cost, including undue litigation. If a case goes to litigation, your out-of-pocket cost will triple. Out of your total claims about 20 percent will involve disability and 9 percent will be litigated. This is the national average quoted from *Business Insurance Magazine*. Also, the largest single category of injury that goes to litigation is back injuries.

Why do attorneys get involved? One obvious reason is that they can make money, but the reason they are able to become involved is the adversarial relationship that exists between the employer and the employee. Unfortunately for the injured employee, the fees for the attorney are subtracted from the disability payment. How and why does this adversarial relationship come about, in particular when an employee is hard-working, loyal, and a valued member of the team?

In most cases it occurs when the employer fails to meet its obligations under the law and more importantly has failed to educate the employee and their family as to their entitlements. This simple lack of caring by a manager for an injured employee can cost a company thousands of dollars annually in workers' compensation, quite apart from the ill-will it creates with all the employees.

Disability management is simply a process for managing a workers' compensation claim so that:

1. Loss exposure is minimized.
2. An employee receives his or her entitlements under the law.
3. An attorney is not involved.
4. Recovery is speeded and the employee is got back to work.

There are other benefits of a sound disability management program, which include elimination of "workers' compensation syndrome," which occurs when people are off from work more than 60 days collecting Temporary Total Disability, and elimination of those who try to take the system for a ride, alias the "malingerer." The cornerstones of disability management are (1) the "We Care" program and (2) the Modified Duty program.

"We Care" Program

Let us illustrate this program with a case study. Ron Jones graduated from Cornell University in Hotel and Restaurant Management. He has a bright future in hotel management and his talents have been recognized. He is married and has one child who is 18 months old. In the hotel, his position is restaurant manager of a very busy and successful outlet. One day in the middle of a very busy lunch rush, he sees a slight altercation between one of the waitresses and a guest. He rushes over and on his way does not notice a lettuce leaf on the floor; he slips and goes down, striking his head on the corner of the salad bar. Paramedics are summoned and he is taken to the hospital unable to move his legs. The diagnosis is paraplegia from a spinal cord injury caused by the fall.

What goes through Ron's head? "Who's going to pay the bills?"

"What is my family going to do?" "Do I have a job?" "What am I going to do?"

This is a million dollar plus claim. From the earlier discussion on workers' compensation, Ron Jones is entitled to full medical treatment, which in this case is lifetime—temporary total disability, permanent partial disability, and with a strong possibility of permanent total disability.

Unfortunately no one went to see Ron, so Ron took the advice that he got from a TV advertisement: "Injured on-the-job? Call the Law Offices of X, Y, and Z. We get you what you're entitled to." What would you do if you were Ron? This is exactly how adversarial relationships get started.

Let us review the simple procedures involved in "We Care."

"We Care"

1. Tell the employees their workers' compensation rights, the policy for reporting accidents, and suggested or approved medical providers.

2. Follow the injury-management program and get prompt and immediate medical attention for the injury. A good diagnosis and quality care go a long way toward alleviating fears and allows you to gear up your disability program. Contact must be made with the physician in order to obtain a complete diagnosis of the disability.

3. Document all conversations, accident investigations, and interviews of witnesses. This is needed should you need to prove a lack of compensability. When I worked in the construction industry, there was a rash of back injuries around hunting season. Documentation of proof is the only way to win a case before the commission.

4. Promptly complete all required reports and notify the claims adjuster within 24 hours. In most states where disability is to be paid, the check must be in the hands of the employee within 2 weeks.

5. Call and visit the employee. Enquire whether there is anything the person needs; it could simply be someone to pick up their prescription. Discuss with them their entitlements, when they can expect their check, and most importantly that you plan to make them whole again and return them to their job. Some companies have a short pamphlet in different languages on workers' compensation

law and what the employee can expect from the company. Document all conversations. Figure 5-4 shows a sample form to be given to the manager for completion as well as to anyone else who has contact with the employee. Contact should be frequent.

6. Human Resources should contact the employee and let them know how to maintain their family benefits during their recovery. This should be done in writing, with a phone call to verify all conditions.

7. The department manager should maintain weekly contact and apprize the Accident Prevention Facilitator or claims coordinator of the employee's status. Additionally, the Accident Prevention Facilitator or claims coordinator should keep in contact with the physician on the recovery process in order to develop a possible modified duty position.

All of this is an attempt to show your concern for your most valuable resource, your employee. You can call the program anything you like, but it works, because the employees do not need an attorney to get what they are entitled to. By eliminating the attorney, the claims cost is cut by two-thirds. "We Care" is that simple—nothing magical just a little old-fashioned concern and follow-up.

Modified Duty Program

This is probably the single most important aspect of an excellent disability program, yet sometimes the hardest to convince a manager to implement. Many articles have been published that expound on the program's cost benefit, from measuring work productivity to calculating costs of lost days versus industry standards (Ratliff and Grogan, 1989). The hotel company I worked for showed a return on investment of around 200 percent. Additionally, there are other benefits that help cut costs.

One involves the elimination of Workers' Compensation Syndrome, which is a documented psychological malady that strikes people who have extended time away from work. The injured employee begins to feel they will never recover or return to any kind of normal productive life. They begin to realize receiving two-thirds of their weekly pay check without having to produce anything is not such a bad deal. So they begin to make excuses not to get up, they complain more and tend to dramatize

EMPLOYEE CONTACT

Date:

Employee Name:

Date of Injury:

Telephone:

	Date of Contact			
Items To Verify				
Condition of Injury				
Projected Disability				
Compensation Paid				
Medical Being Paid				
Employee Disposition				
Any Special Needs				
Manager's Initials				

OTHER COMMENTS: _____

_____

_____

Figure 5-4. A sample "We Care" Employee Contract form that provides a record of the supervisor's contact with the recovering employee.

small problems. When someone falls into this situation it is extremely difficult to get them motivated to come back to work. Eventually they will seek legal council who will shuffle them off to a myriad of doctors in order to get a physician to say they are disabled. This process continues for years until some settlement is reached, usually a "green poultice" (dollars!), applied to the injured area.

Another benefit of the program is the control of those few people who are taking the system for a ride. But remember, the true malingerer exists only in small numbers:

> Never accuse anyone of malingering. Certainly, an effort should be made to controvert fraudulent claims. The workforce should know that it is not easy to fake claims against the company. (English, 1988, p. 58).

However, the benefit of a modified duty plan is that malingers have to come back to work or possibly lose compensation benefits for refusing a modified job that has been approved by the physician. Additionally, a sound medical diagnosis will weed out this small percentage of the workforce who try to fake injuries.

The basics of an effective modified duty program are as follows.

Modified Duty Program

1. Sound injury management. The need for quality medical diagnosis and treatment cannot be overemphasized. Immediately following treatment, a follow-up call should be made to the medical provider to discuss the diagnosis and need for a modified job. If you have set this up previously with the provider, as outlined in the injury management program, the provider will be calling you if a modified job is necessary.

2. There are two types of modified duty: type I, is when the employee can come back to work within 14 days; type II, when the employee will have an extended disability of 14 days or longer.

3. Type I modified duty applies when we have received the information from the doctor that a simple modification to the job is all that is necessary for a period of less than 14 days. The Accident Prevention Facilitator or claims coordinator and the manager need to create a job for the employee. In some cases this may mean working within several different departments doing different jobs so long

as there is no aggravation of the injury. The modified job must be notified in writing and signed off by the physician. Figure 5-5 is a sample of how a modified duty job description should look. One useful practice is to have some pre-developed job descriptions for the most common injuries.

4.   For type I, be sure to contact the claims adjuster and forward a copy of the approved job description. In that way, if the employee refuses to work the claim can be denied and payments withheld.

3A. Type II modified duty is similar to type I except that the employee is on a long leave and may or may not be easy to get hold of. In this case the modified job is developed with the blessing of the physician; however, the claims adjuster should contact the medical provider to obtain information on the extent of the disability and whether any special precautions must be taken. Rehabilitation programs may also come into play on extended disability, thus the claims adjuster needs to be directly involved in cases with lost time over 14 days.

4A. Submit the modified duty job description and the offer letter to the employee via registered mail. The letter should explain that the position has been cleared by the physician and should include a work schedule; it requests a response within 7 days. The letter should not contain any threats or allude to possible job loss. Should the employee refuse the job, notify the claims adjuster and benefits will normally be suspended, bringing the claim to a head. If the employee accepts the job, every effort should be made to bring them back with a pay rate commensurate with their regular position.

5.   Document all calls and all coordination efforts. Figure 5-6 shows a simple tracking sheet to help document that effort.

As an example to illustrate all the steps of how an employee injury should be handled, let us go back to our restaurant manager Ron Jones and start from the beginning. Ron slips and falls striking his head on the salad bar. Security and another manager respond to the scene and begin administering first-aid by checking Ron's vital signs and calling for paramedics. The manager calls the Accident Prevention Facilitator, Food and Beverage Director, and General Manager who respond to the scene and assist in

MODIFIED DUTY JOB DESCRIPTION

Employee: Date Of Offer:

Injury Date: Report To:

Supervisor:

WE CARE

XYZ Company "Cares" about you and your future. We have been in contact with the treating physician on your condition. Your physician has advised us that you are capable of performing a modified duty job. The following is a description of a temporary modified job which has been reviewed and approved by your doctor. "We Care" about you and this position entitles you to full pay at your pre-injury rate. We will be contacting you in the near future to arrange a work schedule. Please sign and return this job description in the enclosed self-addressed envelope.

JOB DESCRIPTION

General: All tasks will be performed in a sitting position. Periodic breaks are provided for prescribed stretching and standing.

Task 1:

Location: Restaurant
Supervisor: J. Smith
Schedule: 7:00 am to 11:00 am
Duties: 1. Fold and stack napkins
2. Stock, clean and fill condiment containers
3. Sort silverware into appropriate bins

Rest Periods:

1. 9:00 to 9:10
2. 11:00 to 11:10

Task 2:

Location: Kitchen
Supervisor: B. Jones
Schedule: 11:10 am to 3:30 pm
Duties: 1. Cut and prepare vegetables and fruit and place on trays

Rest Periods:

1. Lunch 12:30 to 1:00
2. 2:00 to 2:10

Signatures

_____   _____
Physician   *Employee*

_____   _____
Manager   *Accident Prevention Facilitator*

Figure 5-5. A completed modified duty job description.

106

WORKERS' COMPENSATION
CLAIMS STATUS

Location: _____   Date: _____

Name: _____   SSN.: _____

Injury Date: _____   Dept.: _____

Job Title: _____   Supv.: _____

Description of Injury/Illness:

Restrictions:

Projected Length of Lost Time:

Has Initial Contact Been Made With The Employee? _____ Date:_____

Physician:
Address:
Phone:

Claims Management Tracking

1. Date First Report completed and sent to claims adjuster: _____
2. Manager's Investigation completed: _____ Date: _____
3. Benefits and entitlements communicated to employee: _____ Date: _____
4. Modified Duty Job Description completed: _____ Date: _____
5. Physician Approval of modified job: _____ Date: _____
6. Date Employee allowed to return to work: _____
7. Date Claims Adjuster notified: _____
8. Date modified duty offer extended: ____ Accepted: ____ Rejected: ___
9. Copies of signed job description sent to claims adjuster: _____
10. Date employee returned to work: _____ Modified: _____ Full: _____
11. Date disability is over and employee released to full duties: _____

COMMENTS: _____

_____

_____

_____

_____

Figure 5-6. Sample Claims Status form that tracks the history of activities in a particular employee injury case. The form would be placed and kept in the employee's accident file.

stabilizing the area. Ron is rushed to the hospital; the Accident Prevention Facilitator and Food and Beverage Director go to the hopsital in order to take care of the paperwork and follow the status. The General Manager calls Ron's wife and offers to take her to the hospital and arrange for a sitter.

Ron is stabilized and the Accident Prevention Facilitator spends time with Ron's wife assuring her of Ron's benefits and that she need not worry that the management will stand behind him. The Accident Prevention Facilitator calls the claim into the claims adjuster with the current diagnosis and other pertinent details. He begins completing the necessary paperwork and insures that it gets to the adjuster the next day. During the next few days, Ron gains consciousness and is told the tragic news that he has only a 10 percent chance of walking again. As soon as the hospital allows, Ron's manager goes to see him and reviews all of his workers' compensation entitlements with him and the fact management will see to it that he has a job when he is medically able. The Food and Beverage Director, General Manager, and the Accident Prevention Facilitator make weekly visits; 10 days later, Ron's manager picks Ron's first disability check up and delivers it personally. Ron undergoes a full physical rehabilitation program and when he is considered able to leave the hospital a modified job is developed to begin training him in some new skills while he undergoes vocational counseling. Ron decides to crosstrain into reservations and undergoes a development program to make him a Reservations Manager. He excells in this job and eventually works his way through accounting then sales and marketing and today he is a General Manager.

Ron recovered quickly and so will others who are handled with the same concern and caring. People are a very important resource and the supply is getting short as we approach the turn of the century. You cannot afford to take an employee injury lightly. The two very basic processes discussed do work and if they are administered correctly can net up to a 40 percent reduction in workers' compensation costs, and they will foster a sense of good will amongst all the employees.

CHAPTER 6

The Guest Liability Dilemma
HAVE WE BECOME INSURERS OF THE GUESTS' SAFETY?

CURRENT STATE OF THE LAW

Today, we are the most litigious society in the world. As a result, we are having an impact on the whole world by raising expectations and standards. Attorneys who are advertising on TV for workers' compensation claims are doing the same for personal injury claims. But who is to blame—the attorneys or ourselves? People today have the expectation that if they are harmed in anyway, someone else is going to be responsible and they are entitled to recover their loss. With the advent of the "deep pocket theory," damage suits are filed charging several entities for the damages sustained even though they may be only marginally at fault. In this way, if the plaintiff is successful, the person with the deepest pockets will bear the greatest cost. Today

> Suing for some is like buying a ticket to a lottery—but with better odds. With the right ticket you can win big, from whoever has the money. There is a good chance you will not even have to go to court to collect: "Many people with even a frivolous grievance or injury consider a law suit knowing that insurance companies will be likely to settle out of court to avoid high defense costs." (MacHovec, 1987, p. 4)

The future seems assured of a continued steady trend of increased litigation and awards, and so-called tort reform will have little impact. Also there will be more criminal charges filed against officers of companies for negligence in their decisions that affect guest and worker safety. It is apparent that management cannot stand behind the defense that they complied with all codes,

109

as this too is changing with case law. Codes are useful, but they are only minimum standards and the jury wants to know whether those in responsibility did everything within reason to eliminate hazards. Argument can go on indefinitely as to what is reasonable, but what it boils down in the end to is what the jury perceives as reasonable. Where did it all begin?

> Common law is defined as the legal processes and procedures based on custom, usage and tradition "of immemorial antiquity" and from legal precedents (case law) from the U.S. and England excluding laws passed by a legislature. (MacHovec, 1987, p. 135)

Thus, a place of business is required to meet certain conditions in common law as it provides a legal duty to act as an ordinary, prudent, reasonable person. In the case of a hotel, motel, or restaurant, the general duty is to not do something that will cause an injury to its guests or fail to do something that will prevent one. However, that duty is limited to what is termed as "reasonable care."

Besides the general duty owed, the business must also provide reasonably safe premises and this cannot be delegated to another. Lastly, the duty to provide safe premises carries an obligation to warn the guest or patron of any dangers on or about the premises.

If you break this nonverbal covenant, what happens? This is called a *tort*. A tort is a willful act that causes a violation of another's rights, a neglect of one's duty or obligations which results in some harm to another. There are three conditions for tort: (1) there must be a duty owed; (2) a breach of that duty must occur; and (3) the breach must be the proximate cause of the injury.

To prove that a tort has been committed, the plaintiff must show negligence by the hotel, motel, or restaurant. This is accomplished by showing what is termed actual notice, constructive notice, or negligence per se. *Actual notice* involves a foreseeable inherent design defect that is the proximate cause of the injury. *Constructive notice* is the failure to inspect the premises for hazardous conditions. *Negeligence per se* is when there is a violation of a statute such as a building code.

The same degree of care is not owed to everyone who comes into the establishment. For instance, people who enter the premises uninvited or against the wishes of management, such as robbers or prostitutes, are termed trespassers and generally no duty is owed to protect them except from intentional harm. Another group are those who enter the premise to solicit, or sell products. They are termed *licensees*. The duty owed is to warn them of known defects, not to make the place reasonably safe. The final group are guests and patrons. Recently, case law has established that the hospitality industry is held to a very high standard of *reasonable care* to provide safe premises and to warn of all known defects.

Two further legal terms need to be clarified: contributory negligence and the relatively new rule of comparative negligence. *Contributory negligence* means that a guest who is in part wholly responsible for their own injury cannot recover damages against the establishment. This was a major defense strategy used by all businesses for many years. Then the system seemed to break down; contributory negligence was overturned in many cases and plaintiffs were given full recovery for damages. Then came the advent of punitive damages. This was born primarily out of litigation against manufacturers who introduced products into the market that were defective or who failed to warn of the hazards. A classic case was the Ford Pinto and the tendency for the gas tank to explode in rear end collisions.

With the so called tort reform movement, the pendulum began to swing the other way and along came comparative negligence which is now in more than 36 states. This change was accomplished through statutory changes. *Comparative negligence* assigns fault against each party in order to assess damages to be paid. There is the pure form and the 50 percent type. In the latter plaintiffs may recover only if they are less than 50 percent at fault. The pure form assigns a percentage of fault to all parties without restrictions.

A significant result of the comparative negligence rule has been the phenomenal increases in personal injury litigation against the hospitality and restaurant industries.

This discussion of some basic legal terms is intended to aid understanding of the impact management can have on improving guest liability exposure, but legal experts should be consulted for more complete definitions.

Let us again illustrate many of these legal terms through a case history. It is a Saturday night; an older couple, Mr. and Mrs. Jones, arrive at the restaurant for the early-bird special. The hostess seats them at a table approximately 20 feet from the salad bar. Mrs. Jones gets up after they have ordered and heads to the salad bar. There is a piece of lettuce on the floor; her heel hits the lettuce and she slips and falls.

First, the proximate cause of the fall was the lettuce. But do we have a tort? That is for the plaintiff to show and the jury to decide, but we can consider the relevant facts. The restaurant had a duty to protect Mrs. Jones from harm, in this case slipping and falling. But, did the restaurant need to warn her of the potential for foreign matter on the floor? And finally did the restaurant breach that duty? In this case there probably did not need to be a formal warning of possible debris. Generally, consumers are aware of the fact there may be some debris around a salad bar in a restaurant. But as it relates to tort, did the restaurant provide a reasonable safe place? It is arguable that it did not because (1) the floor around the salad bar was found not to be slip-resistant and (2) there was no employee assigned to police the area at regular intervals. Item 1 is actual notice, a design defect, and item 2 is constructive notice, which is inspecting to ensure there are no hazards. For negligence per se, there would need to be the requirement that the code required the floor to be slip-resistant. In this case this would not apply, because the local jurisdiction had not adopted slip-resistant floors as a part of the building code.

So what is reasonable these days? This is a hard question to answer, but it helps to think of it this way: If it were you, and you got hurt or a family member was injured, would you consider the premises "reasonably" safe or would you feel that the owner did not care. Even then case law may have already broadened the definition of "reasonable" for that unique situation. Also, these days it is becoming ever more apparent that in the hospitality industry the definitions are becoming so broad that management are being held to a very high level of care almost approaching strict liability. In fact in some situations I would say that situation has already been reached. As a hotel or restaurant manager or owner, the key to the liability dilemma is still your efforts to prevent the accident. It is a very simple premise regarding accidents that "if you don't have 'em you ain't got to pay for 'em."

If a guest is injured, the first "fifteen minutes" are critical.

THE CRITICAL FIRST FIFTEEN MINUTES

There is one simple truth in liability cases: failure to take care of an incident expeditiously, professionally, and correctly, means loss of most of the liability case. One of the biggest problems occurs when the operator fails to report the incident to the claims adjuster; then, maybe 2 years later, papers are served against him from the guest's (plaintiff's) attorney. It is a proven fact that guest accidents can be minimized by simple but prompt and complete investigation and reporting. Those first 15 minutes immediately after notification by the guest that some form of harm has been sustained, are in a sense a "moment of truth" in true customer service. The impression made on the guest immediately after being involved in an accident can mean not only a favorable outcome on the claim but also that you will have a guest who will return to your establishment and tell their friends of the bad experience that turned out well.

Roles and Responsibilities

As in everything, the ultimate responsibility rests with the general manager of the property, but management must be trained in the proper handling of guest injuries, the "Do's and Don'ts." Each manager on duty has a leadership role to insure that the guest receives prompt treatment and that the accident is properly investigated and reported to the claims adjuster. The actual doing of the investigation and contact of the medical service can be delegated to a position such as Security. If you have Security, they should respond to the scene with the manager on duty to conduct a supplemental investigation of the accident scene and act as an adviser to the manager. In some hotels Security departments take charge of the entire process. There is nothing wrong with this so long as they have been properly trained. However, management and the claims adjuster must always be notified of all incidents. If there is no Security, then someone trained in first-aid must accompany the manager; it is in any case always wise to have back-up.

Procedures

1. *Take care of the injured guest.* Be courteous and helpful, offer immediate first aid as appropriate. In cases of serious injury do not delay in calling the paramedics; be sure to keep the injured person comfortable until EMS arrives—moving the seriously injured can increase your liability. Possible exceptions would be a life-threatening situation necessitating movement or first-aid intervention, such as arterial bleeding, interrupted breathing, or

poisoning. For less serious injuries, offer to contact a doctor or hospital but let the guest decide. It may be a good idea to offer the clinic established for employee injuries. In any case there should be preestablished procedures with a nearby clinic and hospital emergency room for handling guest injuries. Figure 6-1 shows a sample medical authorization form that can go a long way to help the operator's case and help the guest receive prompt medical attention. The company should also assist with arrangements for transportation, but it is not recommended you transport injured guests in company vehicles.

Additionally the company should pay for all initial 24-hour medical treatment. The first question should be "Does the company incur any liability?" This will not mean that the company is admitting any liability; however, it does buy access to medical records which is invaluable in deflating exaggerated claims and eliminates the possibility of the guest passing back to you responsibility for subsequent injury. The payment for these services should be handled by the claims adjusting group.

AUTHORIZATION FOR MEDICAL TREATMENT

Date:

To: _____

Physician/Hospital

_____

Address

This signed form is your authorization to render one time treatment to:

_____

Name   Address

Please forward the medical record and a statement for services rendered to:

_____

Manager   Company

_____

Address   Phone

Signature: _____

Manager   Date

Figure 6-1. Sample form for authorizing initial medical treatment for an injured guest.

The company must pay this initial medical cost on all guest accidents. Consistency is very important. However, for those injuries or situations which involve illnesses not involving property services, injuries from horseplay, self-inflicted wounds, or domestic altercations, or persons injured while committing an illegal act on the premises, you may elect not to pay and only offer to assist them in obtaining medical care. This area should be discussed with corporate council.

2. *Take control of the accident scene.* First have one of the staff obtain the names of witnesses. Disinterested third parties are best but employees' statements should also be documented. Never *call* anyone a witness, simply ask them what they saw and record their name, phone number, and whether they are a guest in the hotel (so that, if the claims adjuster wants to reach them while they are in the hotel he can). If possible try to obtain the personal data from the guest as well as a statement of what happened. Be sure to have someone witness the guest's description of the accident, even an employee will be acceptable. During the conversation do not apologize for the accident or mention insurance or liability; it is suitable to apologize for the fact they are not feeling well or in pain. If the guest asks about bills or who is going to pay and the like, they should be told not to worry about insurance at that moment as the important thing is getting medical attention. If there is an established policy to pay initial medical, they can be assured that the company will take care of initial emergency treatment.

Try to confirm the guest's story. Note any personal factors that may have contributed to the accident, such as eye glasses, horseplay, third-party involvement, drinking and/or drugs, shoes (condition of heels), wet spots on clothing, foreign objects, and the like, defective products or equipment, or physical condition. This list can go on and on; the important point is to inspect the accident scene thoroughly and document only "factual" conditions. This should be on a separate document from the accident report. The reason for a separate report is that in most cases the plaintiff's attorney will request a copy of the accident report and this second report is not immediately discoverable as it is not attached physically to the accident report; and it is labeled "attorney client work product."

Photograph the area and date and sign the pictures. Save all evidence and turn it over as soon as possible to the claims adjuster. Additionally, attach a copy of the guest folio or check to the secondary report. Be alert to the possibility of *subrogation*, which means that the proximate cause of the injury involved some other third party; for example, canned goods causing food poisoning or a new banquet chair falling apart. Obtain invoices, labels, anything that will identify that third party and attach them to your report. Be sure to save the chair, items of food, and so on for the adjuster.

Document and have witnessed all those conditions that are not defective; for example, that the lighting is in good condition, that there is no water on the floor, that wet-floor signs are in place, and so on.

3. *Complete the claims report and call the adjuster as soon as possible.* Many have answering services to receive reports. The company pays them and if it appears important ask them to come to the site as soon as possible. File a complete, factual and accurate accident report—do not "editorialize."

Obtain phone numbers, addresses, employers' names, anything readily available. In most liability cases, the plaintiff's attorney will wait until just before the statute of limitations runs out before filing the suit, hoping that memories will lapse (which they do) and that details will fade.

Negligence must not be concealed from the claims adjuster, otherwise they may be fighting a case that could have settled for far less. Remember that claims adjusters are not knowledgeable about hotel or restaurant operations. They have to be clearly supplied with detailed information that might help the outcome— little things such as rooms inspections, engineering inspections and work orders, safety inspections, warning labels and signs, and sweep logs. Are all the chefs trained and certified in food sanitation—this would be a big plus in the case of an outbreak of salmonella. Training records are very important in many liability cases.

Management knows the operation, the adjuster knows claims. The key to an effective defense strategy is "good faith"—what the company did right in relation to this case. This aspect should be kept in mind when thinking of what might be helpful to the claims person.

4. *Be polite and courteous to the guest.* Give flowers, vist the hospital, charge their meal or room to the house; but document the conversations and observations for the claims adjuster.

Now it is up to the claims adjuster, but the chances of a

case that has been handled expeditiously and properly from its inception going to trial or even having an attorney involved are much reduced if these basic steps have been followed. This is why those first 15 minutes are so important in the control of guest liability claims.

It is worth listing specifically those things that should *not* be done:

DO NOT offer to pay all medical expenses.
DO NOT admit liability, negligence, or responsibility.
DO NOT mention insurance.
DO NOT apologize for the accident.
DO NOT argue the cause of the accident.
DO NOT reprimand employees at the scene.
DO NOT discuss the accident with outsiders, even weeks later.
DO NOT throw away records until the case is settled.

THE SUIT IS FILED

After a complaint has been filed by the guest's (plaintiff's) attorney a series of back-and-forth information exchanges, called *interrogatories*, takes place to clarify the complaint and answer many basic questions. This is called the discovery process.

Here is where the plaintiff's attorney requests information such as who is the owner of the premises; names and addresses of all those involved; whether any outside experts are involved; plans of the building and names of manufacturers of materials; prior incidents or complaints issued; code violations or inspection reports. This is not a complete list of all that is asked. The sole purpose of interrogatories is to discover any and all information that has a bearing on the case and which will establish whether a tort was committed.

These days more and more plaintiffs hire expert witnesses. An expert witness can be defined as anyone who has a specific basis of knowledge on a subject relevant to the case that the ordinary person does not have. The expert witness's role is to investigate the accident to determine whether the defect or action was the proximate cause of the injury and whether liability exists in their opinion. The defense often hires an expert to counter the plaintiff's expert, and the jury has to decide which expert to believe.

The next step is for depositions to be taken on each individual involved in the case. This is a time when an opposing attorney can question the other side's witnesses in cross-examination format but without a judge. Frequently after this occurs cases are settled as it becomes obvious who is responsible and who will have the best odds in court.

With thorough procedure in the first 15 minutes, 90 percent of guest incidents will not reach this point, but at least if they do you will be very glad that you did your homework.

If the case does go to trial, listen to your attorney. He or she is the expert in the court room. At this point, if you have designed safety and security into your facility, trained your employees, followed your safety and security management policies, and acted in good faith, you stand an excellent chance of winning.

Kohr's Rule

> For every case you win, you will discourage many others from filing frivolous suits. Pick your cases wisely and go to the mat on those where you have a favorable pretrial case; however, you should quickly settle those that present a weak defense.

Following this simple rule of thumb will reduce overall litigation exposure.

CASE HISTORIES

An excellent way to demonstrate the principles of liability will be to use some specific cases to illustrate the key points of what must be done to have an impact on the so-called liability crisis. These case histories are drawn from my personal experience in the hospitality industry.

The three cases are examples of situations that can and often do impact hotels, motels, and restaurants all too frequently: slips, trips, and falls; food-borne illness; and liquor liability.

Slips, Trips, and Falls

Slips, trips, and falls account for 40–50 percent of the industry's liability loss exposure. Prevention and building a defensible position are key to avoiding or winning these cases. Chapter 12 is devoted to this subject. This case study will reflect some of the more important qualities.

The location is a business transient type of hotel, fairly new, having been open a little more than a year. The guest, John, was in town for sales calls to some of his clients. John got up at his usual time, around 7:00 a.m. and started to get ready for the day. He went into the bathroom, turned the shower on, placed the terry bathmat on the floor beside the tub, and stepped into the shower. As John was bathing, he noticed a grabbar on the front service wall, just inside the shower curtain. His mind on the day's activities, John dropped the soap, turned off the water, opened the shower curtain, and reached for a towel, which he wrapped around himself. He tried to step out of the tube, not using the grabbar; his back foot slipped on the soap; he fell backwards, hitting his head and wrenching his back badly. He lay for a few minutes stunned by what had happened.

John pulled himself up and out of the tube, and into the bed. He picked up the phone and called the operator. The PBX operator immediately called the Resident Manager and Security. They responded to John's room, knocked, identified themselves, and used a master key to enter. The Security officer was trained in advanced first-aid, he began checking John's vital signs and found them to be stable. The Resident Manager and Security officer recommended to John that paramedics be called to transport him to the local hospital for further examination. John hesitated at first but then agreed and the paramedics arrived shortly thereafter. The hospital had already been notified by the Resident Manager that John was a guest and the initial medical treatment would be picked up by the insurance carrier for the hotel. The Resident Manager also gave John a medical authorization form so that there would be no hassle at the hospital.

When John got back home he went to his supervisor and filed for workers' compensation. He was still having severe back and neck pain from the fall. Once the compensation carrier was notified of the claim, they immediately filed a subrogation claim against the hotel. Subrogation occurs when an insurance carrier or claims adjuster attempts to transfer the cost and responsibility for the claim to a third party. Before we go further, let us go over what happened at the hotel just after John had left for the hospital.

The Security officer got the polaroid camera and shot several pictures of the bathroom in general, tub bottom, and especially the bar of soap in the bottom; he had the pictures and bathroom conditions witnessed by two other hotel employees. The Resident

Manager completed the standard insurance claim report and the Security officer completed his supplemental report. That afternoon the Resident Manager contacted the claims adjuster to report the incident, and then called John to see how he was and whether he needed anything.

Once the hotel's claims adjuster received notice from the compensation carrier, she immediately denied the subrogation request. Some months later, suit was filed by the compensation carrier. They retained a so-called slip-and-fall expert who really did not understand hotels and who failed to inspect the accident scene thoroughly. Defense contacted an expert experienced in falls and hotel litigation, and with the excellent data supplied by the hotel it was easy to put the pieces together to draft a strong defense to the plaintiff's allegations. The allegations stated that (1) the bath tub was not slip-resistant and that (2) a grabbar should have been on the side wall and (3) on the rear nonservice wall.

The claims adjuster and defense expert immediately contacted an independent testing lab, who performed a nationally recognized test for slip resistance on the tub's surface. It passed the test. Next the expert researched local building and plumbing codes and none required slip-resistant bath tubs or grabbars. However, there were national standards such as American National Standards Institute (ANSI) and American Society for Testing and Materials (ASTM) that recommend a non-slip surface and grabbars. In this case the hotel had a slip-resistant tub and a grabbar on the front wall of the tub, which exceeded typical industry practice. This particular state had adopted the rule of comparative negligence and in this case it was found that reasonable care had been met, and that additional grabbars would not have prevented the fall, because John did not use the one that was provided, which could have kept him from falling since it was correctly positioned.

Food-Borne Illness

Joe had just arrived to work at his new job as salad prepper for a new upscale restaurant. Joe had a few cuts on his hands from working in his garden the previous day. His supervisor took him around and introduced him to the kitchen staff, then showed Joe to the prep station and had him get to work on making potato salad. Joe had never attended sanitation classes; in fact this restaurant did not even have a basic orientation program let alone a safety program. Joe jumps right in and wants to make a good impression. Being new he was hesitant about asking too many questions, so he stuck his hands in the bowl to mix the dressing and other ingredients. He took a break before cutting up some more potatoes, rinsed his hands off in the sink and went to the men's room, where he defecated and went back to work without washing his hands. He cut up the potatoes for the salad and mixed them in with the dressing. Once the salad was finished he covered it and placed it in the walk-in box.

The next day the potato salad was put out on the salad bar for the lunch special. It was a busy lunch crowd and at least 50 people had Joe's potato salad. What those people did not know is the salad was contaminated with *Staphylococcus* and *Clostridium perfringens* bacteria. Within about eight hours all 50 people became ill with severe abdominal pain, vomiting, diarrhea, and nausea.

It was not long before the cause of the illnesses was narrowed down to this restaurant. Health Department officials arrived and began the process of identifying the specific causes; also, the press was along to get an eye-witness report. It was not long before suits were filed by all 50 people. Of course, the restaurant owner reported the situation to his insurance carrier as soon as the potato salad problem was identified.

This is fairly clear-cut. This was obviously negligence on the part of the restaurant and the only resource is a good claims adjuster who can keep the settlements low. The key points to remember are:

1. If you get a complaint do not delay in having the health authorities investigate as soon as possible.
2. Pull all food items involved with the complaint off the line; refrigerate them; keep them segregated and covered until the health authorities arrive.
3. Contact your claims adjuster as soon as possible.

Liquor Liability

It was another Friday night extracurricular meeting. Simon the sales manager, as he always did, ordered everyone to go to the local bar to finish the meeting agenda. All the sales people felt obligated to attend; those who balked were intimidated by the possible accusation that they were not team players. This was the case with Sue, who had joined the sales team only 3 months before. She was recently married and was very reluctant to attend these after-hours sessions, but Simon was not one to take no for an answer, especially from a woman.

Simon had been reprimanded in the past for alleged sexual harassment of female subordinates, but the company kept him on the payroll. As the evening progressed people started to leave one by one until around 11:00 p.m. only Simon and Sue were left. Simon had had five scotches over the course of five hours, Sue had had three glasses of wine. By this point you should be asking why Sue is still with Simon. This is a classic case of a dominant personality and a less dominant; in fact, Sue felt that if she left it would affect her career. Nevertheless, Sue excused herself and said she needed to leave and go home. Before she left she went to the ladies' room; when she came out, Simon was there and again talked her into a nightcap. All evening, except for the nightcap, one server was involved. Her name was Linda and she had received formalized training on "serving alcohol responsibly." In fact, at this restaurant and bar the topic was reviewed regularly at employee meetings. The owner/manager had a strong commitment to accident prevention in general. She had even committed to writing a policy and procedures covering everything from nuts to soup as it related to safety. She was well aware of the exposure her operation faced when it came to liquor liability. She maintained active support in the local restaurant trade association in order to keep informed of any legal changes. As a normal course of events, every new employee was thoroughly indoctrinated in serving alcohol responsibly. All activities were documented, including employee meetings.

After the nightcap, Simon and Sue left the bar. It was 1:00 a.m. and Simon again was pushing the issue of possible sexual favours in return for future career objectives, but Sue was able to maintain her composure and fend his advances off. On the way to her car, Simon followed. As Sue got into her car, Simon grabbed her, forced her into the back seat, and raped her. This was a large parking lot; the restaurant and bar was a part of a large hotel. The parking lot lighting was minimal and the area where Sue was parked could not be seen from the hotel as it was over a hilly area. Hotel security routinely patrolled the parking lot; in fact, 15 minutes earlier, they had cruised the area where Sue's car was.

The final outcome was Simon was found guilty of rape and sentenced to 15 years in jail. Sue filed suit against her employer for sexual harassment and mental anguish. Additionally, suit was filed against the restaurant and hotel for lack of adequate security and serving alcohol irresponsibly.

This is a classic case of a "deep pocket" approach to litigation on the part of the plaintiff. Fortunately, the restaurant had an excellent program of liquor control or they probably would have paid the price for a lack of it. One of the ways a defense was established involved the calculation of how intoxicated Simon was at the time of the rape. This was necessary because the plaintiff's expert witness stated figures showing that alcohol is a leading factor in sexual assaults, especially rape, and it was claimed that the restaurant had failed to supervise liquor sales and failed to act on the foreseeability of Simon's potential to cause harm to others. As it turned out, Simon's blood alcohol level was just below the statute maximum. Additionally, there were eye witnesses, including other sales people who were with Simon and Sue, who stated that Simon did not exhibit any unusual behavior.

Other aspects of the restaurant's defense included tabulation of liquor sales versus food sales; the fact of active training and supervision of liquor sales; the fact that a strong policy was enforced; lack of prior violations of the law or prior claims.

As a result, negligence could not be shown because the liquor was not the proximate cause of the rape and the restaurant had done everything it reasonably could to prevent any alcohol-related incidents; thus there was no breach of the duty owed.

However, the hotel was not so lucky because the lighting levels fell below what is considered adequate for safety and security and the plaintiff was able to show that prior incidents had occurred in the lot, including another rape. The hotel's insurance carrier settled the case out of court.

To summarize, guest liability is not a magical mystery tour so long as it is managed and treated with the same emphasis as marketing your establishment to increase sales. You must prepare by doing two things: develop a strong prevention program, and combine prevention with litigation avoidance. The result will be a strong litigation defense and control on the guest liability dilemma.

CHAPTER 7

Things We Have No Choice but to Do and a Potpourri of Special Needs

DEALING WITH OSHA

What is OSHA?

The Occupational Safety and Health Administration (OSHA) is here to stay. In fact, with some of the new standards being issued, such as the Hazard Communications Standard (HAZCOM), employers will probably be seeing them more in the future. The intent of the act, passed by Congress in December 1970, is to assure so far as possible every working man and women in the nation a safe and healthy workplace to preserve our human resources.

OSHA was created under the jurisdiction of the Department of Labor. Its primary functions are (OSHA 2056, 1985):

- To encourage employers and employees to reduce workplace hazards and to implement new or improved existing safety and health programs.
- To provide for research in occupational safety and health to develop innovative ways of dealing with occupational safety and health problems.
- To establish "separate but dependent responsibilities and rights" for employers and employees for the achievement of better safety and health conditions.
- To maintain a reporting and recordkeeping system for job-related injuries and illnesses.

124

- To establish training programs.
- To develop mandatory job safety standards and enforce them through workplace inspections.
- To provide for state programs.

Under the HAZCOM standard, employers are required to provide a place free of recognized hazards and comply with all OSHA standards. OSHA has the right to impose fines upon a company that does not and in some cases to refer the situation to the Justice Department for review and possible criminal prosecution. Also under the act, employees are required to adhere to job safety standards. Under the law it is a violation to punish an employee for reporting safety and health violations to OSHA. In fact, the law states that an employee cannot be discriminated against, fired, demoted, or otherwise penalized for such actions as complaining to the supervisor about a hazard, requesting an OSHA inspection, or participating in union safety activities.

Many operators will never have seen, let alone experienced, an OSHA inspection. The industry is not a high-focus industry like construction or mining. However, employees do complain and numerous inspections have been prompted by those complaints. What is the procedure if OSHA representatives call? The best advice is to ask for ID, and then be cooperative. There will first be an opening conference at which the officer will explain the nature of the visit, the scope of the inspection, and nature of the applicable standards. Copies of the regulations or the actual employee complaint will be furnished. If an inspection is to take place the officer will request an employer representative as well as an employee representative in a union shop or any employee in a nonunion property. If you have an active program this is an excellent time to have the Quality Safety Committee Chairperson and Accident Prevention Facilitator go along on the inspection as an advertisement for the program.

Usually prior to or after the walkaround inspection the compliance officer will check on company recordkeeping. Accurate records must be kept: a surprising number of companies are fined for failing to maintain records properly. The officer will also check compliance with the new Hazardous Chemicals Communications Act. Hotels have been fined $10,000 each for failing to implement the standards.

During the inspection officers can note any hazard and talk to any employee on their way to the specific complaint area.

Everything is fair game for a citation. After the inspection there will be a closing conference. The officer reviews any violations and states time periods for correction. They are required to issue citations for all violations—"No Warnings." The company has 15 days after receipt to file an intention to contest the citations before the independent review board. Sometimes a settlement can be worked out with the area director, but in most cases it is easier to fix the problem.

It is worth knowing that OSHA offers a free consultation service. An OSHA representative will come to your establishment and conduct a free survey with no citations against you in order to assist in identifying workplace hazards and ways to correct them. What better way to help a small operator kick off a program and insure it is in compliance with the law at no risk.

Records: OSHA Requirements

Employers of 11 or more employees are required to maintain records of occupational injuries and illnesses. This is not a voluntary item. Some retail and service industry trades are exempt, such as eating and drinking establishments, industry code 58, but a check should be made with the local OSHA office to verify exemption. Recordkeeping is rather simple; there are two forms that must be maintained. Form 200 is the general summary, which provides a brief description and simple check off to maintain running totals. The summary is posted annually every February so that every employee has visual access; the best place is the employee bulletin board outside the Human Resources office or cafeteria. The other is form 101, which records more detailed information on each specific accident. This can be replaced by the state's workers' compensation report or the Manager's Accident Investigation form, which reduces duplication of paperwork. Additionally the company is required to display permanently an OSHA poster, regardless of the number of employees or the industry.

All employers are required to report within 48 hours any work-related death or five or more hospitalizations per incident to the nearest OSHA office. I recommend that you obtain a copy of the OSHA standards: ask for OSHA General Industry Standards 1910. Copies can be obtained by contacting your local OSHA office or Superintendent of Documents, U.S. Government Printing Office, Washington, D.C. 20402.

HAZARD COMMUNICATION STANDARD

The Hazard Communications Standard (HAZCOM) or Right to Know, and its sister SARA title III, are about letting people know what chemicals are around them in the workplace and the community and what possible effects those chemicals can have on them and their families. Managers will probably say "Oh no, more paperwork and regulations!", but individuals will no doubt want to know whether the cleaner being used or the water treatment chemicals being handled could harm them in any way. The intention is pure but as ever there is bureaucracy involved that has to be lived with.

This section will cover the basics of the federal standard; however, individual states may have expanded the act through their own programs. It is important to check with the regional OSHA office and state OSHA plan office to verify compliance.

The purpose of the act, as stated earlier, is to address comprehensively the issue of evaluating the potential hazards of chemicals in the workplace and communicating that information, including appropriate protective measures, to employers and employees. It all starts with the chemical manufacturers and importers of chemicals. They are required to assess the hazards, and communicate the hazards and precautions to those to whom they sell and distribute their products. This information is in the form of warning labels and Material Safety Data Sheets (MSDS). When buying any chemical product it is important to obtain this information. Some of the larger manufacturers supply labels for those containers used daily, such as spray bottles.

"Right To Know" Program Elements

There are four components in meeting the standard as it applies to the hotel, motel and restaurant industry:

1. Written hazard communication program.
2. Labels and other forms of warnings.
3. Material Safety Data Sheets (MSDS).
4. Employee training.

"Right to Know" Program

The written Hazard Communication Program or "Right to Know" is required at every location of business. A multi-site company should have a corporate-wide program. However, a small operator is still required to have a written program. The hiring of an outside consultant to assist a small operator may be cost-effective. The purpose of the program, which will become part of the operations policy, is to describe how it is intended to meet the standards requirements for items (2), (3) and (4) above. Additional program requirements include:

- A list of the hazardous chemicals, cross referenced to the appropriate MSDS.
- How it is planned to notify employees of hazards associated with nonroutine tasks such as flushing the chiller lines.

As with any other program, a central coordinator should be identified to ensure that all required materials are maintained and to track all training activities. Human Resources and the Accident Prevention Facilitator are probably the two most likely candidates.

Labels and Other Forms of Warnings

Each manufacturer is required to label all chemicals with the following information:

1. Identity of the hazardous chemicals.
2. Appropriate warnings.
3. Name and address of the manufacturer, importer, or responsible party.

The user's responsibility is to ensure the containers are labeled and not to remove or deface those labels. It is a good idea to obtain labels from the manufacturer for all your daily use containers. One manufacturer at least will sell spray bottles and other containers that are already labeled. Also, keep a copy of all labels and have them filed with the appropriate MSDS.

Material Safety Data Sheets

Again this is an item that must be supplied by the manufacturer, distributor, or importer. An MSDS must include the name used on the container label, hazardous chemicals' common and chemical names, physical characteristics, health hazards, OSHA permissible exposure levels, whether the chemical listed is a carcinogen, route of entry, precautions for safe handling, emergency and first aid procedures. MSDSs must be kept at each facility for all chemicals that are used routinely and nonroutinely. They must be located so they are accessible to every employee 24 hours a day.

The amount of paper this involves, depending on the size of the business, can be mind-boggling. This is certainly an excellent reason for controlling what is purchased and used. If you have a central procurement program, it may be worthwhile to adopt a computerized MSDS system. There are several on the market that could substantially ease the burden of maintaining and updating files. With electronic mail also it would be a simple matter of downloading new MSDS information to all facilities. Otherwise a manual system will have to be used. Again it is important to have a person designated as the central coordinator for the program.

Employee Information and Training

The employer is required to provide information and training to every employee regarding chemical hazards in their work areas at the time of hire and whenever a new hazard is introduced. Each employee must be told:

- Pertinent requirements of the Hazard Communications Standard.
- Any operations where hazardous chemicals exist.
- Location and availability of the written program.
- Location and availability of MSDSs and required list of hazardous chemicals.

Each employee must then be trained on detection of accidental releases of the chemicals, physical and health hazards, and what they can do to protect themselves. An excellent way to accomplish some of this training is through the Task Safety Analysis program as well as having the manufacturers' representatives attend employee meetings. The TSA can provide the required documentation that the training took place. Additionally, at new employee orientations the four basic items listed above should be covered along with other accident prevention items. The employee should sign off that they have received this training and that document should be placed in their personnel file. It is advisable also to maintain a log of training dates, content, and who attended the training with the rest of the "Right to Know" materials.

This seems like a lot: it is, but there is no choice in the matter. Already hotels have been cited and fined for failing to implement this standard.

ACCIDENT PREVENTION MOTIVATORS AND INCENTIVE PROGRAMS

Everybody's Ideas Count

Motivators and incentives can work. Recall the earlier discussion of behavior analysis, which is a focus on the positive in order to get people to modify their behavior. Incentives when properly set up are positive motivators. People can be persuaded to commit themselves. Recall the notion of finding someone's "hot button"; once the right button is found, the sky is the limit. On the downside, programs have failed miserably for the simple reason that they lacked a clear-cut measurable objective and they were not marketed to the employees.

A successful program is one that has:

- Clearly defined measurable objectives.
- A marketing plan to give it high visibility.
- A focused "hot button."
- No-gain no-reward component.

The best programs have not come from safety people, they have come from the bottom up, from the employees. Consequently, the various incentive programs listed next are a compilation of those from hotels and restaurants that I have had personal contact with. There is no such thing as plagiarism when it comes to award programs for employees.

Safety Bingo or B-Safe Bingo

For a single facility, one approach is to divide the facility into teams. It is usually best to base the division on accident potential. Kitchen could be one team, housekeeping another, and servers of all types another; alternatively, a lottery could be used to mix the teams. The way the game operates is that bingo cards are handed out to each team. The cards are posted on the bulletin board. Each day a number is pulled from a hat by an employee. The teams that go without an accident get to place a mark on their bingo card if they have that number. The team that completes the card with five in a row, column or diagonal, wins and receives a prize, which could be cash or a catered luncheon or the like.

Another approach involved a whole fastfood chain. The chain was divided into regional bingo games. Here each restaurant received a bingo card and the numbers were chosen each day by the regional offices. Any restaurant that went a day without an accident could mark its bingo card. The restaurant that reached bingo first would receive a $10 cash bonus for each employee. Additionally, any unit that went 70 days without an accident received an additional $10 per employee. Because of the support, clear objectives, and good marketing this incentive reduced the employee injury frequency by 83 percent and cut workers' compensation costs by 75 percent.

Safety Bucks

This program is a sort of points system in which employees earn safety bucks or points for reporting hazards, completing Accident Prevention Work Orders, or making quality/safety suggestions that are adopted by the facility. Employees continue to earn these credits toward selecting various prizes from a catalogue. There are many companies that will develop personalized gifts with a company's logo and help set up a points-type program or other incentive program.

Safety Challenges

Whenever competition can be included in a program, the chances for success are much higher. Examples would be a competition for the best safety record between the various housekeeping departments at all hotels in a chain or pitting one restaurant against another. The winning team is the one that goes the longest without an injury over some specified time. More narrowly, the objective could be the team without a lost-time injury or with no back injuries.

Safety Puzzles or Slogans

These are fairly simple programs that are intended to create awareness and keep up employee morale regarding accident prevention. The slogan is the simplest. The Quality Safety Committee comes up with an accident prevention slogan, which is published and announced to each employee. On some unspecified day a "mystery employee" walks around the property and if any employee knows the slogan a silver dollar is handed out.

Puzzles are a little more involved. They involve the use of crossword or "find the hidden word or phrase" types. A prize is awarded when an employee completes the puzzle. The contests run weekly, but if there are any accidents the contest does not take place for that week.

Another twist to the slogan is a contest based on a game show, retitled "Wheel of Safety". A slogan is selected each week by the Quality Safety Committee. A blank slogan is placed in a high-visibility area with a spinning wheel labeled with letters. Each day an employee from each shift spins the wheel and adds letters. The first employee to guess the slogan wins a prize.

Safety Baseball

The emphasis for this contest is accident-free periods. Divide the property into teams, put up a ball field on the bulletin board. By drawing plays from a box, team players advance around the playing field using the information on the slips of paper. Each day a drawing is made by the team on offense, but should there be an accident it counts as a triple play and the other team comes to bat. There are all kinds of variations to this contest.

These are just a few types of incentive programs. You are only limited by your own creativity. Incentives do work, but take care that they do not place operators in such a position that they hide accidents or try to pay the claims themselves.

TRANSPORTATION OF GUESTS

Imagine you have a van load of IBM executives who have just had a meeting at your hotel; they are on their way to the airport in your hotel courtesy van. The driver, a bellman, who by the way was arrested for driving while intoxicated (DWI) the night before and has a history of traffic violations, fails to stop at an intersection and is hit by a dump truck. What do you think is your exposure? Answer: Get the check book out.

Fleet safety is an area all to often overlooked in our industry. We hand the keys to our vehicles to just about anyone, not realizing we are turning over a loaded gun. Additionally, if you transport more than 15 people in one of your vans this meets the definition of a "commercial vehicle" under the Federal Highway Administration and there are specific laws that must be met with the possibility of fines up to $2,500 in civil penalties per violation. OSHA is now proposing specific driver training and seat-belt regulations. The intention here is not to discuss the laws but to provide a basic outline of activities for preventing loss and minimizing liability.

Driver Screening

When a new driver is hired for the company vehicles it is very important to conduct adequate screening to verify that the individual will not cause problems. Screening should include:

- *Motor vehicle register check.* This is a list of motor vehicle violations over the past few years. They are obtainable from your state division for motor vehicles.
- *Telephone reference check.* It is often difficult to obtain any information from previous employers, but you must make the effort.
- *Road and knowledge testing.* This should be completed prior to employment and cover basic driving skills such as defensive driving habits, signaling, passing, parking, and knowledge of traffic laws. A good resource for a checklist is your insurance carrier.
- *Physical examination.* This should be completed before a position is offered. A guideline examination can be obtained from your insurance carrier; however, let the physician keep the completed form in his or her files.

With all of this information, it should be possible to make an informed decision whether or not to hire this individual. The company cannot afford not to implement some form of strict screening process.

Each driver needs to be trained at initial hire and at least annually thereafter on the following topics:

- Company rules and regulations.
- Equipment use, pre-trip and post-trip inspections.
- Routes and schedules.
- Emergency procedures.
- Defensive driving techniques.
- Traffic regulations.
- Accident procedures.

Additionally, on an annual basis each driver should be re-checked on their motor vehicle register and have a physical.

There are many resources to help in establishing a good fleet safety program. This is a brief guideline to help you begin the process of developing your own program.

SUBSTANCE ABUSE

The National Institute on Drug Abuse has reported that approximately two-thirds of individuals entering the workplace have used illegal drugs at least once. Drug abuse is highest amongst those aged 20–40. Not all abuse occurs before hire; much occurs later during employment and is related to stress. In the hospitality and restaurant industry, where there tends to be a lower pay scale and labor is generally unskilled, the possibility of substance abuse has been shown to be quite significant. What can be done about it? First it must be recognized that a problem exists. However, this does not mean instituting random or full drug screening.

Laws on drug testing in the private sector are still in their formative stages. In fact, cases are before the Supreme Court attempting to make random testing illegal because it is alleged to be a violation of an employee's privacy. The question will probably still be being contested at the time of reading this. Drug testing could very well eliminate so many candidates for the hospitality industry that operators will be hard pressed to fill many already vacant positions.

Substance abuse poses a threat to the abuser as well as threatening others' safety and increasing the company's liability exposure. Most companies have some form of termination policy that includes being caught drinking or using illegal drugs on the job. However, many companies fail to train their managers in recognition of substance abuse or provide some form of Employee Assistance Program to help salvage an otherwise good employee. If a company is in the process of deciding to take a strong stand on this issue and wants to implement drug screening, then the legalities, risks, and whether the benefits outweigh the disadvantages needs to be thoroughly researched. If the decision is to test, experts today recommend uniform testing of all employees, including company executives. A company policy document should define the company's position on all forms of substance abuse, state when and how testing will be performed, indicate that the labs are certified and have a strong program of chain of custody on all samples. Measures should be included for second tests for confirmation on all positive first tests. Never release any information on any unconfirmed tests. Be sure the company sets up a voluntary Employee Assistance Program to refer first-time offenders for treatment. In this way, if they fail subsequent tests and fail to show for treatment, discharge will be looked upon more favorably by the courts. Last and most importantly, check local and state laws to verify compliance.

Drug testing alone does not make a substance abuse program. It is necessary to (1) train management to spot abuse and how to deal with it; (2) implement and promote an Employee Assistance Program; (3) put into place education programs for the work force that discuss the risks involved; and (4) communicate clearly and sympathetically with employees. Substance abuse does have an impact on everyone. A simple caring approach can go a long way to discouraging abuse in the work place and reduce the potential for accidents.

THE NEW THREATS: AIDS AND OTHER LIFE-THREATENING ILLNESSES

AIDS has grabbed all the publicity, but hepatitis A and B demand serious consideration too. It is false and dangerous thinking to assume these things are not part of our environment. AIDS and other life-threatening diseases can impact us at any time.

Consider the security officer who gets caught in the middle of an altercation between a prostitute and client or between two prostitutes. They are cut and bleeding and the security officer is administering first-aid, or perhaps the officer is bitten. It can happen and disease can be transmitted, if blood is transferred to an open wound. An employee who uses a needle to dispense illicit drugs and has contracted hepatitis B can transmit it via a cut if the blood comes into contact with blood of the individual administering first aid. An employee might contract hepatitis A, which is communicable via other modes of transmission such as food. What do you do with an excellent employee who has worked for you for several years and comes to you one day and tells you in confidence that he or she has AIDS? Under federal law, an individual suffering from AIDS is considered to be a handicapped person entitled to legal protection. These are all tough situations, but there are some precautions that can be taken to minimize potential exposure.

All first-aid kits should include a ready supply of disposable good-quality latex gloves. Seek advice from suppliers on what they recommend. Train first-aiders in dealing with the exposure of AIDS and other blood-transmitted diseases. There should be a procedure to transfer employees to nonfood-handling positions if there is a communicable illness that could be transmitted to the public. Lastly, establish a policy for dealing with life-threatening illnesses including but not limited to heart diseases, AIDS, and cancer.

The policy should cover who to contact regarding specifics such as medical people, employee relations, and legal matters, and the extent to which the company will accommodate and modify jobs to fit the medical condition. Maximum confidentiality has to be a part of every policy and case.

Dealing with these issues is not easy and a tremendous amount of sensitivity must be afforded the affected employee by management. These issues, if not properly managed, can result in lawsuits and other employee-relations problems, let alone the liability potential.

TYING UP LOOSE ENDS

The special activities discussed in this chapter are not the minimum, but ones that either must be done because they are required by law and/or because they make good business sense. Accident prevention is not hard to accomplish. What is hard is changing one's attitude and behavior to embrace it as we do other things in our lives. These programs take time and effort but the rewards are great in improving the quality of life for both management and employees.

CHAPTER 8

Measuring Results

Costs must be known in order to allow motivation and setting of performance objectives. If a business did not forecast or measure sales-to-profits ratios it would have a great deal of difficulty obtaining investments or even determining whether it was keeping its head above water. Measuring is essential in business to tell if whether improvement has occurred. The simplistic premise is that "What gets measured gets done."

Quality and safety are really synonymous. Philip Crosby in his book *Quality Without Tears* discusses the importance of measurement as a key element in the quality process. Without it how can one know the cost of change let alone the benefits of change? He goes on to discuss the idea of a "hassle-free" company as one in which employees and management are on the same side, with the creation of pleasant working relationships, a smooth system, and happy employees. The significance is having happy employees, which will make the guest happy also. The following is a quote from Crosby's book—observe how the word *safety* can be interchanged so easily with the word *quality*:

> The cost of quality [safety] has been a subject of discussion for 25 years. However, it has only been used as a means of measuring defects on the manufacturing line. It has not been used as a management tool. That's because it hasn't been presented to management in terms it can understand. (Crosby 1984, p. 85)

He goes on in the following paragraph to talk about how quality is divided into two areas:

> ...the price of nonconformance (PONC) and the price of conformance. Prices of nonconformance are all the expenses involved in doing things wrong. Price of conformance is what is

necessary to spend to make things come out right. (Crosby 1984, pp. 85–86)

According to Crosby, the price of nonconformance is around 35 percent of your operating cost versus only 3–4 percent if you get it right the first time. As a direct corollary, the lack of a good accident prevention program is a price of nonconformance. As soon as an injury occurs, the associated costs of worker downtime, management intervention, equipment failure, and bad press all contribute to the PONC let alone the real dollar price of the injury. Thus, measuring accident prevention is as much a part of business as measuring sales and profit.

FREQUENCY, SEVERITY, AND COST—THE BASICS OF PERFORMANCE

How is performance measured in accident prevention? To begin let us first deal with some basic tenets that all safety professionals are used to seeing but of which management has little understanding. In the classic sense, accident prevention can be measured in two ways: frequency and severity. Chapter 3 reviewed some incident rates published by the National Safety Council. Those incident rates were based on formulas defined by OSHA in its recordkeeping standard. OSHA has specific definitions for classifying various types of injuries for statistical measurements:

Occupational injury is any injury such as a cut, fracture, sprain, amputation, etc., which results from a work accident or from an exposure involving a single incident in the work environment.

Occupational illness of an employee is any abnormal condition or disorder, other than one resulting from an occupational injury caused by exposure to environmental factors associated with employment. It includes acute and chronic illnesses or diseases that may be caused by inhalation, absorption, ingestion, or direct contact.

Lost workdays are those days the employee would have worked but could not because of an occupational injury or illness. The number of lost days should not include the day of injury or the onset of illness. The number of days includes all days (consecutive or not) on which, because of injury or illness: (1) the employee would have worked but could not, or (2) the employee was assigned to a temporary job, or (3) the employee worked at a permanent job less than full time, or (4) the employee worked at a permanently assigned job but could not perform all duties normally connected with it.

Recordable cases are those involving an occupational injury or illness, including death. Not recordable are first-aid cases that involve one-time treatment and subsequent observation of minor scratches, cuts, burns, splinters, etc., that do not ordinarily require medical care, even though such treatment is provided by a physician or registered professional personnel.

Nonfatal cases without lost workdays are cases of occupational injury or illness that do not involve fatalities or lost workdays but result in (1) transfer to another job or termination of employment, or (2) medical treatment, other than first aid, or (3) diagnosis of occupational illness, or (4) loss of consciousness, or (5) restriction of work or motion.

Calculating OSHA incident rates is relatively simple even though the terms and definitions are complex. As mentioned earlier, there are two primary statistical measurement areas. The first is frequency of accidents.

The frequency of accidents is calculated by taking the total number of recordable cases and dividing it by the total number of manhours and multiplying the result by a base of 200,000. The base is supposed to represent the equivalent of 100 full-time workers. The frequency of non-fatal accidents with no lost time or even first-aid cases can also be calculated. Each of these measurements tells something about the health of the program. Many safety professionals have stated numerous negative effects of putting too much reliance on measuring the compiled frequencies of accidents that do not involve payment of lost wages because of management's tendency to circumvent the system and not report these accidents in order to make their record look good (Culbertson, 1981). However, in my opinion they should be measured for the simple reason of comparison with other competitors or the industry at large. On an annual basis, the National Safety Council publishes its *Accident Facts*. That publication provides frequencies of all the various types of industries including hotels and restaurants. This at least gives a benchmark for comparison with industry's norm. Additionally, these frequencies have to be calculated for OSHA in order to comply with its recordkeeping standards. Similarly, the U.S.

Department of Labor, Bureau of Statistics, issues an annual report for OSHA of all reporting units of industries extrapolated to the entire industry for each industry segment. This is a more comprehensive report, as the National Safety Council figures are for member organizations only.

Putting too much emphasis on frequency can cause a lot of petty argument about what is reportable and what is not, but if we believe that safety and quality are synonymous then frequency of even first-aid cases is important. The way to get around the bickering and cheating is to set up a claims reporting system that is tied into the workers' compensation system, because as soon as a claim is filed there is a record and if the manager fails to report it down goes his or her bonus. This is another good reason for centralized first-aid, the New Loss Control Concept, and/or centralized call-in of accidents.

There is another frequency measurement that needs to be taken into account, that is, a tabulation of guest injuries. This should measure the total number of claims (less those closed without payment), divided by the total number of manhours or total sales, the result multiplied by a base of 200,000 for manhours or $1 million for sales.

As with any measurement, there must be a basis for comparison. The best way is to compare with prior years. This gives an apples-to-apples comparison and makes a fair proposition for the managers whose performance is tied to their frequency.

The second primary statistical measure is of severity, probably the most difficult to measure and understand in classical terms. Traditional safety practitioners and OSHA state that severity is a measure of the number of lost work days. Severity is like a roll of the dice. For every slip and fall, one could involve death while hundreds could involve no injury or minor injuries. But severity is a critical measurement because it is associated with dollars lost. Severity should encompass the measurement of all costs, including incurred claims cost, safety program cost, excess insurance costs. In essence it measures the cost-effectiveness of the program. Severity then becomes a measurement that business people can embrace. The numerator should be dollars lost, while the denominator should be whatever is the universal yardstick in the organization (Culbertson, 1981). In the organization I came from, that universal number was dollars of sales; as a result severity was measured as a cost percent of sales. This made it very easy for managers to know where they stood relative to budget, as it became an immediate performance measure and motivator. But severity cannot be taken alone without frequency. For example, if out of total losses of, say, $100,000 dollars, $75,000 was from one accident, does that signify a bad safety program. Not necessarily. Thus, frequency is important as an indicator of program health. In fact, an additional way of measuring severity is to calculate the number of lost-time cases or cases where lost wages were paid as a frequency. This can measure the effectiveness of the modified duty program.

RISK RANKING—WHERE TO TARGET YOUR EFFORTS IN THE COMPANY

For a middle-sized to large company, risk ranking takes on a major importance in order to focus accident prevention efforts toward those facilities that for various reasons need more attention than other properties in the company. The way to begin is to take all of the measurement indices and weight them for importance; this could also include security risks or potential property loss criteria. As an example, let us look at a company with 10 properties and use the following risk ranking criteria:

Total accident frequency. If the company objective was 10, then a property that had a frequency in a given range would receive a Risk Factor Value based on that frequency.

Frequency range	RFV
0–10	0
11–14	1
15–18	2
19–21	3
22 and above	4

Indemnity frequency. These are cases where lost wages have been paid; the company objective is 4.

Frequency range	RFV
0–4	0
5–6	1
7–8	2
9 and above	3

Loss rate as a percent of sales. Actual dollars lost for current year expressed as a percentage of sales; the company objective is 0.35.

Range	RFV
0–0.18	0
0.18–0.35	1
0.36–0.54	2
0.54 and above	3

Number of employee claims over $10,000 in reserves. This helps place an emphasis on controlling the high-dollar exposure.

Range	RFV
0–1	0
2–3	1
4–5	2
6–7	3
8 and above	4

Number of guest claims over $5,000 in reserves. This places a higher emphasis on guest injuries.

Range	RFV
0–1	0
2–3	1
4–5	2
6–7	3
7 and above	4

Now the criteria are established, it is necessary to be specific about what is considered high-risk versus low-risk. The following is a guide for our example:

Low risk = 0 to 5
At risk = 6
At high risk = 7
At very high risk = 10
Big problems = 11 and above

Example

The RFV is calculated by adding up points for each category in the risk ranking criteria. Listed below are the sum totals for each of our hypothetical properties.

Property	RFV	Assessment
A	0	Low risk
B	5	Low risk
C	6	At risk
D	10	Very high risk
E	7	High risk
F	1	Low risk
G	7	High risk
H	0	Low risk
I	2	Low risk
J	8	High risk

For the district manager or safety manager for these 10 facilities who had limited resources, using this type of risk ranking approach would allow focusing of efforts on those properties that really need the help. More than likely, these same high-risk properties would be having other problems.

Properties D, E, G, and J are the high-risk profiles and as such demand immediate attention. One of the first steps would be to schedule a meeting with the Quality Safety Committee at each property. There is no need for an elaborate paper audit exercise; simply talking to the employees will reveal what is wrong. In any case, if performance is tied to the numbers, it is more than likely that this point will never be reached.

Risk ranking is a very valuable tool but how are efforts focused toward a particular type of injury or claim?

TREND ANALYSIS—WHERE TO TARGET A SPECIFIC PROGRAM

Accident Trend Analysis

Accident trend analysis is not new. In a call-in claims management program, the New Loss Control Concept, or even centralized first-aid there is the capability of entering that information into a database program or even manually onto a form that will sort the data by type of accident, location, time, etc. There are off-the-shelf risk-management information programs that can be used with a personal computer. A small company does not need to buy elaborate software; a simple spreadsheet program with database applications can easily be set up to track accident trends and at the same time calculate frequency measures.

The importance of tracking trends cannot be overstated. This information allows energies to be focused on a specific injury cause such as back strains to housekeepers or slips and falls on level surfaces in the lobby. Also, it is important to have someone identified as the coordinator of this data. Again, if the claims coordination is set up properly, this becomes an easy exercise.

Behavior Trend Analysis

Chapter 3 referred to this analysis under the heading "Identifying Accident Causes." Once behavior lists have been set up that describe how a job should be performed safely, direct observation allows you to note the number of *safe* behaviors exhibited by that particular job group. Tracking of these observations allows focusing in on which behaviors need reinforcement and also provides a gauge for measuring the success of a particular program.

Setting up these measurement programs can be a little overwhelming for a small organization. My suggestion would be to seek some outside help because, without measurement of results, there will be no success in motivating managers to perform.

SETTING OBJECTIVES—HOW TO MOTIVATE MANAGERS TO PERFORM

Once the measurement criteria, trend analysis, and so on have been set up, they have to be imprinted into management's consciousness. The way to do this is to make it a part of the business planning and budgeting process. Chapter 1 introduced the idea of management's "hot button"—and that is their pocket book.

Establish objectives in each of the measurement criteria areas. Once top management have put their blessing on those objectives, establish budgets to cover projected accident costs, administrative costs, and prevention program costs. The critical element here is to make accident prevention a management responsibility, a controllable like food costs or labor. Put accident prevention into everyone's job description. Then provide a rating category on whatever is used for a performance appraisal that includes general accident prevention support and meeting of the objectives. Accident prevention thus becomes objective, something management can embrace and deal with and control.

Publish and republish results. Good old-fashioned competition between units can never hurt and is always an excellent motivator for managers and employees. A company I worked for published a document called a "ranking comparison." That listed each facility and its standing in meeting the objectives. The ranking was from best to worst within a region, with a comparison between regions. At the end of the year, President's awards were issued in a big celebration for the best in a region, the best region, and the best in the nation. This type of scheme can be given a lot of press in the company's employee magazine.

Publishing results also lets management know where it stands during the course of the year so that mid-course adjustments can be made. There is power in numbers, especially when they are in the limelight. As Philip Crosby stated:

> Management really has three basic tasks to perform:
> (1) establish the requirements that employees are to meet,
> (2) supply the wherewithal that the employees need in order to meet those requirements, and (3) spend all its time encouraging and helping employees to meet those requirements. (Crosby, 1984, p. 59).

As a result, without measuring progress there is no way to recognize performance or motivate employees to perform. Accident prevention is no different than any other management responsibility. Successful companies display the point—they take conformance to standards and prevention of problems very seriously. They realized early on that without concern for the safety of their employees and guests there is little chance of achieving a quality operation and improving profits in the long term.

In closing, there are six key elements to a successful Accident Prevention *Process*. Note the change from a program to a process: a process is permanent, whereas programs come and go.

- Senior management involvement in accident prevention.
- Reinforcement of safe work behavior at the unit level.
- Effective charge-back system of the losses to the unit.
- Specific pool of funds to correct hazards with no red tape.
- Bottom-up approach to unit-level programs for ownership.
- Adequate professional safety staffing.

Part II

Designing for Safety and Security

CHAPTER 9

The Design Process

Simply put, the design process is the bringing together of all the salient points that comprise the development of a facility—for our purposes the building of a hotel, motel, or restaurant. The design process has many phases, which we will address later. Suffice it to say that this process affects two major groups: the guests or patrons and the people who operate the facility. The best designs not only anticipate the guests' and patrons' needs, and the functional requirements of the staff and management, but integrate all aspects of safety and security. Therefore it is important that the design process should include an understanding of operations, management, and loss control.

There are two basic reasons why it is so important to include safety and security in the design process: litigation defense and prevention. Taken individually or together they can represent large sums of money lost or saved by the operation quite apart from the individual pain and suffering that can be experienced. Loss control design can also make the facility easier to operate and maintain. In fact, some elements can aid in accessibility, making it easier to move luggage carts, service dollies, linen carts, and cleaning and maintenance equipment.

With the potential negative impact certain losses can have, a company cannot afford not to include safety and security in the design of its facility. Unfortunately, the industry is in its infancy in terms of designing out potential hazards. This lack of involvement reflects not so much a lack of concern, as the fact that most are unaware of simple design elements that can be implemented with little or no cost but have a significant impact on loss reduction. But awareness is growing; not only is the industry caught up in a liability litigation explosion, but architects and engineers are facing a rising exposure of professional liability claims related to negligent design and specification of products that may be involved in personal injury litigation.

Recently I was contacted by an architect who was caught up in a situation that could have cost him his business or at least raised his professional insurance premiums or involved the possibility of being dropped from coverage. What had happened is not uncommon these days. The architect was contracted to develop the design and complete a program for a new upscale restaurant. When the time came to draft specifications relative to floor coverings, the architect specified ceramic tiles for the restaurant public area and quarry tiles for the kitchen; both were required to be slip-resistant. However, he failed to set criteria for (1) slip resistance, (2) a method for approving substitutions, and (3) verifying claims of performance. As a result, the tile contractor installed a red body glazed tile with a very minor amount of abrasive grit in both the public and kitchen areas. The manufacturer of the tile, in the sales literature, claimed that it was suitable for use in restaurants and so the contractor and architect assumed that it was a suitable product for both areas. As it turned out, it was not suitable in either location. Within the first few weeks of opening, 12 patrons had fallen on the floor as well as several employees. The owner and architect naturally became very concerned.

In this situation the architect actually had more to lose financially than did the restaurant owner. The architect's insurance company had already begun sending very nervous signals about the impact this situation would have on his insurability as a professional. Very few architects can remain in business without professional liability insurance. This was a case where if the architect or the owner had utilized the skills of a Loss Control Consultant or safety engineer they would probably not have been facing the problem.

The most significant future challenge for the hospitality and restaurant industries will be lack of manpower. We have an aging population in which soon there will not be anyone to flip the burgers or make the beds. According to population experts, in the U.S. population the older consumer represents the fastest-growing segment in the market place. By the year 2000, 31 percent of the population will be aged 55 or older. These are the people with the disposable income: for example, the over fifties purchase 80 percent of all luxury travel. As the market continues to evolve more in line with older affluent consumers, as well as an older work force, the result will be an increase in liability and workers' compensation risks. With this increased risk exposure, and as states continue to be more liberal with benefits and with the continued increase of personal injury litigation, safety and security have to be planned before the doors are opened. Chapters 10 and 11 will outline some specific suggestions for achieving the inclusion of loss control into the design objective. First we need to know how to get involved.

ROLE OF THE DESIGN TEAM

A simple definition of a design team is: A team of professionals in charge of overseeing and coordinating the design and preparation of construction documents as well as managing the construction and operation of the facility (Kohr, 1990). The following list portrays the typical design team as outlined by Rutes and Penner in their book *Hotel Planning and Design*:

Owner The owning company, which may also be the developer, an equity investor, operator, government, or a combined joint venture of any of the above.

Developer The entity initiating and actively managing the overall development process.

Operator The hotel company that holds a management agreement and, normally, a technical services agreement with the owner or joint-venture partner or developer.

Franchisor The hotel company that holds a hotel franchise agreement with the owner (or franchisee).

Lender Institution providing primary debt financing; may also be an owner or joint-venture partner.

Construction lender Institution providing temporary financing until construction is complete.

Feasibility consultant Independent accounting or similar professional firm recognized in the field of hotel development and finance.

Design consultants Owner controlled versus architect controlled.

Lender's inspecting architect Architect independently reviewing design and construction for the lender.

Contractors   All trades.

Construction manager   Consultant employed by the owner to manage the construction and equipping of the hotel if not managed directly by the owner or operator. (Rutes and Penner, 1985, p. 234)

The various types of consultants are:

Owner-controlled

Architect
Interior designer
Food service equipment
Laundry equipment
Graphics
Geotechnical
Site surveyor
Environmental impact

Architect-controlled but approved by owner

Structural engineer
Mechanical, electrical and elevator engineers
Civil engineer
Fire protection
Audiovisual
Acoustical
Traffic and parking
Landscape architect
Estimator

Interior designer-controlled but approved by the owner

Lighting
Graphics (Rutes and Penner, 1985)

However, where is the loss control consultant or the safety and security engineer? The world is changing, and with that change so too will the design team of Rutes and Penner. Every day higher and higher standards are being demanded. As in the case of the architect discussed earlier, not enlisting the services of a loss control consultant can be a serious mistake on both the owner's and architect's part. This kind of consultancy need not be from outside; it could easily be services provided by the owner's or operator's Loss Control staff if that expertise exists (Sinnott, 1985). As stated by Rutes and Penner:

The techniques developed to effectively deal with design and
construction of hotels [and in my opinion motels and
restaurants], require special coordination procedures among the
owner developers, operators, architects and consultants....
Extensive guidance is provided by the operator... during the
design process to assure that the structure complies with
standards required by the operator or franchisor. (Rutes and
Penner, 1985, p. 233).

With all the changes and refinements in operations and systems,
as well as the risk exposure faced, the operator needs to participate
fully in the design process and that needs to include safety and
security. The more safety and security can be designed into the
facility, the easier it will be to operate, and the lower will be the
investment and operating costs. To illustrate, imagine what it
costs to retrofit a major system such as fire or security or replace
a lobby floor because it was not properly planned into the facility.

If the Loss Control Consultant was fitted into the Rutes and
Penner design team, it would be slightly offset from the design
team and other consultant teams. This is due to the dual role this
professional plays whether the individual is an employee of the
owner/operator or an outside consultant hired with the other
consultants. Those roles are:

- Staff function, technical advisor to the owner, operator and
  design team.
- Technical consultant to the architect's and interior designer's
  respective teams.

As a staff function to the design team, the Loss Control Consultant
conducts risk assessments, evaluates loss exposures, recommends
systems and products, and establishes the safety and security
design criteria for the facility which then become part of the
overall design objective.

As the technical consultant, the Loss Control Consultant
actually communicates the safety and security design criteria to
the architect and interior design teams. This communication takes
the form of plan reviews or plan checks. The Loss Control
Consultant assists these teams in interpretation of the safety and
security design criteria and how to apply it to the specific project.
In the world of security this would involve defining systems, their
functions, and their locations to the electrical design engineer.

Involvement by the Loss Control Consultant should begin at
the preliminary design phase as concepts are being discussed and

changed. This involvement should continue into construction document preparation. Finally, concluding that involvement at acceptance, systems are tested and turned over to the operator. The next section will deal with each phase of a project's development and discuss what happens at each phase as well as the role of the Loss Control Consultant.

STAGES OF DEVELOPMENT FOR A TYPICAL PROPERTY

Feasibility and Development

It is at this stage that the proposed new facility is studied for marketability, competition, site, and financial projections; it is also called a proforma. A consensus of objectives and design goals must be achieved. The facility is defined by a facility program (Rutes and Penner, 1985), which is a listing of all spaces and their associated square footage. Additionally, the overall operations are described to insure that the facility has an overall philosophy of how it will function. Lastly, an estimated project budget is developed that includes construction, systems, furniture and fixtures, developmental costs, opening expenses, and working capital.

A Loss Control Consultant should input space needs for security, first aid, and secure storage, and should also be involved in establishing the system budgets. However, before this can be accomplished, the Loss Control Consultant must complete a thorough analysis of the potential risk factors that the facility will face, including property and people loss.

This analysis is called a *risk assessment*, or *threat assessment* in the case of security issues. For the in-house Loss Control staff this should be fairly routine as all the data and track histories of like facilities are readily available. But if an outside consultant is being used, these records need to be made available. These would include things like accident reports, insurance inspections, insurance requirements, and any data that would assist in assessing all loss-producing exposures. The next step is to contact local officials including fire, police, and building code officials. Here information should be obtained on local conditions, crime potentials and the like. Competitors in the area should also be checked, not only those next door but all around town. One of the big issues in liability litigation is industry norms and practices—did the facility across the street experience high incidents of crime and increase their security? This information is extremely valuable in establishing the safety and security design criteria for a particular facility. It also allows for the fine tuning of the types of security hardware and operations for the facility. By these means, realistic estimates of costs for the total project budget are established.

After all this study and refinement of costs and the facility definition, funding is obtained in all sorts of ways and, if successful, the project gets underway and the preliminary design phases are entered.

Development of Design Criteria: Setting the Design Directive

Before any new facility can be designed and built, it must be quantified what the facility will be when completed. Without this knowledge architects cannot complete their job. Design criteria are the body of information which clearly outlines how each space is related to other spaces and how that space is defined in physical terms. The development of design criteria which then translate into the "design guide" is paramount to the success of any major development of more than one facility. Usually development of the criteria is accomplished by in-house personnel with the help of an architect. Each operational discipline inputs its needs for space, mechanical, electrical, plumbing and special systems, and its relationships to other areas. At the same time, members of the architect's and interior design teams assist the operator put all of the data into perspective. The Loss Control Consultant should be involved in the review and development of this very important document, with the role of specifying those design and system items that will minimize loss-producing events that apply to the particular product under development. Once the guide is complete and everyone has signed off its content, the next step is the design directive.

A design directive is exactly what its name suggests. It describes the parameters of what is required for a particular project and includes design criteria that have been interpreted and applied to the project. The role of the Loss Control Consultant is very clear: to develop specific interpretations of the safety and security criteria to fit the specific project—for example, the use of CCTV cameras, which should not be used in remote areas if it is not planned to have a security person watching the monitors 24 hours a day. However, some criteria cross all project lines; for instance, slip-resistance flooring and handrails on stairs.

The key to this whole process is bringing everyone together before beginning serious development to gain a consensus as to where the directive is headed. Anyone who has tried to retrofit a major system or replace a lobby floor will appreciate the point. Chapters 10 and 11 will offer some specific loss-control design criteria for hotels, motels, and restaurants.

Preliminary Design Phases

It is at these early stages that the Loss Control Consultant can have a dramatic impact on the overall design. Here refinements are continually being made to the overall design in order to meet the design directive. It is also the time to refine estimates for project completion. Many projects die at this phase for a variety of reasons, usually related to project costs versus projected returns. There are three phases that fall within the area of preliminary design: conceptual design, schematic design, and design development. Each is a continuing saga of getting the facility to meet the design directive and at times modifying the directive to meet changing conditions.

The conceptual design phase is a basic layout of the facility including gross floor space allocations, elevations of the structure, an artist's rendering, and a site plan. During this process the operations people sign off on the "look" of the new property. The Loss Control Consultant should be evaluating the overall design for materials handling flow problems, inadequate storage, blind and remote areas, site access, handicap access, parking layout, and so on.

At schematic design, the facility program is finalized and all of the square footage is assigned. Walls begin to subdivide the larger spaces and tradeoffs are made to further refine space allocations on the micro scale. At this point a project kick-off meeting is called by the architect in order to acquaint all the outside consultants with internal operations and specialists. Also the architect will have received final comments relating to gross design concerns. At this phase, the Loss Control Consultant needs to become more specific as to requirements for stairs, ramps, work flow, security systems, locking hardware, and so on. These concerns are then transferred into the next phase.

The design development phase is the "last chance" phase. This phase finalizes the facility's design from the site to every public and back of house area. Generally a project at this phase has received all approvals and a green light for construction. For the Loss Control Consultant it is the last opportunity to make changes that will not appreciably affect the cost of the project. Yet, as a Loss Control Consultant, I see many people skip this phase, thinking the architect has read their mind and their requirements will magically appear on the drawing during construction document phases.

How should the Loss Control Consultant communicate to the architect? The process is called *design review*. Here drawings are given to the Loss Control Consultant by the architect for comments. The first such review begins during the conceptual phase and continues on through construction documents. In my own work I have found the use of a check sheet that lists the loss prevention criteria by area an excellent means of commenting on the design. It also saves having to look the criteria up. At these early stages the types of security systems need to be identified so that a rough estimate can be made of the costs. In the case of hotels and motels, the type of guestroom locking system should be decided. This is the purpose of the risk assessment—to assist operations in deciding which systems are needed. Upon completion of these reviews, the design criteria is then applied to the project and areas needing refinement or change are noted and modifications are made by the design team.

At this stage, the building has substance and the other consultants on the design team are beginning their heavy involvement in development of construction documents.

Construction Document Development

This is the time when systems of all types are shown on the drawings. Specifications for every component of the facility are drafted and the Interior Designer is readying a presentation of the "look" of each space. At this phase the project is generally a go project, though there may be a few delays due to code approvals, zoning appeals, and the like.

This phase is broken down into four segments: 30, 60, 90, and 100 percent document development. The ultimate goal is to produce drawings and specifications that fully describe the facility to be built so that contractors can competitively bid the project and there are no surprises because, say, someone has forgotten to show a telephone outlet in the guestroom.

During the plan review process, it is the responsibility of the Loss Control Consultant to "watchdog" the documents to ensure everything meets the safety and security design criteria. Coordination meetings usually take place amongst the various consultants and operations personnel, including the Loss Control Consultant, to ensure that the documents are clear as to product expectations and scope of work by each contractor. For example, a typical recessed door magnetic contact alarm, costing all of $7.50, requires no less than coordinating the work of four different contractors in order to get the device installed; in this case, security system installer, electrician, door supplier, and the hollow metal frame contractor. It is also the case that any changes after this last design stage will cost significantly in what is endearingly termed as a "scope change." This is where contractors make their money, because they know from past experience that the drawings and specifications are not always correct or in sync.

The Loss Control Consultant must pay close attention to all details, including reviewing finish schedules, door schedules, elevation details, specifications, and so on, in order to ensure the safety and security design directive has been met. Another specific duty of the Loss Control Consultant is to draft job-specific security systems specifications and provide them to the electrical consultant for inclusion into the Division 16 Electrical section of the job specifications, or at least to guide the electrical consultant as to the types and the basic functions of the systems so they can research systems or hire a specialty contractor/ designer to handle the whole piece.

Once construction documents are complete, they are turned over to construction management for solicitation of bids by various contractors. In some cases, the owner/operator could be the general contractor or a general contractor may be hired. In any case, the time for designing is in essence over and it is time to build.

Construction

During this phase the Loss Control Consultant acts as a technical resource to the construction manager and operations by:

- Reviewing security bids for technical accuracy.
- Reviewing and approving substitutions of products, like floor surfaces.
- Reviewing and approving shop drawings.
- Conducting site inspections.
- Overseeing final acceptance of the systems.
- Completing a final physical punch.
- Coordinating and conducting opening training.

Site inspections are very important for the Loss Control Consultant. They help establish a liaison with the contractors and help dispel confusion about systems by answering Request for Information Transmittals and keeping a handle on construction methods. The fact that something is correctly shown on the drawings does not mean that the execution will be right. I have visited many a job site and have seen first-hand stairway concrete finishes that were wavy on top, sloped too much, or had varying riser height. The time to catch problems is at the beginning, not a week before opening.

Getting Ready to Open

At this point in the development there is significant overlap of duties performed by the Loss Control Consultant, which were covered in the previous section. However, opening a new facility is like watching a birth take place. There is pleasure in the fact of having a new facility but there is pain in getting those doors open and the first customer inside. A primary role of the Loss Control Consultant is to support operations staff by ensuring that (1) the security systems are functioning, (2) management has been trained in basic accident prevention, (3) the first-aid program has been set-up, (4) the claims program is established, and (5) deficiency items are in the process of being corrected.

Clearly, the need to have a Loss Control professional as a contributing member of the design team and as a resource to operations has become a necessity rather than a desirable option. This position is worth its weight in gold in the number of times code officials have been satisfied because of a simple creative idea to rectify some on-site problem that allows them to issue an occupancy permit. If there is no Loss Control staff when new facilities are being built, an independent Loss Control Consultant should be hired. Chapter 2 discussed the role of an outside consultant and how to find one. Safety and security must be designed into the facility before the doors open.

Remember the two basic tenets or paradigms for any loss control endeavor: prevention and litigation avoidance and defense.

CHAPTER 10

Safety and Security Factors in Designing Hotels and Motels

GUEST AND EMPLOYEE SAFETY AND SECURITY ISSUES

The Design Objective

Integration of safety and security into building design can at times be difficult and the two can conflict. Take for instance the life safety code, which requires an exit to remain unlocked for emergency egress to the outside. This exit also serves as an exit for employees not wanting to be noticed leaving the building with hotel property. Here is a classic conflict between security and life safety. However, there are ways of accomplishing both objectives. Take for example the installation of magnetic door locks on the exit with an electronic panic device. Egress can be delayed by up to 15 seconds. After that time or during a fire alarm condition, the door will release. Place a CCTV camera at that exit, tie it to a VCR and a magnetic door alarm or motion sensor, and when someone attempts an exit, they will be automatically video recorded.

However great the difficulties may seem, they are not insurmountable. In this example, a little creativity accomplished two objectives that were apparently diametrically opposed.

In hotels and motels, the first order of business is to establish the design objective. But first it is necessary to anticipate the kinds of problems the operator can expect. The following breakdown of accident types by costs is fairly typical in the industry:

Guests

Slips, trips and falls	42 percent
Security related	40 percent

Figure 10-1. Convention hotel—in many ways safety and security concerns are the same as for a convention center, resort, or budget hotel.

Figure 10-2. Resort hotel.

Figure 10-3. Budget hotel.

Other (struck by objects, defective products)	15 percent
Food-borne illness	3 percent

Employees

Slips and falls	42 percent
Materials handling	35 percent
Struck against or by objects	13 percent
Other (chemicals, fights, etc.)	10 percent

The National Safety Council's latest annual *Accident Facts* for accidental deaths by type of accident shows falls to be the number one killer in the home with fires and drowning next.

It is apparent that design can have a significant impact in reducing accident costs simply by (1) designing out slips, trips, and falls, (2) improving security, and (3) concentrating on how materials flow and are stored. For the other types of accidents, as well as improvements over design considerations, commitment from management is necessary as discussed in Part I.

Given the nature of the opportunities, how are design criteria established and who is responsible for implementation?

Responsibility for the Design

The ultimate responsibility for any new facility rests with the designer of record, usually the architect. He or she is charged with ensuring that the facility meets standards and codes for design and construction. The problem is it is too easy to hide behind the veil or rely on a false sense of security about meeting building costs rather than effect good design decisions based on a sound design objective. The excuse is often heard that some feature would detract from the aesthetics or form that the designer is trying to achieve. As stated by Ralph Sinnott:

> The designer must not allow the pursuit of artistic achievement or other objectives to obscure the need for safety. A mother expects her home to be a safe place for a small child to play in. The elderly expect to be protected against their infirmities if they remain housebound. The public in general expects not to be put at risk unnecessarily in the buildings they use. It is the designer's duty to meet these expectations. (Sinnott, 1985, p. 7)

Costs associated with improved safety and security do not have to increase the design and construction costs of the facility. Many ideas can even cost less. For example, to improve security from illegal entry to a building via a fire exit, simply eliminate the exterior hardware, provide an "exit only" panic device and a full astragal. This design actually reduces the costs of that opening while improving security.

Because the designer is the ultimate responsible party, it is the owner and his or her representatives that must establish with the designer the design directive and approve, or at least review, the designs to insure that they incorporate safety and security. Thus, we have a partnership between the designer and the end user and as a result a sharing in the safety and security of guests and employees. As discussed in Chapter 9, the role of the Loss Control Consultant to both the owner and the designer is paramount to the success of any project in achieving safety and security design objectives.

Using History to Establish Criteria

When it comes to safety and security design, history is the best teacher. The mistake most designers and owners make is to assume that building codes and standards are the maximum they must accomplish. In today's environment this could not be further from the truth. Design criteria should be established as a minimum standard unless local codes are more stringent. Criteria should be developed to meet codes and standards nationwide and be based on your claims history.

There is no better barometer for the success of design criteria than actual claims history or incident records. Throughout the rest of this chapter will be listed some basic design criteria that were developed as a result of many years of safety and security claims experience, as well as operational history. Also, some of the design elements are directed toward the future, when safety and security design criteria will need to evolve for the hotel and motel industry.

This chapter is subdivided into the major areas found in hotels and motels. Specialities such as various resort amenities and systems will also be in order to cover all the possible lodging segments. Chapter 11 will continue the process by covering design criteria for restaurants. However, it is not intended to supplant the creative processes. Some of the suggested design items may need to be modified to fit particular environments and should be tempered by a thorough review of local codes and standards. In some cases there may be a better way—the intention is to make readers think about integrating safety and security into their facilities in the same manner as providing matching drapes and bedspreads.

SITE DESIGN

Access to the site is the first thing a guest encounters. Access to a 20-room motel will be quite different from that to a 1000-room resort. However, at either facility there are basic safety and security design concerns that apply. Guests and employees should be able to gain access, know where they are going, park, unload, register, get to employee areas whether it be night or day and whether they are walking or in a wheel chair. And most importantly they must be able to do it safely without fear of an incident occurring.

The mention of people in wheel chairs should not suggest that they are the only ones with a handicap that need to be addressed as part of the overall accessibility program. Handicap access in many ways affords safer access to people who are not handicapped. In any case, the population experts tell us the traveling public is graying and improved accessibility will become a matter of customer preference and expectations. Not to mention the passage of the Americans with Disabilities Act, which makes accessibility a requirement in law.

Specific accessibility issues will not be covered here unless there is a definitive overlap with safety and security. It is highly recommended that anyone involved in hotel and motel accessibility obtain a copy of the book *Design for Hospitality, Planning for*

Accessible Hotels and Motels by Davies and Beasley (1988). Their work will be referred to as it applies to this discussion.

Site design is the first thing a guest and employee sees: what are some of the basic safety and security concerns?

- Directions on how to get around (signage).
- Separate service and public entries.
- Lighting.
- Elevations and surface transitions.
- Access aisles.
- Cover from the elements.
- Adequate parking spaces and turn radii.
- No slip, trip, or fall hazards.
- Nothing that goes bump in the night.

Entrances and Driveways

All main entries and driveways should be a minimum of 26 feet wide if two-way traffic is anticipated. If not, then the minimum width should be 12 feet for a single vehicle. Entries should be clearly marked to show the direction to the major areas of the facility such as the lobby entry, ballroom, restaurants, and service areas. In many instances it is highly advisable to have separate service and public entries, which will help reduce congestion and minimize possible vehicle accidents. As vehicles enter the property there should be posted speed limits of 5–10 m.p.h. Landscaping should not inhibit vision of the drivers. It is wise to have "children playing" signs for extended-stay, resort, and all suite properties that have activity areas and playgrounds.

Two-way traffic requires a painted center line with directional arrows painted on the driveway surface (Figure 10-4). Department of Transportation traffic control signs are necessary throughout the site. Speed bumps are a catch-22; you are damned if you do have them and damned if you don't. On the one hand people trip and fall on them, but on the other they do slow traffic down. The operator has to make a personal choice.

For large resort hotels, with long entries, a "gatehouse" is worth considering. Its function is to provide a welcoming point by having an employee greet guests and visitors and give them directions around the facility. It also improves site security. A gatehouse has psychological value in removing the perceived

Figure 10-4. Traffic flow signage and directional control are key design concerns for all sites.

opportunity for any would-be malefactors. The design of the gatehouse should provide canopies on each side with 20 to 30 footcandles of lighting and 12-foot wide lanes. Adequate heating, ventilation, and air conditioning (HVAC) as well as sun screening are required for the employees.

Site Parking Lots

Parking areas can be divided into two spaces: for vehicles and for pedestrians. Unfortunately, most lots are configured for cars not people. Thus, walking across a large parking lot can be like navigating through a maze of obstacles. People who are walking always seem to walk in the middle of the driveway. To avoid potential injuries and suits, designate crossing areas whenever pedestrians are required to cross traffic to enter your facility (Figure 10-5). Many jurisdictions have design standards for parking lots. The maximum slope is usually 6 percent, which is relatively level. This slope lessens the risk of skidding when surfaces are wet and icy. Parking spaces are usually 8 to 10 feet wide and 18 to 20 feet long, with driving aisles 22 to 24 feet wide. Angled parking allows one-way traffic; the minimum aisle width

Figure 10-5. Pedestrian crossing points should be designated.

should be 12 feet. Handicap spaces should be located near the hotel lobby entry and avoid necessitating the handicapped person to cross traffic to reach the entry. Wheel stops should be avoided if at all possible; people trip over them and maintenance hits them with snow plows and lot sweepers. If they have to be used, they should only be on the periphery of the property, clearly out of the pedestrian travel paths.

Providing for landscape areas and pedestrian ways in the design of parking lots can not only improve safety but enhances the aesthetics as well.

From a security point of view, CCTV cameras may be deemed necessary during the risk assessment. They can be of great value in deterring crime in parking areas. However, the most important security device is adequate lighting (Figure 10-6). According to the Illumination Engineering Society's 1987 lighting handbook, parking lots with high activity and slight hazards should have a minimum footcandle reading of 0.9. That figure is for every spot, curb to curb, and measured with a lightmeter at ground level. Considering pedestrian safety, I suggest that all lodging types should be a minimum of 1 footcandle evenly lit over the lot with a good uniformity ratio to eliminate high spots and dark areas (high-pressure sodium is preferred). This allows your eyes to

Figure 10-6. Site lighting is a crucial security design element in deterring crime.

adjust to surroundings and focus attention on more brightly lit areas such as sidewalks, ramps, steps, and entry points.

Walkways and Changes in Elevation

Closer to the building there will be changes in elevation at stairs and ramps or sidewalks with curb ramps. Extra care is required in their design. There are codes and handicap standards that must not be violated. Figure 10-7 is a drawing of a good curb ramp not only for the handicapped but for other pedestrians as well. Figure 10-8 shows an alternative with landscaped areas. Curb ramps are too often of the wrong slope, or with no tactile warning or built out into the lot (this is allowed in accessibility standards but people trip over them constantly). Ramps and curbs should not be painted with thick yellow highway paint; this becomes super slick when it rains and people are likely to slip and fall. A good finish is staining of concrete, thus maintaining the coarse broom finish that should be on all exterior concrete pedestrian areas. Another alternative is provided by some of the new latex resins that can be sprayed on the surface, making them nonslip. Curbs along walkways should be a minimum of 4 inches and a maximum

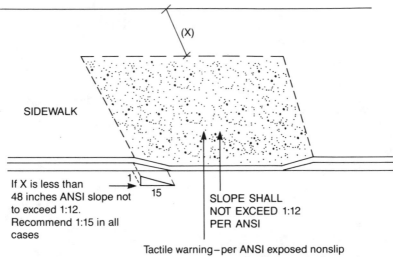

SIDEWALK

(X)

If X is less than
48 inches ANSI slope not
to exceed 1:12.
Recommend 1:15 in all
cases

1
15

SLOPE SHALL
NOT EXCEED 1:12
PER ANSI

Tactile warning–per ANSI exposed nonslip
aggregate concrete, or raised
strips, contrasting color

Figure 10-7. Typical handicap curb ramp.

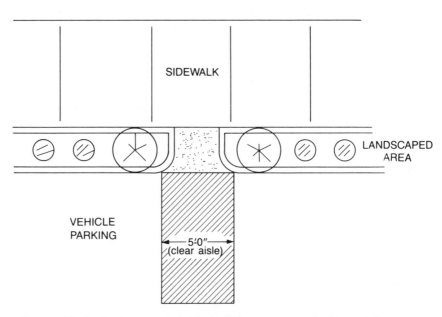

SIDEWALK

LANDSCAPED
AREA

VEHICLE
PARKING

5'-0"
(clear aisle)

Figure 10-8. Curb ramp with landscape area (adapted from a
design by Davies and Beasley, 1988).

of 6 inches high and should be a contrasting color to the walkway and vehicular area. Curbs and sidewalks should be of monolithic construction to eliminate heaving of walkways during freeze–thaw cycles.

Trees with metal tree gate covers should not be placed in walk paths. Inevitably a woman with high heels will get caught in one and fall (Figure 10-9).

All walkways should have a maximum slope of 5 percent. They should be a minimum of 5 feet wide to allow for car overhang. These areas should be illuminated at a minimum 2 footcandles. All steps need handrails on both sides; those that are 88 inches or wider require an intermediate rail and built-in slip-resistant treads and nosings. Treads should be around 12 inches deep with risers around 7 inches high. There should be a minimum of three risers (Figure 10-10). Codes should be checked for stair geometry and single-riser stairs should be avoided—people always trip or fall on them. Ramps, not including curb ramps, should have handrails on both sides and a slip-resistant surface. Retaining walls need 42-inch high guard rails with a 4-inch spacing between

Figure 10-9. An example of proper locations for trees, allowing sufficient width for pedestrians of all types. Note the grassy rest area.

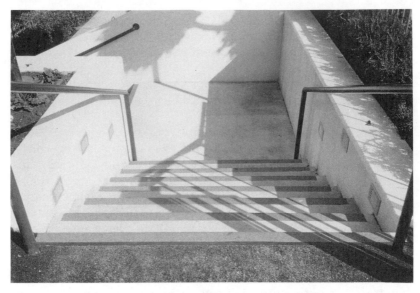

Figure 10-10. This set of exterior stairs has all the key elements of good design, including additional tread illumination.

balustrades and these should be vertical to stop children climbing them like a ladder.

At the main entry of the hotel, provide a flush transition of around 40 feet in length (Figure 10-11). This not only takes care of the accessibility requirement but makes it easier to roll luggage carts in and out and keeps guests from tripping over the traditional curb. At all transitions, provide contrasting color and/or a change in paving material to separate vehicular and pedestrian traffic. Planters and bollards (vehicle barrier) can be used to help in this separation. Color the curb at each end to highlight the tapered area of the curb (Davies and Beasley, 1988). An additional feature for safety and guest comfort is canopy or porte cochere, which helps keep the main lobby entry dry and free of ice and snow. Lighting should be a minimum of 6 footcandles, and 5 footcandles at remote entries. At many facilities, guest keycard access should be provided to improve security after hours by restricting entry to registered guests only. Any stoops or stairs should be avoided at remote entries. However, if they become necessary ensure the stoop or landing is at least 1.5 times the width of the door. The edge must be clearly defined on all stoops and landings. Stairs should be designed to follow code requirements but particularly

Figure 10-11. Provide a flush transition between paving and walk-ways at all main entries.

ensure that handrails are reachable and graspable on both sides, and have a slip-resistant tread with uniform risers and treads.

Outside activity areas require special consideration and will be covered under Resort Amenities. However, walkways in and around activity areas should follow the criteria already discussed.

Parking Structures and Garages

Parking structures and garages have become more prevalent and larger these days. In many cases they are big revenue producers. However, they have attracted vandals, car thieves, muggers, and rapists in recent years. In most cases garages and above-ground parking structures receive very little design effort. This can be a serious mistake. Courts are holding owners, operators and even designers responsible for higher levels of safety for patrons. The intention in this section is not to design the structure but to provide awareness of some basic safety and security design issues.

Parking facilities are an extension of the road system of a community. As a result, in the early design phases a study needs to be completed to determine the level of service and the security risks. A level-of-service study establishes by quantitative means factors such as, safety, maneuverability, convenience, comfort, and delay, and allows the designer to tailor the facility to specific needs (Chrest, Smith, and Bhuyan, 1989). The type of parking can be chosen to be valet, self, monthly, free, or some combination. The overall risk assessment conducted for the property should establish a level of risk for the parking structure. For instance, if there have been physical assaults or car thefts from valet operations in the area, additional active security measures may be warranted.

Security Design Criteria For Self-Parking

Access control design is the first consideration. Who do you want to use the facility and who not. There are numerous revenue control systems on the market which allow operators to do just about anything. Obviously, with free parking there is no need for a cashier, computer, or gates. Some hotels have had gate controls that were operated by the guestroom keycard or by having the driver contact the front desk via an intercom, whereas the clerk would push a button and the gate would open. This is very minimal security, if any. However, where parking is a premium and it is required to restrict it so that only guests can take advantage, this concept will still work without adding labor cost (see Figure 10-12).

A PARC (parking, access, revenue, control) system then is a system for keeping some people out and getting revenues in. The type of system is dependent on the type of facility, the amount of revenue, honesty factors, accurate counts, type of parker, and capacity.

Security measures are either passive or active. *Passive* measures are a physical part of the structure, like open stair towers and elevator lobbies, while *active* security measures include CCTV cameras or a PARC system cashier.

The first rule of thumb is to design the facility to be as open as possible with as few obstructions to visibility as possible. As already mentioned, stair towers and elevator lobbies should be left open (Figure 10-13). This is much easier to accomplish in above-ground structures. Try to convince code officials of the security importance. Barring that, use glass walls and vision panels in doors to provide visibility. As a part of access control, locate attendant booths in such a way that activity at pedestrian and vehicular entry points can be monitored. In some high-risk

Figure 10-12. PARC system using a guest keyboard reader and an intercom to the front desk.

Figure 10-13. Elevator lobbies in garages should be open.

cases, security screening or fencing may be necessary at any grade accessible point of entry on parking structures. Landscaping should be kept to a minimum and kept away from the edge of the structure to eliminate hiding places.

In high crime areas, CCTV and intercoms may be necessary. At least provide a conduit for systems, even if you do not purchase and install the equipment. As a result, the systems can be added at any time in the future should conditions change, which they often do. Another good active design is to use a guestroom keycard electronic reader on the elevator lobby entry doors or at the elevator to activate the call buttons. This is an excellent way to maintain security, especially if the elevator serves guest floors in addition to the lobby and garage levels. In most cases, though, in parking structures I would recommend providing only shuttle elevators that empty onto the hotel lobby level in view of the front desk. This way the person entering must physically get off the elevator and cross the lobby to another elevator bank that serves the guest floors.

The second rule of thumb is not to skimp on the lighting. Lighting is considered the number one deterrent to crime. Table 10-1 shows a comparison in lighting levels recommended by the National Parking Association (NPA) and the Illuminating Engineering Society (IES) *Lighting Handbook*, 1987.

One area not covered is elevator lobbies. Lighting in this area should be 10–15 footcandles. Uniformity of lighting is very important to eliminate dark spots or bright spots. One way to improve and brighten the lighting is to stain the concrete ceiling

TABLE 10-1. Recommended lighting levels for parking structures.

	Footcandles	
	NPA	IES
Entrance	40	50
Stairwells	20	10–15
General parking	6	5
Ramps and corners	—	5
Roof and surface	2	0.8–3.6

Notes: NPA measure lighting levels at 30 inches above the floor, while IES measures lighting levels at the surface.

white, which will help the uniformity. Additionally, ensure that fixtures are glare free.

Rule number three is provide good graphics. This can help eliminate confusion and delays for the guests and get them safely in the hotel. Color coding with level designations can be very effective in guiding the guest to the right floor. In a large structure it may be wise to label areas on a given floor to assist in locating one's vehicle. Always provide a disclaimer for valuables and property left in the vehicle.

In some very large facilities, the PARC system should be designed to provide electronic directional graphics for drivers in order to get them to empty spaces as well as tell the cashier when the lot is full.

Rule four is the use of systems such as emergency call and CCTV. Emergency call systems are the exception rather than the rule. However, some form of emergency communication should be provided at elevator lobbies. This can be an intercom or even a house phone. In high-crime areas some people have placed panic buttons in the structure every 100 to 150 feet. Any form of two-way communication is preferable because it allows you to talk directly to the victim and locate them faster. The big problems with these systems are pranksters and maintenance but in a high-risk area there may not be an option. One way to protect the equipment and improve security is with CCTV systems used in conjunction with emergency call systems.

Provide hold-up buttons or foot-operated devices at cashier booths. It may be wise to include a CCTV camera to monitor the area including the driveways.

As mentioned earlier CCTV should be used judiciously; however, the minimum should be monitoring of the elevator lobbies with a camera, so long as there is someone available to watch the monitor. The use of CCTV in the other areas identified earlier depends on the level of risk and should therefore be carefully reviewed and planned into the design as needed.

Security Design Criteria For Valet Parking

Many hotels valet-park guests as an amenity. In this system a new loss exposure presents itself—car theft.

If you have never been involved in valet services before, take time to really study the idea. Remember that if that Jaguar or Rolls Royce you parked is stolen or damaged then *you pay*! If you are going to valet-park vehicles, try to do only that. Mixed parking (self and valet) is a big mistake and one that is difficult to orchestrate. Unless you are able to totally secure a level to protect the valet-parked cars, I would recommend not mixing parking types.

The prime concern in designing valet parking is obviously access control. But when a major function is breaking up and everyone wants their car, security can be tough. Here is where operations management must have good people with sound policies and programs. When things are slow the metal doors can be dropped (Figure 10-14) and card access or radio-control garage door opener devices can be used to allow access. Another good operational security measure is a special locking device which looks like a tube. The device lets you insert the ignition key into it then close it up, and the only way to open the tube is with a special high-security type key. This provides a way of leaving the keys in the unlocked vehicle although no-one can steal the car using the car's keys. This really speeds up the valet turnaround time.

CCTV and good lighting are a must for valet parking areas. All perimeter access points should be alarmed and authorized

Figure 10-14. A motorized gate to protect access to valet parking.

entry provided at as few locations as possible and only by use of a card or other electronic access control device.

Safety Design Criteria For All Types

Some design features that enhance security also enhance safety. One of the biggest concerns is slips, trips, and falls, but one often overlooked accident potential is head strike hazards. In Figure 10-15 the head strike hazard is obviously the water pipe; also note the ductwork. Most garages should be designed with a clearance of 7 feet; areas designated for handicap parking must have a clearance as high as 8 feet 2 inches, as recommended by the National Parking Association (Chrest, Smith, and Bhuyan, 1989).

Wherever there are clearances less than that required, they should be identified with the international hazard symbol, which is alternating diagonal bars of yellow and black. Also, a "Low Clearance" sign should be posted that states the actual clear height.

At all entry points to the facility, clearance bars made of PVC should be suspended from chains and labeled with the exact clear

Figure 10-15. A lack of coordination during design caused this head-strike hazard.

height. When clear heights change inside, usually when changing from handicap parking to standard parking, the transition must be clearly marked.

Conflicts between vehicles and people are common in these facilities but there are some basic things you can do to minimize the problems. People take the shortest route possible, so if a walkway is provided or designated it should be a realistic expectation that people will use it. At all costs avoid requiring people to walk down ramps.

Any drop-offs or openings must be protected with guardrails; again local codes should be consulted. Balusters must be upright and spaced no more than 4 inches apart. Codes are not very explicit when it comes to garages, so good professional judgment should be used in placing barriers and vehicle restraint mechanisms.

Vehicle restraint systems are used to prevent out-of-control vehicles from breaking through exterior and interior railings. Chrest, Smith and Bhuyan (1989) recommend following the NPA Parking Consultants Council (1987), standards on vehicle restraint design. That standard recommends the following:

> Vehicle restraints should be placed at the perimeter of the structure and where there is a difference in floor elevation of greater than 1 foot. Vehicle restraint systems should not be less than 2 feet in height and should be designed for a single horizontal ultimate load of 10,000 lb applied at a height of 18 in above the floor at any direction.

Slipping, tripping, and falling hazards can easily be avoided with good planning and design. In ice and snow belt areas, there are additional design elements. Good drainage is the first consideration. However, some areas, like uncovered ramp junctures, may be subject to constant freeze–thaw cycles. Trench drains in these areas are quite helpful but sanding may be the only effective control.

All concrete should be broom-finished, which provides good traction and a durable surface. All stairs should have good stair geometry, handrails on both sides, and slip-resistant treads and nosings.

Be sure to avoid wheel stops in areas where pedestrians may walk, including short cuts.

Also to be avoided are raised areas around elevator areas or to connecting bridges. If the design is right the first time there is no need to create problems. In any case, if an area is elevated it must be made accessible to the handicapped and that will involve considerable extra construction costs.

Codes cannot be relied upon to cover every instance to avoid safety and security hazards due to the unique elements of a parking facility. This is where experience and attention to details will minimize the risks and keep the liability exposure to a minimum.

PUBLIC SPACES

The common saying that first impressions are lasting could not be truer when a guest enters a facility for the first time.

Main Entry and Approaching Lobby

At all entries the first thing a guest should walk on is the built-in walk-off mat area (Figure 10-16). This product comes under many different names. The slab area where it is placed is recessed to form a pan and the mat is placed over the top and fastened. The mat is constructed with grooves and holes so that when a person

Figure 10-16. Recessed walk-off mats reduce slips and falls as well as maintenance costs.

walks across it, it scrapes dirt and other debris off shoes, which falls through the holes to a pan below the mat. The mat will dry pedestrian shoes before they enter the hotel, which eliminates the need for those temporary walk-off mats that everyone seems to have in their vestibules and which create more of a hazard because they are never maintained. Walk-off mat areas have the added advantage of reducing maintenance costs for lobby floors and protecting their finish.

Many facilities have double entries to create a vestibule, especially in cold weather areas. This is the perfect location for the built-in mat. Revolving doors, which are common in these entries, should be equipped with governors to restrict their speed. When automatic doors are used, ANSI/BHMA 156.10-1985 should be consulted. Manual doors should be labeled as push and pull and the force necessary to open them should comply with handicap standards of a maximum of 8 lb pull force. Alternatively, a special power-assisted mechanism to facilitate access for the handicap and elderly guests could be contemplated. Any sidelights should be protected by a guardrail or at least decal to warn the pedestrian that they are about to walk into a glass wall. Thresholds should not extend above the surface more than a $\frac{1}{2}$ inch and anything over a $\frac{1}{4}$ inch should be beveled on both sides. Stairs and steps in these areas should be avoided. One good reason for avoiding them is that a ramp or small wheel chair lift will have to be provided to comply with accessibility codes. Avoid all stoops at any entry; if there is a grade difficulty, use a ramp approach instead. However, if there must be a stair system, proper design is critical in this high-traffic area. If a stair is put in, in most localities a wheel chair lift or ramp will be needed for accessibility.

Stair design throughout the facility should meet the following basic criteria as stated by Jake Pauls, a leading stair expert in a paper presented at the First World Conference on Accident and Injury Prevention held in Stockholm, Sweden:

- Steps that can be readily seen (see Figure 10-17).
- Treads large enough to provide adequate footing.
- Reachable and graspable handrails. (Pauls, 1989, p. 8)

In more detail:

- Uniform riser height of not more than 7 inches.
- Uniform tread width of not less than 11 inches.

Figure 10-17. This set of stairs meets the safety design objective. Notice the transition from a patterned carpet to a solid color on the treads.

- Nosing should project no more than $1\frac{1}{2}$ inches and the underside should be sloped, beveled or rounded.
- Avoid open-riser stairs.
- Treads should be uniformly slip-resistant.
- Provide handrails on both sides and intermediately on stairs over 88 inches wide. Do not exceed $1\frac{1}{2}$ inch diameter cross-section and use only correct shapes.
- Provide tread edge definition through color, materials, or lighting (see Figure 10-17).
- Handrails should extend beyond stair landings at the top and bottom and return to the wall or supporting post.
- The top of handrails should be 34 to 38 inches above the tread. Provide a lower handrail, 24 inches above the tread for children. (NFPA Life Safety Code, 1988)
- Step lighting should be on emergency power and non-dimmable.

Consider the counsel of an experienced safety engineer on the "evils" of architects and their undying love of multilevel entries or the ever-popular unplanned grade level mistake which, of course, necessitates providing ramps for wheel chair bound guests: "If you think about it, had the grade of the site been the same as the main entry or lobby, you wouldn't need ramps or stairs and you will have fewer people fall."

However, we do run into ramps at entries and they should meet the following basic criteria (see ANSI A117.1):

- Any walking surface with a slope greater than 1:20 is a ramp.
- All ramps require handrails on both sides.
- Ramps shall not exceed a 1:12 slope.
- Walking surface must be slip-resistant and more so than a level area.

Automatic swing-opening doors can be a real trap if the sensing devices are not calibrated properly; either someone runs into the door because it has not opened or it opens and smacks them in the face. Balanced doors pose another potentially hazardous situation. These doors pivot open from a point several inches from the typical hinge side of the door. As a result, when open the door has a 6- to 7-inch gap between the door and frame. A child playing can get an arm caught and have it severely damaged if the door swings closed.

From a security point of view, main entries attract a lot more than just guests. Robbery of the night clerk is a real event to the roadside motel just off the interstate. For the luxury hotel downtown, the threat can be pickpockets or the ever-popular "grab the luggage and run" routine. Obviously, the security of the main entry, though important, is difficult to achieve. A guest keycard reader and intercom can be placed on the doors, to be activated by the evening crew, but if the clerk fails to turn it on or does it to such a routine that everyone knows that the lobby is locked at 8:00 p.m., then it will be of little value. However, for a hotel or motel of less than 200 rooms, the main entry should be designed to be visible, open, and with lots of light. To be more specific, provide at least (1) 15 footcandles of illumination; (2) a bullet-resistive teller window for afterhours check-in; (3) maglocks with a release button at the desk, and possibly a guest keycard reader, especially if the hotel is designed with interior corridors; and (4) intercom for use by a guest if the clerk is located away from the entry area (Figure 10-18). Obviously if there is a teller window the front desk must be positioned on the opposite wall of the entry vestibule. Walls surrounding the teller

Figure 10-18. Teller window provides secure access for afterhours.

window must also be bullet-resistive. With technology rapidly changing, remote check-in machines are now a reality. Guests can check-in with their credit cards and be issued a key without the need of a clerk. This can be a real plus in curtailing night-time robberies and speeding up check-in at larger hotels.

The typical luxury hotel should have the main entry under surveillance by locating the bell stand and luggage room in close proximity with a full view of the area, and CCTV camera surveillance may also be warranted especially at downtown facilities or in high-crime areas.

Lobbies of All Shapes and Sizes

Many hotels today use marble and other natural stones on their floors. Polished marble is not slip-resistant, but an interesting phenomenon occurs when people encounter polished stone (Figure 10-19). Because they think it is very slick they sub-consciously change their stride to compensate. Also, because the lobby is so important to first impressions, hoteliers tend to tell housekeeping personnel to constantly attend to its cleaning. My

Figure 10-19. Polished stone is not slip-resistant; however, few falls occur in main lobbies.

own experience is of very few falls in lobbies on polished marble; however, from a litigation point of view an operator should settle early if a fall does occur.

Small motels, moderate-priced hotels, and extended-stay hotels should avoid polished materials and use carpet or tile rated as slip-resistant, not only for safety but also for reduced maintenance costs. All public space floors should have a minimum slip resistance value of 0.6 wet and dry (see Chapter 4). These criteria will differ for restaurants and pool decks because of other conditions that affect those walking surfaces.

Entering the lobby area should provide a sense of where one is. The front desk should be in view. Directional graphics should indicate where all the services are located. The elevators to the guest floors should be in full view of the front desk for added security; in fact, some locations may require a guest keycard to activate the elevator call buttons. Again, stairs should be avoided as people are always distracted and thinking of anything but where they are walking. The designers can't be stopped from designing, but it must be insured that elevations are marked and guarded and that stairs and ramps are designed for safety (Figure 10-20).

Figure 10-20. Beautiful and unusual lobbies can be a major distraction. Attention to the safe design of walkways and stairs is critical.

Escalators are very common in larger hotels. As a people mover they have enjoyed a relatively low accident frequency. But it is known that they can seriously maim people by entrapment or by throwing them off when suddenly stopping. Entrapment potential exists at comb plates, tread edges, at the point where the step riser converges, and where the handrails converge. Various approaches to reducing tread edge entrapment include raised step edge on the sides of the tread, pressure switches behind the skirt panel, side panels of low-friction material. The most promising according to John Fruin, an expert on escalator safety, is the use of internally lubricated thermoplastic side plates, which reduces the skirt running clearances (Fruin, 1988).

For comb plates, lamps located below the steps with light shining through can help the pedestrian distinguish edges. Brightly colored comb plates can provide improved definition at the interface between the treads and landing platforms.

Lastly, proper location of the emergency stop button can aid in saving a toe or a life. Codes now require stop buttons to be conspicuous and one way to avoid vandalism and pranksters is to have the escalators under electronic surveillance (Fruin, 1988).

Many luxury hotels have lobby bars. These areas are usually elevated above or sunk into the floor. The basic safety design principles for guarding elevated or sunken areas, stairs, and ramps must be followed. Waitress/waiter pickup areas should not conflict with customer traffic. Also, the floor area behind the bar needs to meet the same criteria as for kitchens and service areas; for seating areas carpet is preferred (see Chapters 3 and 4).

For the budget and extended-stay hotels that serve a breakfast or just have a coffee station, slip-resistant flooring and location of the area out of heavy traffic areas are important in eliminating the falls exposure.

There are other critical areas in lobbies which serve an important security function. A luggage storage room may seem insignificant, but unless there is adequate storage for mass checkouts, you could be buying some new luggage and dealing with some very unhappy guests. Of course there are other ways of securing luggage, for example, in a vacant meeting room, or using cables and locks. Consider and plan for any likely event. The bell captain's stand should also be located to give a wide view of the lobby and exterior approaches.

Location of elevators in relation to the guestrooms and garage shuttle elevators is a very important security concern. All elevator banks should be positioned to be visible by front desk personnel. It is highly recommended to provide separate elevators from underground parking areas that discharge at the main lobby only. If for some reason the elevators cannot be in view of the front desk, use of CCTV cameras and/or guest keycard activated controls may be required.

Circulation Areas, Ballrooms, Meeting Rooms, and Exhibit Halls

Circulation areas include corridors, prefunction assembly, restrooms, public telephones, and any other ancillary area excluding food and beverage outlets and retail areas. General criteria for these areas include:

- Slip-resistant flooring—0.6 or better wet or dry, carpet preferred.
- Minimum of 15 footcandles of lighting except in the washroom, where more light will be needed around the sink areas.

- Wall sconces should not project more than 8 inches into the walking areas and should ideally be located at 6 feet 4 inches AFF (above finished floor). (California requires a 4-inch projection.)
- Remote areas should be under some form of surveillance and remote entries should be securable and alarmed after hours and/or guest keycard-activated if necessary.
- Artifacts, paintings, and the like should be securely fastened to the substrate.

Public restrooms require a few unique considerations. First the entries to the restrooms should be separate and distinct. This means that the entries are designed to preclude inadvertent entry by opposite sexes. Besides this obvious concern, this design also acts as a psychological deterrent to would-be criminal opportunists waiting for their victim to enter the common entry area that is typical in the design of a lot of facilities (see Figures 10-21 and 10-22).

Other important concerns include insuring that soap dispensers are located over sinks and that paper towel dispensers and hand dryers are located so as to minimize dripping of water across the floor (Figure 10-23). All wall-mounted fixtures and privacy screens should be secured to blocking that is firmly attached to studs (Kira, 1976; Kohr, 1989).

Toward the meeting rooms and ballrooms, an area designated as a prefunction space or assembly area is designed to allow people to congregate before, during, and after a function. There is usually a registration area, coatroom, and restrooms in the vicinity. Here the concern is more operational, in setting up coffee breaks and displays, for example. However, there is a security concern and if security staffing is available CCTV surveillance should be provided for this area. Many facilities lose artifacts, plants, and anything else not nailed or tied down. And at many large facilities these areas are remote from the mainstream, inviting unwanted individuals to look for opportunities. Added security in these areas can also provide a sales amenity to a group booking a show or a conference.

Meeting rooms and ballrooms should be securable to prevent theft. Many hotels are installing electronic locking hardware on the doors similar to that on the guestrooms so that they can key an area for a particular group's needs while offering a high level of access control. As a minimum, use a removable core keying

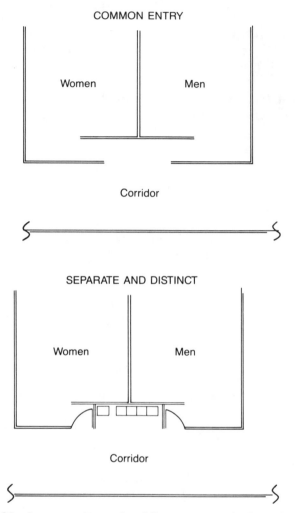

Figure 10-21. A comparison of public restroom design; the design labelled Separate and Distinct is a preferred design for security and privacy.

system with a restricted key way. After that, it is a management problem to maintain key control. Another interesting but over-looked problem is decorative wall sconces projecting too far into the space creating head-strike problems. These should be selected and located with that danger in mind.

Exhibit halls lend themselves to a security opportunity of a different type, given that their purpose is to allow groups to

Figure 10-22. Separate and distinct entries to restrooms.

Figure 10-23. Restrooms and washrooms need attention to the little details to minimize fall hazards.

display anything from boats to computers. Here a simple design enhancement can provide conduit, cable, and power so that a CCTV camera can be installed in any area. Also, alarming all the perimeter doors or use of motion sensors to detect afterhours intrusion provides a value-added service that can allow the security staff to become a profit center. This is not a new idea; many facilities are being set up and run in this way with very little risk to the hotelier.

Health Clubs and Pools

These amenities have become a permanent fixture in all lodging segments as a simple result of demand by the consumer, but the liability has increased disproportionately to the demand. In fact, liability has grown geometrically versus arithmetic growth in demand.

Safety is of prime importance in designing pools, whirlpools, exercise areas, locker rooms, saunas, and steam rooms. The discussion here will be of additional items that should be considered in the design of these areas. Special help on a per case basis is needed in planning water slides, swim-up bars, or free-standing health spas. However, some of the aspects of safety design will remain the same.

An excellent recourse is the National Spa and Pool Institutes Standards. There are several others also, but the key is to hire a reputable pool design consultant.

Pool and whirlpool criteria should include the following:

- Diving boards should not be allowed; they should be removed in a facility that still has them in place.
- Minimum depth should be 3 feet with a maximum of 5 feet. A good recommendation is $4\frac{1}{2}$ feet at the main drain to avoid any transition marking from shallow to deep areas.
- Landscaping and walkway layouts should direct the guest to the shallow end.
- A barrier at least 4 feet high, with the capability of securing the pool area, should be provided (Figure 10-24).
- Major paths and walkways should be a minimum of 5 feet wide.
- Access steps into the pool should have tread widths and risers that meet ANSI requirements, be nonslip, provide a contrasting color on the nose, be recessed in at the shallow end, and have

Figure 10-24. All pools must be securable after hours.

handrails that extend beyond the top and bottom treads (Figure 10-25). (Davies and Beasley, 1988)

- In whirlpools with narrow steps, place handrails on both sides (Figure 10-26).
- All deck surfaces should provide a minimum slip-resistance rating of 0.7 wet and dry.
- The attendant's area should be located to give a view of as much of the activity areas, including locker room entries, exercise room, and so on, as possible.
- Indoor/outdoor pool connectors should have a plexiglass divider for winter use that is marked by a decal or other designation to warn swimmers (Figure 10-27).
- Copings must be slip-resistant.
- Depth markings should be whole number locations on the deck and at the scum line.
- Beside each depth marking provide a "No Diving" graphic, preferably the international type symbol shown in Figure 10-28.
- All outlets around any wet areas, including the attendant's office should be on GFI (ground fault circuit interrupter) protection.

Figure 10-25. Note the recessed steps with handrails, nonslip deck, and depth and "No Diving" markings.

Figure 10-26. Handrails and nonslip contrasting-color nose tile on steps and bench.

Figure 10-27. Plexiglass divider between the indoor and outdoor pool is etched to warn swimmers.

Figure 10-28. Keep depth markings to whole numbers and use an international "No Diving" symbol beside each marker.

- Furnish life-saving equipment—life ring with throw line, shepherd's hook, first-aid kit, and so on.
- Provide required regulatory signage plus signage for CPR procedures and No Diving warning.
- Lighting around the outdoor pool after hours should be at 1 footcandle; however, if the pool is open at night this should be increased to a minimum of 10 footcandles.
- Provide a house phone in view of the guests for assistance calls.
- Furnish a 15-minute timer control on the whirlpool jets and locate it so the guest must exit the pool to activate.
- In older whirlpools with a single output drain on the bottom the cover should be replaced with an antivortex cover. This will prevent long hair from trapping an individual.
- Do not provide a separate vacuum system in the pools with outlets under water. Plug up older pools' outlets and use the skimmer system instead. Young children have been known to get their hands trapped in these outlets and if the attendant fails to turn off the vacuum system, this can be disastrous.
- In many smaller hotels and motels, or wherever the pool cannot be secured, use of one of the new water vibration alarms should be considered. These float in the pool and sound an alarm to a remote monitor station to alert management that someone is in the pool.

Health clubs come in all shapes and sizes and here we will deal only with the typical hotel type, which usually includes locker rooms and showers, sauna and/or steam room, and exercise room.

Liability is certain to become a bigger issue. As the fitness craze continues, and with the recent surge in health clubs, it becomes a simple case of the law of large numbers. The more facilities there are the greater is the likelihood of accidents and injuries. Injuries can be caused by several factors, including improper maintenance or design of equipment, lack of proper supervision during use of the facility, and improper use of the equipment.

The primary concern in these areas is the fact that they are usually remote from the mainstream and the watchful eye of a hotel employee. Concern involves the need for emergency response to falls or even a heart attack and the possibility of assaults and, even worse, rapes.

In exercise rooms, the focus should be on the selection of

well-made and well-designed equipment. Manufacturers today are very concerned with product liability. Newer equipment has detailed instructions on use and warnings of dangers already attached. If you have older equipment, contact the manufacturer and obtain this valuable information and post it (Figure 10-29). The entry door and even the wall facing out should be a glass storefront to provide a full room view. A central issue for the entire complex is to provide an emergency call system or at least a house phone that rings directly to the hotel operator. Lastly, posted rules and precautions are essential in all areas. One other item not related to design is the necessity to ensure routine patrols of these areas by hotel staff. An excellent way to secure the spa is to use a guestroom keycard reader to allow access only by authorized persons.

Locker rooms, showers, saunas, and steam rooms are usually all located within the same space. In Europe, many of these areas are shared by both sexes. Although this might work there, I would not recommend it in the United States. Safety hazards in these areas include slippery floors, electric shock, scalding water,

Figure 10-29. Insure that instructions are posted on all equipment.

unsecured wall-mounted fixtures. Listed below are some design guidelines for each area:

General

- Make all entries accessible with minimum 3-foot widths.
- Floors should have a minimum slip-resistance rating of 0.6 wet and dry.
- All electrical outlets should be on ground fault protection.
- Furnish an emergency call system or house phone.
- Wall-mounted fixtures such as towel racks, dispensers, and privacy partitions should be secured to blocking that is attached to studding with a pull force of 300 lb in any direction and grabbars of 350 lb pull force (ASTM F446 cites 250 lb).
- Insure good lighting (25 to 50 footcandles) and ventilation.
- Provide separate hot-water system from commercial areas; temperature at source 120°F, at tap 110°F.
- In security risk areas, entry may be controlled by guest keycard reader devices.

Toilet and sink areas

- Locate soap dispensers over sinks.
- Place paper towel dispensers and/or hand dryers beside the sinks.
- Use only hair dryers with coil and fan unit, mounted on the wall.
- Use self-activating water controls or those that need the minimum contact of the user, with automatic shut off after 45 to 60 seconds.

Dressing and locker area

- Benches should be smooth, preferably with a polymer coating.
- Mirrors should have a vinyl scrim backing or be of laminated glass, and secured by adhesive and clips.
- Carpet is preferred in this area.
- Lockers should be of solid construction and lockable.

Shower stalls

- Water valves should be specified as pressure and temperature compensation type (ASTM F444). The hot-water system for these areas should be separate from the kitchen and laundry systems.

Figure 10-30. Slope the floor to the back of the stall and eliminate the curb for safety and accessibility. Furnish a grabbar.

- Slope floor toward side wall and provide trench type drain. Avoid curbs; this will give greater accessibility to the showers. If there must be a curb, it should be in a highly contrasting color.
- If the shower door is glass, it should be tempered safety glass.
- As a minimum, furnish a grabbar on side wall, mount it 40 inches AFF in a horizontal position (ASTM F446) (see Figure 10-31).
- Recess the soap dish, and locate it at least 40 inches AFF and in a location where spray from the shower does not hit it.
- Optionally, provide a seat that can fold up out of the way to assist those who may need a resting spot, a hand-held shower nozzle, and an emergency call pull cord.
- Specify showers with non-slip bottom according to ASTM F462 test method. If ceramic tile is used, the slip resistance should be a minimum 0.6 wet and dry.

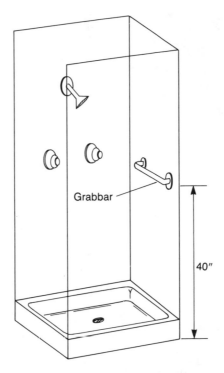

Grabbar

40"

Figure 10-31. Shower stall with horizontal grabbar.

Saunas and steam rooms

- Benches should be of smooth materials with good edge definition and securely anchored to the floor.
- All controls should be on outside of the unit, with automatic cutoffs for temperature variations above limits.
- Heat cycles should be limited to 10 minutes with automatic cut-off requiring guest to exit to reset.
- Post manufacturers' instructions and other precautionary graphics.
- Furnish emergency call buttons.
- Adhere to manufacturers' temperature requirements; for steam rooms do not exceed 120°F room temperature.
- Insure that all heat sources are properly guarded.

BACK-OF-HOUSE SPACES

There is no more important area than the back of house, which consists of all the support areas that make the public spaces work. It is puzzling that architects, developers, and owners spend little effort in designing these areas for people who are the key to the very success of the facility. The answer may lie in a lack of knowledge or in cost. However, there do exist excellent examples of concern and caring on the same order as shown in public spaces.

The following sections cover some basic criteria and common-sense design issues that will assist in reducing employee injuries, increase productivity, and reduce security-related losses.

Remembering that the primary causes of employee injuries are slips, trips, and falls and also materials handling, the design focus for each space should concentrate on minimizing or eliminating these injuries.

The back of house comprises:

Loading dock	Employee lockers and toilets
Receiving	Cafeteria
Security, first aid, and	Human resources
"cool-down" room	Front office, administration,
Service circulation	and related
Housekeeping and laundry	Kitchen and related
Engineering and related	Catering and related

Loading Docks and Receiving

Sizes of loading and receiving areas vary with the size of the hotel. Most hotels will need a minimum of three bays while facilities with fewer than 200 rooms will only need a drive-up area at grade. There should be adequate maneuvering and turnaround space for anticipated types of vehicles. Pedestrian areas must be completely separated from loading and unloading areas. The following criteria are for hotels with a dock.

- Dock should be a minimum of 10 feet deep to allow all types of carts to maneuver easily.
- Surfaces should be slip-resistant-coated or light broom-finished with a granular oxide additive.
- Guardrails should be located adjacent to compactors and there should be separate pedestrian walkways from the dock.

- Trench drains should be located to catch dock runoff with a separate drain for the compactor.
- Half-inch angle-iron cart stops should be placed on the edge of the dock.
- Locate dock rubber bumpers on face of wall.
- Use portable dock plates or levelers for odd height trucks.
- Steps to dock must have handrails and slip-resistant treads.
- Lighting should be a minimum of 15 footcandles; for large convention facilities there should be movable directional lights to view inside trailers.
- Employee entry should be a ramp with a 5 percent grade, completely separate from the dock area, and with a distinct entry door.
- Dock entry doors should be 6 feet wide by 7 feet high with vision panels 5 inches wide by 20 inches high.
- Allow space for laundry holding if it is processed offsite.
- Convention and major resorts should provide separate receiving office and storage room for parcels.
- Provide a house phone, single bathroom and pay phone for drivers.
- Furnish chock blocks or, better, electronic dock locks that lock the trailer in place to prevent forklift accidents.

Control of the dock 24 hours a day is very important. If there is a 24-hour security person on duty in the office, this is a simple matter. However, there are only limited security staff or none at all, then consider using controlled access after hours.

Controlled access of the dock entry doors is easily accomplished by using maglocks on each door tied to an exterior mounted card reader to allow access with a valid card. On the inside, the maglocks are released by a button or motion sensor. For fire codes, simply wire the maglock power supply to the fire alarm system. The dock is now secured. Be sure that the local fire marshall is informed of this. This configuration also allows elimination of mechanical panic hardware, which in the long run can make substantial savings on maintenance due to cart damage. This is advisable whether there is dock security or not, since it can always be shut off during rush hours (see Chapter 5).

Employee entry control is important no matter what the size of the facility. The same card access system can be used on the

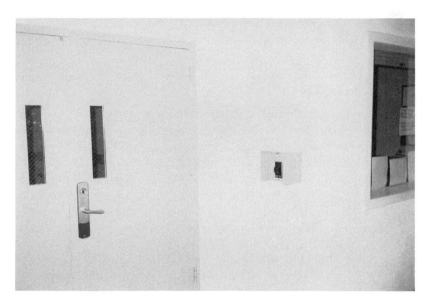

Figure 10-32. Electronic access control is important on the employee entries to control who has access. Also note the vision panels and the window from the security office.

employee entry as on the dock doors (Figure 10-32). Also insure that the employee entry is located so that employees must go past the security office for screening. This will facilitate package inspections and handing out of keys, pocket pagers, and the like. However, avoid if possible combining the dock and employee entries. This will minimize congestion at shift changes and reduce the likelihood of slips and falls due to debris and water.

Hotels and motels without docks have some similar concerns. Good drainage is still needed away from the entry doors and for the dumpster or compactor. Employees should enter via a different entrance. The dock should be secured 24 hours a day and an electronic access system on the employee entry should be considered. In some hotels in Europe the electronic access is coupled with the payroll time-recording system. Avoid elevated platforms and stoops, which are nothing more than trip hazards. For a grade problem, use a gently sloping ramp. Lighting should be 5 footcandles with additional lighting for deliveries.

Avoid a double door if possible, because panic devices with vertical rods are a maintenance nightmare. Use a 48-inch-wide door with heavy duty hinges and good mortise lock and an electric strike if electronic access is used. Provide an exterior house phone for drivers to contact the operator to open the doors for the deliveries. Put a vision panel in the door.

Human Resources

This area deserves some Interior Design attention. This is the place where the prospective employee forms a perception of the operation. If these people are brought through the dock and made to sit on half-broken banquet chairs in the service aisle, are they likely to want to work in such a place? Provide a separate entry from the exterior of the building to Human Resources for applicants and employees who need to come back to the property after hours or on days off to pick up pay checks or deal with benefit issues. This limits traffic in the primary service corridor to essential people and materials traffic only. Depending on the location of the facility, it may be wise to place duress alarms (push-button type devices) at the receptionist's and manager's desks in case emergency assistance is needed.

At larger facilities, a separate room set up as a payroll office within the Human Resources area may be beneficial. This area would include all of the payroll computer system terminals and records. Additionally, a teller-type pass-through window should be provided to a low-traffic corridor so that pay checks can be distributed without disruption to other activities. All Human Resources areas should be on their own submaster key system using a minimum of restricted-keyway removable-core locking systems.

Engineering and Related

Owing to the nature of the job, the designer should preplan the needs of the workshops with Operations in order to elucidate the various hazards, such as:

Flammable and combustible liquids storage
Mists and fumes from spray-painting operations
Dust collection from woodworking
Welding sparks and fumes
Landscape equipment fuel storage
Electric shock
Compressed air and freon in refrigeration repair

The degree of care is directly proportional to the size and volume of work planned in that area. For instance, flammable liquid storage can be simply an approved storage cabinet that holds less than 25 gallons of material or an explosion-proof room. Some excellent resources are OSHA 1910 regulations and NFPA standards. Lighting is very important in the shops; it should be from 35 to 50 footcandles. If fluorescent fixtures are used, lens covers over the bulbs should be provided.

Required ventilation of these areas depends on the hazards involved. Some areas such as spray painting will require special ventilation systems, which must be localized and explosion-proof. Insure that there is clear aisle space in all areas in order to reach main gas valves, water valves, fire pump, electrical distribution center, and emergency generator.

Most engineering departments should be provided with two-way radio communications not only for emergency calls but for faster service to guests.

Traditionally, key making and key control have been located in engineering. It is my opinion that this should be a Security function and space as well as system control should be provided in the Security area. Of course, if there is no security staff, and with the use of restricted keyway or electronic lock systems, key making equipment becomes obsolete. As a result, when replacement keys or cards are needed they are ordered precut from the hardware distributor or security-system vendor. Administration of the system should be by the property manager, with troubleshooting and any maintenance of the hardware by engineering.

Housekeeping and Laundries

Irrespective of the size of the facility, housekeeping areas are roughly the same. The major injury potential for the housekeeping employee seems to relate to materials handling, whether it be back strains or chemical burns. Good equipment, adequate space, and proper procedures for handling chemicals can significantly reduce these injuries. The following are some basic concepts from a design point of view:

- Flooring should be slip-resistant, indoor/outdoor carpet, or safety sheet vinyl.
- Illumination should be 35 to 50 footcandles.
- Valuables storage room or cage with walls extended to

understructure above; removable core deadlock; and latch set or electronic card access with audit trail.

- Automatic chemical mixing equipment for all bulk handling.
- Adequate storage for all supplies, including guest amenities.
- Vision panels in main entry doors.
- Restricted keyway; removable core lockset; keyed to housekeeping submaster or electronic card access.

Laundries pose other issues entirely. At small hotels that send their laundry out to bulk plants, all that is needed is bulk clean linen storage and bulk dirty linen storage areas. These should be located in close proximity of the dock. The ideal would be to have a set of doors to the dock and an interior set to the service corridor. As theft is a big issue, access control to these areas should be routinely accounted for, using as a minimum a restricted keyway with removable core deadlock and latch set. All exterior entries should be alarmed. These areas are definite candidates for electronic access control.

Larger hotels that have their own laundry facilities pose some unique design issues:

- Slip-resistant flooring, safety sheet vinyl, or tile. This will also cut down on staining from bare concrete.
- Illumination 35 to 50 footcandles; cover all tubes.
- Separate HVAC system to keep temperatures even year round. A lot of accidents can be attributed to heat stress.
- Linen chute should terminate 5 feet AFF and have a top hinged door with a fusible link (Figure 10-33).
- All pipes to the ironers, including valves, should be protectively wrapped.
- Locate an interconnected trip beam under the ironer, to automatically shut-off the ironer should an employee crawl beneath to retrieve dropped linen.
- Entries should have deadlock and latch set with removable core, restricted keyway, and be on the housekeeping submaster.
- All exterior exits should be alarmed.
- Entry doors should have vision panels.
- Use bright colors and if possible provide natural light.

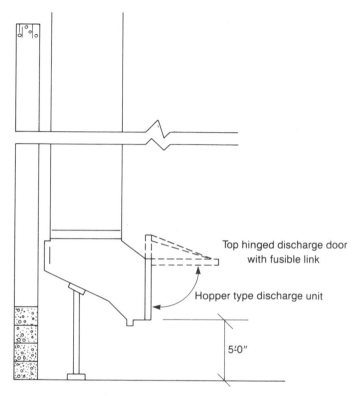

Top hinged discharge door
with fusible link

Hopper type discharge unit

5'-0"

Figure 10-33. Linen chute elevation.

Security and First-Aid Areas

Not every hotel and motel requires a security area but all do need a first-aid area.

The first thing to ask is when a security area needs to be defined in the facility program. There is no clear-cut answer except that after a risk assessment has been completed or due to the size and complexity of the operation, the necessity of a security force often becomes apparent.

Typically the area is located on the dock in any leftover space and with no thought as to the functionality of the space. Security areas generally perform the following functions:

Package inspections
Receiving parcels and express mail

Monitoring systems from CCTV cameras to refrigerator and
freezer alarms
Screening visitors and applicants
Handing out keys, pagers, and radios
Dispatcher for patrol officers
Key control
Administering first-aid
Issuing lockers and parking decals
Interviewing for investigative purposes
Meeting with everyone from a guest to the secret service

With these functions in mind, some basic design guidelines are
as follows.

- Locate main office so it has a view of the dock and employees
  are required to pass by it on their way to and from locker
  room areas.
- Ideally locate all areas together as a suite:

  Main office, minimum 150 ft^2
  Supervisor/manager office, minimum 100 ft^2
  Key control room, minimum 80 ft^2
  Storage minimum, 50 ft^2
  First-aid minimum, 120 ft^2

- Locate time clocks in service corridor adjacent to the security
  suite in view of the officer.
- Involve interior design in ergonomic layout of main office;
  also provide some decor since guests are often brought to this
  area.

Figure 10-34 is an example floorplan layout. Furniture in the
main office should be millwork or, in some cases for housing the
various systems, pre-fab ergonomic work stations may be a better
solution. Figure 10-35 shows some typical elevations, including
work surfaces. Note the half-height sliding window to the dock.
The idea is to keep people out of the service corridors and facilitate
a smoother transaction between the officer and delivery person.
The office entry to the employee service corridor can be either a
dutch door with a shelf or a full leaf door with a half-height
sliding window located in an adjacent wall. For larger hotels, the
layout of Figure 10-36 seems to work quite well in separating the
monitoring areas from visitors.
Some facilities may require satellite offices and these should be

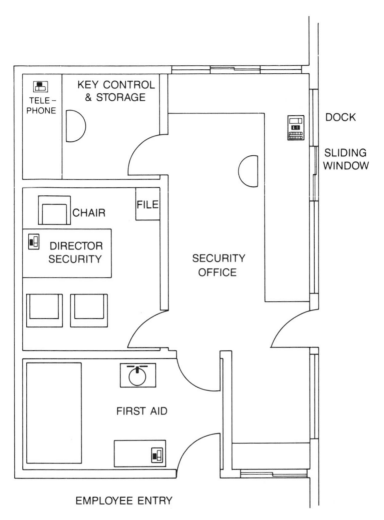

Figure 10-34. Security suite layout.

scrutinized for their intended functions and designed accordingly. The first-aid room in Figure 10-34 has a corridor entry plus entry to the security area suite. This keeps people out of the main office. The needs and functions of the first-aid room are addressed in Chapter 5.

A first-aid room in the security suite should be provided with the following:

- Design to ANSI accessibility standards.

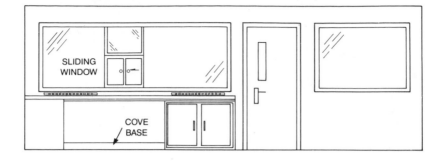

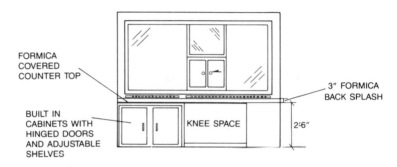

Figure 10-35. Security office elevations.

- Millwork storage cabinets with built-in sink.
- 50 footcandle illumination.
- Treatment table or chair that is adjustable.
- Telephone.
- Portable stretcher.
- Blankets, sheets, and pillow.
- Chair and magnifying lamp.
- Basic first-aid supplies depending on size, including oxygen and other equipment. Consult with local physician and/or local chapter of occupational health nurses, insurance company, and/or independent consultant.

For the very small hotel the minimum should be a well-stocked first-aid kit based on the number of employees and the type of operation and an area for "cool down." There are numerous first-aid supply companies that can assist in selection of the right kit and put the facility on a routine maintenance program. The cool down area function is discussed in detail in Chapter 5. It

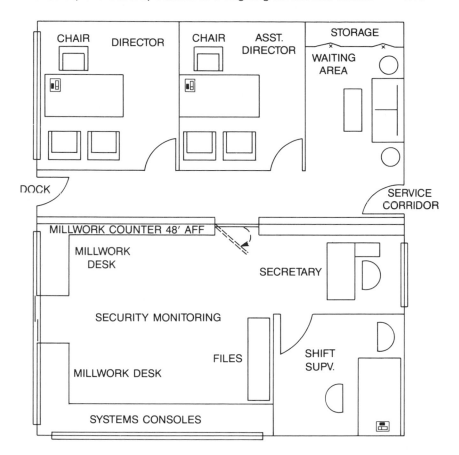

Figure 10-36. Megahotel (1000 or more guestrooms) or resort security suite. Hotels of this size have a medical unit instead of a first-aid room. Key control can be located within suite or elsewhere, as the hotel will have electronic control for guest rooms; key control will be for back of house.

simply is a place where the injured employee can rest and get over the shock of the initial trauma. An office or small room with a cot can serve this function. However, if there is space to design a first-aid room into the program, it will pay dividends.

Full-Fledged Medical Unit

If you are able to take advantage of this program, the benefits will outweigh the costs many times over. A thorough discussion of when to include this type of facility in your program is given in Chapter 5. Figure 10-37 gives a basic layout for a typical unit. The following are the absolute minimum square footages.

Nurse's office, 110 ft^2
Waiting and storage area, 160 ft^2
Treatment/examination room, 120 ft^2
Rest/examination room, 120 ft^2
Water closet, 50 ft^2

This amounts to 560 square feet of space to allow for a smooth functioning unit. A facility of this size can serve a typical hotel of up to 1000 guestrooms. If the hotel is any larger or if the facility is serving more than one hotel, motel, and/or restaurants, additional space may be necessary. A good rule of thumb is half a square foot for each employee served up to 1000 square feet maximum. Depending on the needs of the consulting physician, a doctor's office may be needed, which will require another 120 square feet. Some other general criteria include:

- Millwork cabinets with built-in sinks and refrigerators.
- 50 footcandle illumination.
- Telephones.
- Emergency call buttons in rooms.
- Use of interior design for colors, softgood and casegood selections in all areas except examination, rest, and treatment rooms.
- Bathroom and all areas designed to ANSI accessibility standards with non-slip flooring.
- Nurse and physician to decide layout and specify equipment and furnishings for examination, treatment, and rest rooms.

Catering and Related, Service Circulation, and Storage

There are two major concerns in these areas: (1) slip, trip, and fall prevention and (2) safe movement of people and materials. When goods and people come in through the dock and employee entry, there must be adequate widths and lighting, and there must be no sudden surprises like ice production in the middle of the walkways.

Catering is considered in relationship to the set-up and staging areas. The banquet kitchen, plating, and warewashing areas have

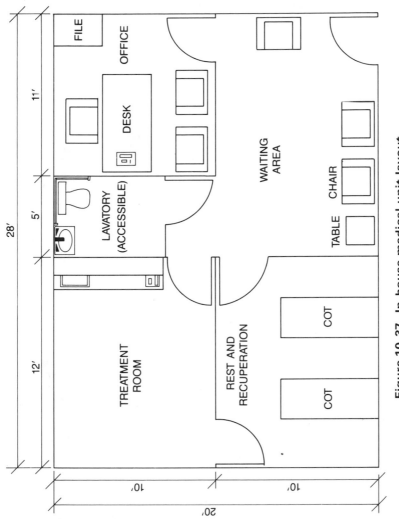

Figure 10-37. In-house medical unit layout.

the same basic requirements as the main kitchen except that if they are on different levels of the building a communicating stair is needed (at least 48 inches wide) and also access to service elevators without having to jog all over the building. Chapter 11 deals with standard criteria for kitchens.

Service circulation refers to the corridors that connect everything together; for example, entering the back of house through the dock or employee entry is entering a service corridor.

The primary design of the circulation should be related to the movement of people and materials. With this as the focus, dry storage rooms do not get stuck in a far-off corner of the main kitchen complex, requiring materials to be moved long distances around corners and through other areas. As already mentioned, bulk dirty linen storage should have a set of doors directly to the dock and an interior set to a service corridor, unless there is an in-house laundry, and properly near the service elevators. The idea is to minimize distances traveled, sharp turns in corridors, blind corners, doors opening into the corridors (see Figure 10-38), equipment such as ice machines projecting into the corridors, and traffic in the banquet corridor.

Some other ideas include positioning room service near the service elevators so that waiters and waitresses do not have to cut across the main kitchen (Figure 10-39).

Accomplishing these design objectives will reduce the exposure to materials handling accidents and improve the operating efficiency of the facility.

Adequate storage is vital, because without it "stuff" will be placed in every nook and cranny, including blocking the fire exits. A good rule of thumb for catering is to provide 12 to 15 percent of the net meeting and ballroom space for storage of dance floor, chairs and tables, and so on. If the allowance is anything less than this, equipment gets damaged from abuse and can pose a hazard to the guest, and the life cycle to replacement will obviously diminish.

To reduce slip and fall exposure, utilize a slip-resistant safety vinyl type product (minimum 0.6 wet and dry in all areas and 0.28 slip resistance with grease at preparation areas), which also cuts down noise and can help improve the appearance and cleanability of the corridors. Most facilities have hardened and sealed concrete floors, which may suffice if there is little potential for water on the floor. Some facilities use vinyl/composite tile (VCT), which can cause a slip problem; however, slip-resistant

Figure 10-38. Use vision panels in all high-traffic doors, especially those that swing into a corridor.

VCT has been introduced and this should be investigated. Another idea is to provide clean-up stations every 50 to 100 feet. These stations could contain mops, paper towels, and wet-floor signs.

The primary *security* concerns involve employee theft and unwanted visitors in the back of house. The way to implement security is to limit access as on the dock and employee entry. All other exits, which are usually fire egress points, should have full astragals and no exterior hardware, and be alarmed. This will help prevent unauthorized access. To prevent employees from using these same egress points to bypass the security checkpoint, use door alarms, both local and wired to a monitoring system. Additionally provide conduit and video cable to these same locations so that a CCTV camera can either be installed at the outset or added when the need arises.

Figure 10-39. Locate roomservice near service elevators but out of main traffic patterns.

Is all this equipment really necessary? A chapter will deal in depth on security systems, but in the present instance the CCTV camera is tied to the door alarms so that when someone exits that door the alarm activates the camera and video records the individual. If a camera is not provided, a hard copy of alarm events will allow management to know which doors are being used without their approval, and a security person or manager can be posted at the location to observe anyone using the exit at the recorded times. Obviously, for a small motel with only an office and lobby area and exterior entries to guestrooms, this system would not be realistic.

To control access to storage areas, a minimum of a restricted-keyway removable-core locking system should be used. On high-value inventory rooms such as those for liquor and silver storage, an electronic access device may be advisable in order to provide an audit trail of all entries for future theft investigations (Figure 10-40).

Employee Areas—Locker Rooms and Cafeteria

Despite the difficulty of attracting good workers and retaining them, employee areas generally receive very little in the way of

Figure 10-40. High-value storage areas should have electronic access control.

decor or design to enhance their value, so it is little wonder that not much is included in the way of safety and even less in accessibility. But surely it is a waste to have an employee in the cafeteria on lunch break slip and fall and perhaps be off work on workers' compensation.

Cafeterias are usually reserved for medium to large hotels. Smaller hotels have a breakroom. Obviously, the exposure to accidents in a small breakroom is far less than in a cafeteria serving, say, 1000 employees.

The breakroom should have plenty of light and good ventilation. Additionally the floor should have a minimum slip-resistance of 0.6 wet and dry. All appliances should be a commercial grade with GFI protection on convenience outlets.

Much larger facilities with a cafeteria require the following basic design elements.

- Separate in and out entries with vision panels for employees.
- Separate entry with vision panel from kitchen area or service corridor for servers and cooks.
- Area behind serving line should have the same floor surface as the kitchen.
- All other floors should have a minimum 0.6 wet and dry slip-resistance (Figure 10-41).
- Natural lighting from windows wherever possible.
- All entries should allow for wheelchair access and thresholds should be beveled on both sides.
- Illumination of 35 footcandles in general; 50 at work surfaces.
- An alcove for dish breakdown and trash disposal (floor the same as in kitchen). Large cafeterias provide a dishwashing area adjacent to the cafeteria.
- Secondary egress exits to the outside should be alarmed.

Employee locker rooms and washroom facilities can pose a significant safety hazard, of about the same degree as in a private

Figure 10-41. Employee cafeteria serving line needs nonslip floors and queuing rail.

Figure 10-42. Employee locker areas should be clean, well lit, and ventilated.

bathroom. There are many potential hazards, such as slippery floors, electric shock, scalding water, and unsecured wall fixtures.

Consider how often a restroom is used, what is expected of it, and what kinds of hazards users are exposed to each day, and they can be made safer. Employee washrooms and locker rooms should be designed with the same care as discussed earlier for the health club area (Figure 10-42). The safety design concerns are directly related, with the only difference that if an employee is hurt, the case is covered under workers' compensation.

Front Offices, Administrative, and Related Areas

These areas are considered back of the house however many are in direct view of the guest. Administrative areas refer to the executive, accounting, sales, and catering offices. The safety design of these areas is rather straightforward:

- Adequate task illumination.
- Ergonomically designed secretarial stations to reduce repetitive motion injuries from typing on computers.
- Sufficient outlets to eliminate extension cords.

- Vision panels in doors and no thresholds except where there is dissimilar flooring. Thresholds should be beveled on both sides.
- Ability to secure area after hours; restricted-keyway removable-core locksets.
- File cabinets should be anchored.
- Carpet throughout.

Front office and related areas refer to front desk, general cashier and count rooms, guest depository, PABX operator, computer room. The front desk is the single most important area to the guests. It is where they register, pay the bill, get messages, get directions and information, and store valuables. When guests come into the facility they may be awed by the lobby interior design but the first thing on their minds is getting checked in and up to their rooms. Because of this the front desk should be positioned for maximum exposure and visual control of the lobby, main entry, and elevators. This is also an important security design parameter. As mentioned regarding lobbies and main entries, there may be the need to position the desk so that a teller-type window for afterhours check-in can be arranged while still keeping the area secured; this works well for budget hotels.

In most hotels access behind the desk is through a single door. This door should be locked 24 hours a day and access gained via a card or pushbutton access control device. Also, at most smaller hotels that do not have a private guest depository, the required safe deposit boxes should be behind the desk in view of the guest during usage. As a deterrent to robbery, it may be wise to provide a CCTV camera, provided it can be monitored by a hotel employee. If using a camera, also use a time-lapse video recorder to tape all activities. Depending on the location and how the lobby is controlled after hours, hold-up alarms may be provided at the front desk. This automatically summons the police when activated by an employee. There should also be a small closet for coats, a first-aid kit, and oxygen. The desk should be designed to provide one section where a person in a wheelchair can approach and use the desk. Also keep in mind all the equipment that must fit into the desk, including electronic and card key equipment, property management system (PMS), credit card verifiers, and so on.

At many resorts and larger hotels there is a need for a separate guest safe depository room (Figure 10-43). This room is designed to provide a secure area for guests depositing valuables into a

Figure 10-43. Private guest depository room with a pass-through window to clerk and safes.

safety deposit box in privacy. Generally the area is comprised of two small rooms with a separation wall and a pass-through window. Entry into the side provided for the guest is through a solid wood or hollow metal door with a passage lockset. The guest throws a deadbolt to secure the door. The door is also provided with a vision port. The employee side has direct access off the front desk. The safes are positioned inside the room in view of the guest standing at the pass-through window. The box insert is pulled by the employee and passed to the guest; the guest deposits valuables, and the insert is returned to the safe and secured by the employee; the key returned to the guest. *Never* have more than one key to a safety deposit box, except of course the guard key, which is needed to open the box along with the individual box key.

Another area that is usually an afterthought is the PABX operator's space. Although this is the primary communications network it is rarely taken into account that employees are shut off there for an eight-hour shift and have to work in this environment. As this space is also the location of fire alarm equipment and sometimes TV monitors and security alarm panels, the need to design this space ergonomically is paramount to an efficient operation.

Next is where the buck literally stops: The design of the general cashier's office and the employee count room is critical to the protection of assets. In a very small facility this area is usually combined with a space identified as a workroom. It is usually behind the desk but out of view. There should be a securable door on the room so that employees can secure it while counting their banks to make their shift drops. Safety deposit boxes are located in this room for the employees' use (Figure 10-44). A box is usually assigned each employee involved with cash handling. For their drops a safe is provided with a specially designed hopper on top to allow for envelope drops. A more elaborate safe that dispenses change at prescribed times via an operator password or other secured entry control might be considered. These safes are used quite extensively in the convenience-store world to minimize the amount of cash a robber can access. The safe should be equipped with a door surface-mounted burglar alarm. Additionally, hold-up alarms in the room may be warranted in certain circumstances.

The more traditional set up for larger properties involves a space similar to the workroom but fully devoted to employee use in maintaining their individual banks and making drops into the general cashier's safe. The difference is that the room has vandal-proof walls that extend from the floor to the understructure above and is separated from the general cashier's office via the same type of wall. In order to get to the general cashier's door one must go through the count room. There should be electronic access on the count room entry door in order to provide an audit trail. In the count room there should be a CCTV camera tied to a video recorder. The cashier's safe should be built through the wall with the hopper facing the count room and the safety entry door positioned in the general cashier's office.

Entry to the general cashier's office should be via electronic access. There should be a teller-type pass-through window so that change can be dispensed (Figure 10-45). The entry door should

Figure 10-44. Count room for employee safes and drop safe with reverse doors to general cashiers office.

have a steel plate to protect the cashier. The office should have a motion sensor for afterhours burglary detection, a hold-up alarm, and vandal-proof walls.

Computer rooms house the essence of your accounting and room-control systems. With the increase in security-related computer vandalism and losses, it is vital to control access to these sensitive areas. Place these rooms on the electronic access system.

A Final Point

Keeping in mind the basic Loss Control Triad discussed in Part I, many risks can be avoided by sound design principles. How people relate to their environment and how they subsequently use the

Figure 10-45. General cashier entry door, solid core, electronic access control, and vandal-proof walls.

equipment to accomplish their work are all interrelated in accident prevention. For the back-of-house areas, if there is a lack of design commitment, not only will it show to the guests through less than optimum services but employee accident costs will skyrocket.

GUESTROOM AND RELATED SUPPORT AREAS

To a guest, whether on vacation or business travel, nothing is more important than a clean, safe, and comfortable room in which to rest and relax. Despite the importance of attention to lobbies, atriums, and the rest, 80 percent of the profit is from rooms revenue. From a safety and a security point of view the design criteria for a guestroom is the same for a 5-star luxury hotel or a roadside motel.

General Criteria

1. If at all possible, have interior corridor access.
2. Remote access points leading to the guestroom corridors from outside should have controlled access via a guest key-card (Figure 10-46).
3. Keep nooks and crannies to a minimum.
4. Illumination of corridors should be minimum of 10 foot-candles.
5. Any change in elevation within a corridor should be accomplished by a ramp not exceeding a 1:12 slope.
6. Fire exits to the outside should terminate flush with grade. When this is not possible, use a ramp not exceeding a 1:12 slope.

Figure 10-46. Remote guest area entry using electronic guest-room keycard reader.

7. Floors should be carpeted.

8. Wall sconces should not project into the corridor and pose a head-strike problem.

9. Provide good contrasting directional graphics to point safe ways out in emergencies and location of elevators and other service areas.

10. Furnish house phones at elevator lobbies.

11. For fire exits directly to the outside that do not have guest keycard access, furnish door contact alarms and use exit-only panic hardware. (In certain high-security areas it may be prudent to use the delay-type panic hardware tied to the life-safety system to deter theft and other security problems.)

Guestrooms and Suites

One of the key functions of the loss control expert is to assist your design team in uncovering potential hidden design hazards. For example, when selecting furniture for guestrooms, pointed corners on night stands should be seen as a potential hazard. It would be very easy indeed for a guest to sustain an eye injury when tossing and turning in their sleep. Telling the manufacturer to ensure that all corners on all furniture are rounded is simple and costs nothing, but it may save an eye (Figure 10-47).

Sliding glass doors are put on rooms with balconies and some grade-accessible rooms. Because of the possibility of water coming into the room, such a door is specified with a 3-inch high base, which creates a major trip hazard. Such a high threshold is not really necessary. Some say that the higher lip prevents people from lifting the door out of the track and gaining entry to the room. However, door manufacturers say that this is not the primary purpose but a side-benefit. Preventing water from entering the room is the primary function of the lip. In fact, the higher lip may not help at all with forced entry if the sliding door is an exterior sash type, which does not allow for the installation of a charlie bar because the leaf that actually slides is on the outside, making entry very easy by lifting the door out of its track. For sliding doors specify the following: (1) interior sash; (2) charlie bar; (3) positive-action latch; (4) self-locking on grade level doors.

Figure 10-47. Notice the rounded corners on the end tables.

The list can go on and on of the things that could eliminate many injuries had someone put a little thought into the design and specifications.

Standard safety and security criteria for guestrooms are as follows:

Security

- Mortise lockset, grade I, with a 1-inch deadbolt, $\frac{3}{4}$-inch latchset, lever handle, reprogrammable on all levels (preferably after each guest on the guest level); it is highly recommended to be electronic with an audit trail capability (Figure 10-48).
- Wide-angle door viewer with at least 120° view (accessible rooms will require two).
- Security chain or door guard (hoop type door guard is preferred for accessibility standards).
- Self-closure or spring hinges (self-closure preferred).
- Welded frames, 16-gauge, securely anchored, or certain knockdowns as long as a stud-supported anchor is provided at the strike location to prevent jam spreading.

Figure 10-48. The guestroom entry is the main security defense.

- Entry door should be at least 3 feet wide.
- Lighting should be very good outside the entry door to assist in lock operation and identification of visitors.
- Post-emergency evacuation and security instructions should be on the back of the entry door. They should graphically depict the room location and exit route.
- Connecting doors should have exit-only type latch set, door guard, and/or deadbolt.
- Sliding glass doors to balconies should have positive action latch set. Grade-accessible, provide self-latching, positive-action latch set and charlie bars. Post "how to use" instructions directly on the glass door for operation of the charlie bar.

- Avoid communicating balconies and direct sight-lines between guestrooms.
- In-room safes can be provided. This is an excellent idea for resorts.

Safety

- Window openings, if required by code, should be restricted to an opening no wider than 4 inches, and have the opening at the top of the window and opening outward.
- Balcony sliding or swinging doors should be designed to ANSI standards for clear width, maneuvering space, threshold, and hardware.
- Balcony guardrail design should meet minimum code strengths and ensure that openings of upright balustrades are no wider than 4 inches with the first horizontal opening no wider than 2 inches. Do not create a ladder.
- Post a stick-on label on sliding glass doors to warn parents not to leave children unattended on balconies and to insure that the door is secured.
- All furniture should have rounded corners.
- All head boards, artworks, and any other wall-mounted items, should be secured to blocking that is attached to studs.
- Mirrors, especially mirror doors to closets, should have a vinyl scrim backing or be made from laminated glass or plexiglass and secured by glue and clips to the wall if wall-mounted.
- With new adaptability standards being promulgated by the federal government, audible and visual fire alarm signals may be required in every room.
- Pantries should have slip-resistant flooring, 0.5 wet and dry or greater.
- Fireplaces should be avoided. If they are provided, strict control of materials burned in them should be maintained. Adequate warnings should be placed on the fireplace itself.
- Use illuminated wall switches or touch controls to operate all lighting; provide cover plates over outlets and plugs.

Kitchenettes

- Kitchenettes should have the following:

  1. Slip-resistant floor, 0.5 wet and dry or greater.

2. Fire extinguisher, minimum 10 lb ABC.

3. Posted operating instructions for all appliances.

4. GFI protection on all outlets.

5. Warnings on microwave equipment relating to pacemakers and the like.

6. Safety latches on cabinets that are reachable by small children.

Guestroom baths

- Guestroom baths should have the following:

    1. Overall lighting should be at least 30 footcandles.

    2. All outlets on GFI protection.

    3. Any hairdryers should have coil and fan assembly mounted on the wall.

    4. Vanities should be shallow and provide adequate knee space for accessibility. Sharp or abrasive surfaces and hot-water pipes should be protected.

    5. All wall-mounted fixtures must be attached to blocking and withstand a pull force of 300 lb. Avoid towel racks within the tub or shower enclosure.

    6. Use lever fixtures and clearly identify hot and cold controls.

    7. Entry doors should swing out and be 3 feet wide if possible, with lever handles. (Out-swing doors eliminate the possibility of the door being blocked internally in the event of an accident.) (Davies and Beasley, 1988.)

    8. If heat lamps are used, they should be located so that the bath door cannot come directly below the lamp.

    9. Provide a telephone in the bathroom for emergencies.

    10. Floor slip resistance should be a minimum of 0.5 wet and dry.

    11. Hot-water system should not be integrated with those of kitchens and laundries. Hot water should not exceed 120°F at the source and 110°F at the tap.

    12. All bath and shower valves should be specified as pressure and temperature compensation types, so that the valve will maintain a preset mix of hot and cold water and automatically adjust to system changes (ASTM F444).

13. If at all possible, provide showers and avoid bathtubs. Many hotel suite bathrooms offer both types of fixture.

14. Specify shower stalls and bathtubs with nonslip bottoms (ASTM F462). For ceramic tile bottoms specify at least a 0.6 wet and dry slip resistance.

15. Provide grabbars with a 350 lb minimum pull force in any direction. Grabbars should be located to assist in entering and exiting the tub and in changing position from sitting or standing or when moving in the bath area. ASTM F446 describes the parameters for a bathtub (Figure 10-49) and separate shower (Figure 10-50). However, because most falls related to tub/shower combinations occur when entering/exiting the bathtub, a minimum of a 24-inch grabbar is recommended in all nonaccessible rooms (Figure 10-51) for tub/shower combinations. Because of its placement on the front service wall, the grabbar can assist a person when sitting or standing. For showers, locate a grabbar on the side wall in a horizontal position about 40 inches above the floor. Bathroom grabbar placement is covered by ANSI A117.1.

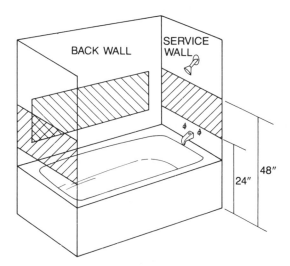

Figure 10-49. Combined bath and shower grabbar placement according to ASTM F446. Grabbars are located in the critical support areas. A horizontal grabbar is required on the back wall and either a vertical or a horizontal grabbar is required on either the service or nonservice wall.

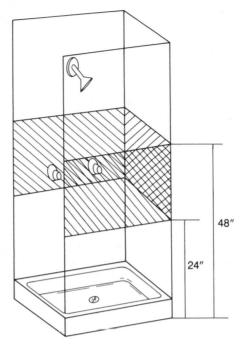

Figure 10-50. Shower stall grabbar placement according to ASTM F446.

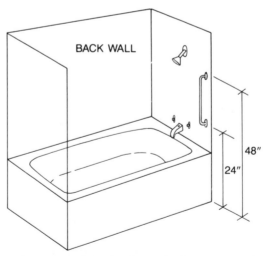

Figure 10-51. Nonaccessible bath and shower vertical grabbar placement.

16. Curbless showers are the best approach. Avoid shower doors; use curtains. If glass doors are used they must be safety glazed with tempered glass.

17. Provide recessed soap dishes and locate them so that water from the shower will not strike the dish.

18. Specify all bathtubs with the drain flush-mounted so that the tub floor is close to the elevation of the bathroom floor. (Try to avoid tubs; use oversized showers instead.) (Kohr, 1989)

Whirlpools in bathrooms are another story. Alexander Kira, a leading authority on bathroom design, stated in an article for *Kitchen and Bath Concepts*:

> In an attempt to presumably celebrate the tub and make it the feature of the bathroom, the tub is either sunken, or more commonly, set into a massive platform, generally marble or tile covered, with a flight of steps leading to the top of the platform. And naturally, there are never any grab bars, or any other type of hand holds available, since they would detract from the important image of fantasy and sensuality. Unfortunately, such installations represent a high potential hazard, that should carry a warning label: LOOK BUT DO NOT USE! (Kira, 1987, p. 11)

Consider Kira's scenario and add to it a set of steps that do not have good geometry and are covered with high-gloss marble, and water controls that are located so that the user must step over them, and you have the makings of a major law suit. To make this safer:

- Put the water controls on the front wall, foot end of the tub, and mount them 30 to 34 inches above the floor.
- Eliminate the step-up. If there must be a step, use a slip-resistant tread and nosing with edge definition, good riser/tread dimension, and a handrail/grabbar installed from the bath floor vertically above the tub and fastened to the horizontal surface on the tub or surrounding structure (Figure 10-52).

Guest Laundries

These require essentially two simple design items. Floor slip resistance should be 0.6 wet and dry minimum. There should be a half-glass entry door for security (Figure 10-53) and a house phone for emergencies. Depending on the area it may be desirable to make access via guestroom keycard and provide a panic button.

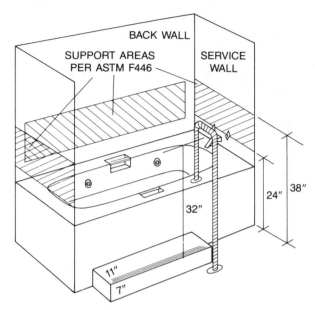

Figure 10-52. Grabbar placement for a whirlpool tub.

Vending Areas

These should have a slip-resistant floor, minimum 0.6 wet and dry. Ice machines should be of the self-dispensing type; the traditional bin types are major harbingers of unsanitary conditions, broken glass, and other nasties (Figure 10-54).

Concierge Lounge

This area should be able to be secured after hours. Provide a slip-resistant floor in the pantry and bathroom. Additionally install duress alarms at the concierge desk and in the pantry to deal with late-evening feisty guests. If you are doing major check-in services, provide the same security protection as the front desk.

A Final Point

The guestroom areas are the most sensitive areas from a liability standpoint. The direction of case law today is such that access to a guestroom is being held to such a high standard of care that it closely approximates the concept of strict liability traditionally reserved for manufacturer's and product liability. You cannot overdesign safety and security of these areas. It will reap many

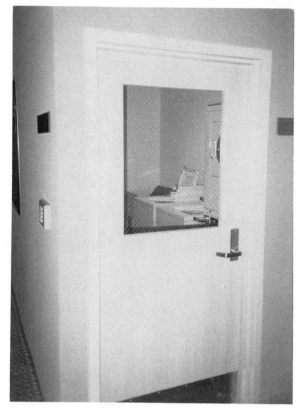

Figure 10-53. Provide a half-glass door in guest laundries; keep in view of staff.

benefits, including providing greater accessibility to those who have special needs. If a guest has a negative experience, that one individual will affect 25 others as to whether they will use your facility again.

RESORT AMENITIES AND OTHER PASTIMES

In the resort world there all kinds of facilities to entice guests to spend their vacations there. Typically these facilities include golf courses, tennis courts, jogging paths, health spas, bowling alleys, recreation rooms, handball and racquet ball courts, water slides, boating, scuba diving, parasailing, and day-care centers. Each has a unique risk exposure that requires special analysis beyond the scope of this book. However, consideration will be given to some basics in designing and protecting health spas, play

Figure 10-54. Self-dispensing ice machines provide sanitation and safety from foreign substances.

grounds for day care, club houses and pro shops, and briefly to jogging paths.

Health Spas

A health spa facility is usually a free-standing building that provides a very expanded health club concept such as is usually associated with standard hotels. The focus is on catering not only to hotel guests but to the general public as well through a membership program. Some of the expanded services include personalized health and fitness analysis; personalized counselors and exercise instructors; massage; loofah; steam and sauna rooms; plunge pools; whirlpools; lap pools; and aerobics. These are not all of the many services that can be provided. Many provide complete nutritional services and offer a complete total-fitness program.

A prime requirement in these facilities is top-notch management and a well-trained staff able to handle all types of emergencies. With the exposure to sports-related injuries, it is highly desirable to have a small medical unit staffed with a registered nurse skilled in treating the typical injuries. From a safety design point of view, all of the criteria covered under health clubs need to be included and expanded throughout the spa facility. Other unique design criteria for a spa include:

- A basic nurse-call system for all areas, to be monitored by attendants and the medical unit.
- A perimeter burglary system tied to the main hotel's security system.
- Alarmed temperature-sensing devices on all heating equipment for the steam room and sauna to alert staff of malfunctions in thermostats.
- Special shock-absorbent flooring designed for aerobics rooms.

Golf Clubhouses and Pro Shops

These facilities usually have the same guest accident trappings as have already been discussed: parking, main entries and lobbies, as well as restaurants. For general safety criteria refer to those sections as the same principles apply. Some unique problems that exist in unusual areas include burglary, shoplifting, and golf-cart battery handling and storage. For the intricacies of battery handling consult NFPA, OSHA, and EPA regulations.

It is wise to install a burglary system with hold-up protection and in some cases CCTV surveillance. Because of the high value items in the pro shops, if they are of significant size an article surveillance system may be a worthwhile investment.

Day Care and Playgrounds

These types of service are becoming more and more popular. The managerial and operational details for these need thorough researching, but this section will endeavor to provide some basics in laying out a play area for children and a few other design tidbits.

The center itself is usually housed within the hotel and adjacent to an outdoor area. Inside, the area should all be on the same level and include an open play area and children's chairs and work tables. Everything should be kept simple and on the same elevation. As in a private home, childproof cabinets, electrical outlets, and fixtures are required and sharp or abrasive materials must be removed or avoided. An adult as well as a children's bathroom will be needed. The main entry to the facility should be a glass-type storefront so that individuals can be screened by staff; the area must be kept open so that staff can see all of the children. It may be worthwhile fitting a door chime tied to the entrances and exits to alert staff of anyone entering or leaving the facility. The best type is one tied to a door contact so that children will not play with the electric-eye or mat type.

The play yard should be surrounded by at least a 4-foot high fence with no gate if possible, or alternatively a gate that is childproof. If there is nighttime activity, insure at least 15 footcandles of illumination.

Design of the play yard and equipment is critical in reducing child injuries. According to the Consumer Products Safety Commission (CPSC), four out of five playground injuries are suffered by children under the age of 10 years. Seven out of ten injuries, however, are caused by falls—the most common playground accident. The type of surface on the playground is a major factor affecting the number and severity of injuries associated with falls.

General design guidelines for safe play areas

- Surface treatment is difficult because all surfaces require maintenance to varying degrees; organic and inorganic materials such as bark or pea gravel require the most, while outdoor rubber mats and synthetic turf require less but are more expensive. The CPSC recommends testing the surface according to *Impact Attenuation Performance of Surfaces Installed Under Playground Equipment* published by the National Bureau of Standards, NBSIR 79-1707. The pass criterion for the test is that the surface should not impart a peak acceleration in access of $200g$ to an instrumented ANSI headform dropped on to the surface from the maximum estimated fall height.
- Provide adequate space around each piece of equipment, taking into account the equipment's use zone.

- Paths, fences, gates, and buildings should be at least 8 feet from the use zone.
- Keep the site free of visual barriers.
- Allow for maximum drainage so that the yard can dry out quickly.
- Buy only equipment that has been extensively tested to CPSC standards.
- Reduce the possibility of entrapment by eliminating angles or openings that could trap any part of a child's body.
- Accessible parts of moving devices and sliding surfaces should be designed so they do not catch children's clothing.
- Equipment should present no accessible sharp edges or protruding points.
- Elevated areas must be properly guarded and graspable rungs and handrails should be provided.

These are not all of the issues involved in safe design of day care centers, but they comprise a base from which to begin to look at these areas carefully before proceeding with implementing this kind of service.

Jogging and Fitness Trails

This area can easily be overlooked. Significant liability arises when a jogging route is provided for guests. In many instances, failure to notify guests of potential hazards while running around the block will be held to be negligent. The same applies for a jogging path on your property. All the fitness areas should be built with the same concepts mentioned above for playgrounds and the course must be properly maintained.

A uniform surface is required for running on. Many facilities use blacktop with the new rubberized shock-absorbent coatings. Pathway lighting should be provided at a 1 footcandle minimum; alternatively, close the track down after hours.

All fitness stations should have clearly written instructions and precautions. Lighting in these areas should be 5 to 10 footcandles. It may be a worthwhile addition to include rest stations with benches and water fountains. Landscaping should be kept out of the path zone. From a security point of view, landscaping should not be used that could conceal intruders from the view of the guest. It may be wise to have the entire property fenced to deter intruders. Obviously, this is an area that should be patrolled regularly by hotel security.

GETTING IT RIGHT

It might seem that operators cannot do anything without inviting trouble. The answer is to be sure to get the design right in the first place. Many of the suggested design items will not cost a lot in up-front investment, but they will impact operating costs by reducing risk exposure. And it should be stressed yet again that if a guest has a good experience they will come back. There is no more winning combination than good design and good management.

CHAPTER 11

Safety and Security Factors in Designing Restaurants

CUSTOMER AND EMPLOYEE SAFETY AND SECURITY ISSUES

The Design Objective

For the restaurant industry, the challenges to integrating safety and security into the building design are no less complicated than for a hotel or a motel, even though the facility is less complex (Figure 11-1). In fact, in many instances, with the rapid pace of development, design, and construction, it can be more difficult.

A colleague who worked for a major fastfood chain has told me, "If you miss it in review or the contractor fails to provide it as designed, many times the operator will accept the situation as is." Why? "Because a typical fastfood restaurant will lose around $30,000 a day in revenue for every day it's not open."

Considering this scenario, it becomes imperative that the construction documents reflect the safety and security design directive. It is the only way to minimize job site problems and being forced to accept surprises. As in the case of any new structure, the responsibility for the design and the end product rests with the designer of record. However, in order for the designer to perform as intended, clear cut design directives and criteria have to be established.

To accomplish this goal, the designer needs to understand the problems that the operator faces in day-to-day operation. It is a well publicized fact that the food service industry in general is clamoring for the limited pool of relatively inexpensive labor.

Figure 11-1. Integrating safety and security into restaurant design is no less complicated than for a hotel.

Add to that the rise in the minimum wage in the next few years and increased competition and the price cutting wars, and top management will be squeezing overhead to try to make profits.

There is a significant shortage of qualified labor, so in the press of business the property manager is forced into hiring the "warm body." The typical manager is also working 70 to 80 hours a week. These restaurant managers are burned out, so it is no wonder safety and security takes a back seat to the day-to-day operations. This is why designing the facility to improve operating efficiency, safety, and security are paramount in reducing losses.

What are some of the problems that can be expected? The following is a breakdown of accident types, as a percentage of the total claims cost for a typical restaurant operation:

Employees

Slips, trips, and falls	43 percent
Lifting	14 percent
Cuts and burns	9 percent
Struck against or by an object	22 percent
Security related	12 percent

Customers

Slips, trips, and falls (inside)	43 percent
Slips, trips, and falls (outside)	23 percent

Struck by an object or defective equipment   22 percent
Food-borne illness and foreign objects   11 percent
Security related   1 percent

Slips, trips, and falls are broken down into two areas, indoors versus outdoors, for customers to illustrate that site design is a very important consideration in the overall design. Yet real practice contradicts this concept; the building is squeezed onto the site and everything else is stuck in around it.

Another interesting statistic is security related: this category refers to injuries received during a robbery attempt or altercation. Unfortunately, people are killed during these events. A review of some recent cases will illustrate the point. In *Nelson* v. *Church's Fried Chicken* (1987) a settlement was reached. In this case a man was shot in a parking lot, causing him to become quadriplegic. The suit alleged inadequate security because of previous crimes [foreseeability] and failure to hire a guard. Another case (*Taco Bell* v. *Lannon*, 1987) involved a patron being shot in a fastfood restaurant during a hold-up. Negligence was found because of a previous history of robberies and lack of management action to prevent these acts or warn of the danger. Several other factors were also cited, including improper cash-handling procedures, poor lighting, lack of employee training for robberies, and a failure to lock remote entries. Could a design change have helped to prevent or mitigate the lawsuit? It is more than likely in the first case; lighting was an issue, and also access to the lot from perimeter areas. In the second case, perhaps a lower settlement would have resulted from provision of trim banks, adequate lighting and automatic locks, or use of exit-only hardware.

Another interesting tidbit, according to the National Restaurant Association, is that four cents of every dollar earned in the food service industry goes to theft, usually by employees.

In the case of redevelopment areas downtown in major cities or in marginal neighborhoods, the need for increased security is a major concern in order to draw customers to the establishment. Here again establishing the design directive and criteria will impact the profitability of the restaurant operation.

This chapter is divided into shared elements such as kitchens and site considerations and then into the various restaurant types, which are free-standing theme restaurants, fastfood restaurants, restaurants and bars in hotels, and lastly food courts. There are numerous other types, but the criteria are not significantly different.

Site Design—Parking and Entries

Unlike a hotel, at a restaurant patrons will usually be parking at the facility near the main entry, but the basic safety and security design concerns are the same.

All entries, if traffic is two-way, should be 26 feet wide. They should be clearly marked and well lit. Landscaping should not inhibit drivers' vision. In many cases owing to tight sites it may be advisable to have separate entry and exit drives remote from each other, with one-way traffic around the site. Lanes should be a minimum of 12 feet wide. Double lanes should have painted center lanes. If the restaurant sits in the middle of a mall parking lot the situation is more difficult, but the basic principles still apply. In most cases guests will not encounter a sidewalk until they are adjacent to the building.

Most free-standing restaurants have a sidewalk that surrounds the structure on at least three sides (Figure 11-2). The biggest problem is achieving accessibility. Because there is such little space to work with, the strangest, steepest, oddest curb ramps are used. These ramps are claims and lawsuits waiting to happen. Monolithic curbs and gutters should be used to prevent heaving due to freeze–thaw cycles.

Handicap spaces should be located near the front entry and there should be curb access or even better a flush pavement main entry to the building. Stoops and single risers should be avoided

Figure 11-2. Achieving accessibility while maintaining safety for other pedestrians can be a challenge with free-standing restaurants.

at all costs; not only do they defeat accessibility but they are tripping hazards. Chapter 10 has an in-depth discussion of how to handle this design item.

In the early stages planners need to work with the civil engineers to plan site accessibility so as to meet minimum ANSI A117.1 standards (Figure 11-3). Details of the entries, curb ramps, steps, and other areas must be shown clearly on the civil drawings. Avoid having wheel stops except, if necessary, on the perimeter, where people will not be walking.

Lighting is a critical element for security and safety. The Illumination Engineering Society quotes a 0.9 footcandle reading measured at the surface. In my opinion, there should be 1 footcandle minimum for the general site with lighting on sidewalks increased to around 2 footcandles, and 5 footcandles minimum at all entrances. For fastfood facilities, the general site lighting value should be about twice these figures.

Lighting is also important for marketing purposes, to draw attention to the building. Conversely, if the restaurant is located in a marginal neighborhood, insufficient lighting creates a sense of insecurity for patrons and could turn them away.

For all free-standing and fastfood restaurants, a covered entry

Figure 11-3. Site design is complicated at times because of a lack of space.

and double vestibule area is desirable. This will not only increase the comfort of the customer but it reduces energy consumption and allows an area for built-in walk-off mats, sometimes called pedimat. This arrangement will go along way to reducing slip and fall exposure in inclement weather.

All walkways should be broom finished. Curb ramps should have a contrasting color (see Chapter 10). Some operators like to have curbs of a contrasting color; this may be required by code for such things as fire lanes. Avoid heavy deck paints or highway type paints; either stain the areas or use a nonslip, sprayed on, water based, latex resin coating.

For a facility in a tough neighborhood, some added security measures are:

- Having a fenced parking lot that is well-lit, with security officers.
- Valet parking is an option; however you must protect the vehicles from theft (see Chapter 10).
- Cab stands located close by; alternatively, have arrangements for availability at short notice.
- All exits should be well-lit.

Again, use of a qualified expert to assist in assessing the risk so that adequate design directives can be produced is crucial to avoiding a catastrophe, and can help sales.

Kitchens in General—Most Hazardous Places

Kitchens are among the most hazardous areas for employees to work in and yet the exposure to cuts, burns, strains, and sprains can be significantly reduced through some very simple design techniques (Figure 11-4). Besides good design, proper training, supervision, and the right equipment are equally important to a total loss control program.

From a security point of view, the obvious concern is internal theft through access to high-value storage areas such as meat lockers and liquor rooms. Besides the usual management techniques (inventories, key control, package checks, and honesty tests), technology exists that can control who enters these areas and, should a loss occur, indicate who the individuals were that had access and at what time. It may sound expensive, but it costs less than a $1000 per door. It can also eliminate the all too frequent

Figure 11-4. A kitchen with a safety conscience, and the quality is likely to be outstanding.

key duplication at the local hardware store. There are systems that can control access to the entire facility, act as a time-recording system, and monitor alarms of all types. Obviously these are rather expensive, but in certain situations they may be cost-effective for large operations or operations within a hotel.

More and more restaurant operations are using sophisticated, computerized point-of-sale (POS) systems to control when and how food is issued from the kitchen and to track inventory and food costs. Bar code technology has also slowly crept into the control process, scanning deliveries, then inputting the data into a database system and running comparisons with physical inventories and POS output data. However, even with these new tools, good management is still the key.

As discussed in Chapter 13, even video surveillance systems can be of a tremendous value in deterring and detecting theft through video recording of day-to-day activities.

Kitchen safety is also important to customer safety. One of the less frequent claims, but one that can be devastating to reputation, is a food poisoning or illness claim. The best prevention method is enforcement of good sanitation rules—foods properly stored, hands washed regularly, good housekeeping, no-one handling food with open sores, and so on. From a design perspective, the following should be considered:

- Adequate hand-washing facilities, foot treadle activated with automatic timed cut-off.
- Sufficient cold storage and temperature alarms.
- Proper racks for keeping goods off floors.
- Specific segregated preparation areas.

There are many more. An excellent resource is the local health department. Get them involved before the plans are being drafted and consult them throughout the design process. Always remember the three C's for wholesome food: Keep it Clean, Cold and Covered.

Now let us review the basic design criteria for kitchen areas.

General Criteria for Kitchen Areas

- All flooring should:
    1. Be of a minimum 0.7 wet and dry and 0.28 grease slip resistance.
    2. Pass the Robinson wheel abrasion test.
    3. Have breaking strength of at least 450 lb.
    4. Have water absorption below 0.5 percent.
- Floor drains should be located so that they are no more than 40 feet apart. They should be flush with the floor and secured. Openings should be no greater than 1 inch by 1 inch.
- Locate trench drains in front of all ice machines and around dish machines to prevent water from running across the floor (Figure 11-5).
- Provide drains in front of all tilt kettles, tilt fryers and other equipment which is hosed down (Figure 11-5).
- Provide glass vision panels 5 inches wide by 20 inches high on all high-traffic doors.
- Where doors open into an aisle, protect the swing area by a railing or wall.
- Locate all compressed gas cylinders in a low-traffic area and secure cylinders to the wall by chains or racks.
- Store glassware away from food areas.

Figure 11-5. Trench drains are needed in front of tilt kettles, fryers, and ice machines.

- All light fixtures shall have full lens covers to prevent shattered glass from falling into food areas.
- Furnish separate cleaning supply storage away from foodstuffs.
- Meat slicers, choppers, and other like equipment must have interlocks so that equipment cannot be operated if guards are not in place.
- Tops of soup warmers should be no higher than 3 feet above the finished floor to facilitate ladling and prevent burns.
- Open and top-burner equipment should not be located at the end of the line because people coming around a corner quickly could inadvertently place a hand on the equipment.
- French-fry holding stations should be next to the fryer and on the same side of the aisle, so that grease is not tracked across the floor.
- All wheeled carts and other portable wheeled equipment should have wheel locks.
- All floor-mounted mixers need a separate panic disconnect switch for quick shut-down in case clothes or other objects get trapped.

- All counter-top ovens and microwaves should have baffles on vents to vent heat away from people.
- All equipment should have National Sanitation Federation (NSF) and Underwriters Laboratories (UL) labels as applicable.
- Lighting should be 50 footcandles in all cooking and preparation area; 25 footcandles in storerooms and service corridors.
- Use vapor-sealed lighting fixtures inside coolers and hoods.
- Furnish GFI protection on all convenience outlets especially in or near wet areas.
- Garbage disposal should have offset neck to prevent hand contact with blades.
- Walk-in boxes should have a flush entry and glass vision panel in the door. Compressors, condensing units, and coils should be located in a machine room remote from boxes.
- Provide mop and sink stations in easily accessible areas.
- Locate breakdown and warewashing so that waiters, waitresses and bus personnel have easy access on their way to and from dining areas but do not locate them so that food spills and water can occur in main traffic points.
- Work surfaces should not be higher than 36 inches. However, for preparation areas, adjustable work surfaces are desirable for workers of different heights. Allow space for feet to go under work tables and lines to prevent slouching or leaning over tables.
- Height above the floor for ice bins should be designed to help reduce the amount of bending by an employee while transferring ice into another container.
- Shelving should be able to hold a minimum of 200 lb per square foot.
- Utilize a restricted keying system with commercial cylindrical locksets, deadlocks, and in certain instances electronic access control.

Specialty Support Areas

High Dollar Inventory Storage Areas These areas include dry storage, meat lockers, freezers, liquor storage and silver storage. Access control is an effective tool to reduce the opportunity for theft. The following is the bare minimum from a design standpoint in order to help curtail theft-related losses:

- Vandalproof walls.
- Commercial grade, removable-core latch set with restricted keyway or electronic card/key reader.
- Hollow metal door, 16-gauge welded metal frame.
- Vision panel in door leafs.

For safety, the primary concerns are:

- Non-slip flooring (same as kitchen).
- Shelving and racks designed to sustain 200 lb per square foot.
- 25 footcandles of light with plastic lens to protect bulbs.
- Walk-in boxes with flush entry and vision panels.

Warewashing and Breakdown Area   The most often overlooked area is where the dishes and pots get cleaned. Some of the key design concerns are:

- Adequate space for breakdown of soiled dishes and soiled and clean dish carts and glass/cut dollies.
- Sufficient dolly and rack storage so dripping racks are not carried around the kitchen to storage rooms.
- Mop sink and clean up station.
- Hand sink, towel, and soap dispenser.
- The area should be located to be in close proximity to service exits from the restaurant to facilitate breakdown, but out of normal traffic patterns so that water and debris are not in main walking paths to kitchen lines.
- Garbage disposal should have offset throat to prevent hand entry at the blades.
- Drain boards at pot sinks to prevent dripping water.
- Lighting should be around 50 footcandles.
- Furnish GFI protection on all convenience outlets.

Liquor Service Bar   Security is again the prime concern (Figure 11-6). The space should have walls from floor to the understructure above. Entry should be through a hollow metal door and welded steel frame. Use a high-security, removable-core latch set with a restricted keyway. Many restaurants are using the automatic

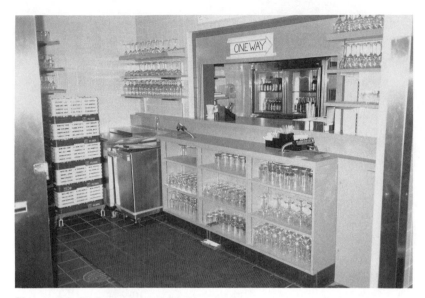

Figure 11-6. Security of high-value inventory areas is critical to the assets-protection effort.

dispensing systems for liquors and soda; access to the main equipment should be in a separate secure area. Lastly, provide a metal roll down door to secure the counter areas after operation.

When designing the service bar, keep in mind limitations regarding reach and employee comfort. Not everyone is six feet three inches tall. Some of the greatest complaints from bartenders are that the glass racks are too high, that bottled liquor storage is too deep and too high to reach, or that the counter is too wide with all the equipment, and that they can't get the kegs out without straining their backs. Bear these things in mind before grabbing any "spare" space.

Additionally, provide a non-slip floor, task lighting, and a hand sink. At the waitress pick-up, adequate space for drinks, checks, glasses, ice, and condiments is needed.

Service Stands   Service stands are places where service personnel obtain coffee, ice and water, condiments, table linen, silverware, and other items to keep customers happy. They are also used for staging service to the tables and in some cases for cash handling for reconciliation of the checks and for credit card verification.

For a space the size of a closet, this area services a multitude of functions. Basic criteria include:

- Nonslip tile, minimum 0.7 wet and dry, 0.28 grease
- 15 footcandles of lighting at the counter
- Depending on location, a duress alarm
- GFI protection on convenience outlets

HOTEL RESTAURANTS AND LOUNGES

Fundamentally the safety and security criteria for any type of restaurant are much the same. However, there is a very important distinction in the case of hotels. In essence it derives from the fact that the restaurant and lounge are located within this greater structure, so now services are shared as a part of the total operation of the facility. Even in those hotels that lease or hire management companies to oversee the food and beverage operations, service areas, dock access, and ice production are generally shared unless specific arrangements are made for separate facilities during the design phases. With the passage of the Americans with Disabilities Act, all restaurants and lounges will need to be accessible.

Some of the advantages of shared services include a security staff and built-in systems to help reduce employee theft or various other types of security incidents, and a Human Resources department to help in screening and recruiting new employees as well as training, and lastly a full maintenance staff to repair equipment.

Restaurants

Safety

- Dining room aisles should be a minimum of 3 feet wide.
- Main entry vestibule and hostess area should be of a nonslip floor material, minimum 0.6 wet and dry. If marble is used, it should have a honed finish.
- Avoid multilevels; however, if desired they must be accessible. If stairs are used in conjunction with ramps, for non-handicapped persons there should be a minimum of three riser steps with reachable/graspable handrails, uniform slip-resistant treads (minimum 12 inches) and risers (maximum

Figure 11-7. If steps are needed, use safe design principles.

7 inches), edge definition and step lighting (nondimmable and on emergency circuit) (Figure 11-8).

- All multilevels should provide handicap accessibility via a ramp or lift (Figure 11-8). Ramps should have a maximum 1:12 slope, slip-resistant surface (carpet), graspable handrails, and down-lights or side-lights (nondimmable and on emergency circuit).
- Buffets need sneeze guards according to health requirements (Figure 11-9). Ensure that glass is tempered glass or plexiglass and that all edges are rounded and protected.
- Buffet floors should meet the same criteria as kitchen floors except that they can be a little less stringent on the grease slip test.
- Provide adequate storage for children's seats and highchairs so that they do not block aisles.
- Service entries to the kitchen should be a minimum of 42 inches wide and separated by a center mullion with opposite swinging doors that have vision panels. Avoid sharp corners and placing ice machine or service stands directly in the path of travel.

Figure 11-8. Design of safe access to multilevel areas for the handicapped is crucial in the early stages.

Figure 11-9. Buffet lines need nonslip floors and sneeze guards.

- All service area flooring should achieve the same criteria as for kitchens.
- Pendant lighting should only be used over fixed seating and should dangle no lower than 64 inches AFF and be made with rounded edges and lightweight materials.
- Wall sconces should be selected with care for location and projection into the space so they do not create head-strike problems.
- Avoid elevated banquets at all costs.
- Seating areas should be carpeted or have flooring that achieves a slip-resistance of a minimum 0.6 wet and dry and is suitable for heavy traffic.

Security

Taking full advantage of the fact of being within the hotel structure, security of the restaurant after hours can be accomplished simply by making use of the hotel security patrols and CCTV if necessary. It would be ideal to be able to secure the main entry and service doors after hours. This helps prevent theft of silver, place settings, and artifacts. Rear exits required by code that egress directly to the outside should be locally and remotely alarmed and labeled for emergency use only. Wine storage should be securely locked and access to the key should be restricted.

As already mentioned, many restaurants are using computerized point-of-sale systems. With the increasing use of electronic guest-room lock systems, it may be desirable to provide verification readers that will confirm whether a card key is valid and whether the patron is able to make room charges.

Lounges

Lounges come in all shapes and sizes, from the small club or piano bar to the high-action entertainment type. With the concern these days about serving liquor responsibly, more and more lounges are doing food service. As a result, it is probably wise to situate bars with service access to the kitchen or provide a food production pantry within the lounge itself.

From a safety and security standpoint, access to the hotel's basic back-of-house services is also a big advantage. However, in a leased establishment separate facilities may be desirable from a control point of view.

Many of the restaurant safety and security criteria apply to all lounge designs. Listed below are criteria unique to a lounge.

Safety

- Avoid hinged bar tops as they will inevitably cut someone's fingers off when they free-fall.
- Dance floors should be of wood or a material that allows gliding. However they should be clearly distinctive in color from other walking surfaces.
- All other walking surfaces should be carpeted. Any hard surface materials should be used sparingly and achieve a minimum of 0.6 slip resistance wet and dry as well as being suitable for heavy traffic.
- Design the bar storage and glass racks for the 95th percentile or greater population anthropological requirements for reach and functionality (see service bar criteria).

Security

- Furnish duress alarms to summon security at main bar POS terminals.
- The entire lounge should be securable after hours.
- Secure DJ booths and sound equipment rooms with full-height walls, solid wood or hollow metal doors, and restricted keyway removable-core commercial latchsets and deadlocks (motion sensors may also be desirable).

FREE-STANDING THEME RESTAURANTS

These restaurants have waitress/waiter service but they can be anything from a pizza shop to a family-style restaurant or a gourmet restaurant. The primary difference in this class of restaurants is that they are generally a free-standing structure with site parking or are within a mall or office complex. This section deals with unique design elements not covered already in site, kitchens, and hotel restaurants and lounges that apply directly to this classification of restaurant.

As the support services of a hotel setting are not available, it is necessary to provide that kind of service in the design. The receiving and employee entry to the rear of the facility is the only entry for getting foodstuffs and other materials into the restaurant, unless the front door is used. The door should be hollow metal with a welded steel frame securely anchored to block walls. The opening should be at least 42 inches wide with a view port, commercial removable-core latchset and deadlock with a high-security restricted keyway. The threshold should be beveled on both sides and the surface outside should be sloped away from the building, but avoiding stoops. There should also be a doorbell. Lighting should be a minimum of 5 footcandles for safety and security with additional controlled lighting to 15 footcandles outside for evening deliveries.

Many facilities, because they are tight on space, locate walk-in boxes outside. It may be desirable to create a fenced yard entry to help improve the security access to this potential high-value loss area. The walk-in door should be alarmed as a part of the total burglar protection.

Inside, flooring throughout the service areas should meet the same standards as for general kitchen areas. Avoid standard VCT tile to avoid slips and falls. If a type of vinyl tile is favored because of cost, there are at least two manufacturers of slip-resistant tiles that do not require any dressings and have a nonslip surface.

Kitchen and service areas should be designed in accordance with the criteria already covered. However, there is usually less space in which to accomplish them, and that is a challenge in itself.

In the dining room and lounge, attention must be placed on floor materials and lighting. I ate at a restaurant which is part of a chain and caters to the young professionals. The interior design was rustic, with gas lamps and dark woods. Between the banquet sections the flooring was very dark stained wood. Over each banquet was a downlight with a very narrow beam that illuminated only the table top. The rest of the restaurant lighting was dimmed very low. I observed two people slip on dripped water that could not be seen. Fortunately they were young and their reaction time kept them from falling. However, an elderly couple who came in literally could not see the floor. The hostess unfortunately did not offer any assistance to the couple but walked two steps in front. The restaurant was lucky that the couple eventually made it to their seat. The point of this anecdote is that there is no reason for such things to occur. A couple of simple design solutions, by providing downlights overhead or mounted on the table support and directed into the walkway, would have eliminated the problem. Wood can be treated to provide some slip resistance, but in any case it is probably not the best surface for seating areas. A lighter stain and better lighting would have helped the situation.

Most people at some time have hit their head on a swag lamp when standing up after eating. Many small claims can be avoided by following simple rules:

- Swag lamps should only be used over fixed seating.
- The lowest point of the lamp should be a minimum of 64 inches above the finished floor.
- The lamp should be made of lightweight materials with rounded edges.

Public restrooms should be designed to the same basic criteria discussed in Chapter 10. Some of the basics are:

- Entrances should be separate and distinct, if possible viewed by host/hostess stand or cashier.
- There should be doors on all entries.
- Slip resistant flooring, minimum 0.6 wet and dry.
- Soap dispensers should be located over sinks.
- Take care with line of sight problems caused by mirrors.
- Towel dispensers or hand dryers should be beside sinks.

Another important concern is physical security. Install a security alarm system that includes perimeter alarms, motion sensor trap, hold-up alarms, safe alarm, and central station monitoring. Additionally, use commercial-grade latchsets and deadbolts that have a restricted keyway and are the removable-core type. If employee theft is a serious concern, use one of the new electronic access control devices, which will provide an audit trail of all entries. Remote fire exits from the dining and lounge areas should be specified as exit-only with hard-wired local alarms to help deter skipping and employee theft. Chapter 12 will go into detail on various types of security devices that are appropriate for use in all types of restaurants.

FASTFOOD RESTAURANTS OF ALL TYPES

As society has become more mobile, with two wage earners, the need for quick service and inexpensive food has become a billion-dollar industry. Because of our fast-paced life style, people no longer even bother to sit down inside the establishment. Today's weekly family event is to jump in the car, head to the nearest fastfood restaurant, go through the drive-through, pick up dinner, and eat on the way home or to the movies. However, people still come inside, especially if there is a ten-car wait at the drive-through.

This section will concentrate only on those design issues that are unique to this type of outlet. Many of the design concepts in the previous discussions apply directly to the fastfood restaurant.

Fast food is what the name implies. As a result the most significant hazard inside is slips and falls, while outside in the drive-through it is property damage. But the overall loss exposure is still the same as with any type of restaurant.

Drive-Through

Most fastfood restaurants have at least one drive-through, but a new trend is to provide two because many people do not want to come in and sit down. The biggest problem is space. Most restaurants are situated on tight sites and it is difficult to accomplish even minimal safety design considerations. As Figure 11-10 shows, a drive-through consists of the following different

Figure 11-10. Drive-up lane and order station; notice the steel gate that blocks off receiving drive-up.

components: drive-up lane, order station, pick-up window, and exit lane.

Drive-up lanes are the initial approach to the order station. The drive-up lane begins as a normal traffic lane in the parking lot. At a point before the order station it splits off from the parking lot lane and becomes the drive-up lane. It is very important to segregate this lane if at all possible (Figure 11-11). As the lane is usually on a curve, try to maintain a minimum width of 12 feet with an outside radius of 30 feet and an inside radius of 18 feet, and flare the lane in at the window to a width of $9\frac{1}{2}$ feet. To segregate the lane, use either a curb or painted lane markings. Allow a sufficiently large staging area for two to three cars before they enter the order station, so that they do not interfere with other lot traffic. Many facilities put up concrete bollards at these turn areas, but these should be avoided because people will always hit them. Lighting of this area should be higher than the general site lighting, possibly twice as much.

Order stations are giant lighted menu boards that have an intercom built into them so that drivers of vehicles can place their orders with employees inside the restaurant. If the sign is properly located there is no need for bollards to protect it from being struck. In high-crime areas, consider installing a CCTV camera in the board so that employees can screen it and be aware of potential problems. Exits from the restaurant, including rear receiving exits, should never empty directly into the drive-through

Figure 11-11. Lane to pick-up window separated from general lot traffic by curbs and landscaping.

area. They should always direct pedestrian traffic around the area as much as possible or give sufficient visibility and warning to the pedestrian and driver that a crosswalk exists.

As the name implies, the pick-up window is where drivers pay for the food and receive their completed order (Figure 11-12). Some obvious considerations are the height of the window and how far it sticks out into the lane. The best approach is to position a curb below the edge of the window which surrounds the perimeter of the building, thus eliminating the problem of someone running into the window. The bottom edge of the window should be located so that there is easy transfer to the driver with minimal strain on the employee. Many facilities are using hands-free communications sets for the employees so that they can take orders as well as fill them in the same motion. The window should be made of safety glass and be easy to open and close. Many facilities use bullet-resistant glass in high-crime areas. There are even bank teller type windows, where a drawer is used to collect money and place the order and the window is of fixed bullet-resistant glass set in heavy masonry walls.

The last component is the exit lane (Figure 11-13). Here the most critical design aspect is visibility and a smooth transition into the normal parking lot traffic flow. The lane curbing should continue until just past the building's edge and allow a smooth flow into oncoming traffic. In most facilities, pedestrian exits usually come out into this lane area. A guardrail should be located

Figure 11-12. Drive-up lane, order station, staging area, and pick-up window.

Figure 11-13. Exit lane, pedestrian exit with guardrail, and cross-walk.

just prior to the curb edge and direct pedestrian flow down the sidewalk parallel to the lane. This will provide for the safety of pedestrians and give the driver good visibility should someone attempt to cross the lane at some point down the sidewalk.

Playgrounds

Playgrounds were a very popular addition to many restaurants some years ago. However, with the increase in litigation and the tremendous exposure they present in terms of child injuries, most facilities have removed them from their restaurants. Considering our changing dining-out trends, playgrounds are probably more of a headache than they are worth in marketing value. If a playground exists as is planned, follow the basic criteria discussed in Chapter 10.

Dining Areas and Ordering Lines

It seems ideas abound about how the order line should be set up. There appear to be two main approaches: counter with many order-taking stations, or queuing rails directing flow to where food is picked up and leading the customer to a cashier's station (Figure 11-14).

In the first set-up, the concern will be adequate space for handling the load during rushes so that there is some semblance

Figure 11-14. Queuing rails direct people traffic and keep crowded areas organized.

of a straight line to the counter. The second requires an adequate width between the queuing rails. They should be 42 inches AFF and properly supported to handle loads from people leaning on them. Accessibility must be provided for. In both scenarios the potential for food and drink spillage is high and nonslip flooring to a minimum 0.7 wet and dry. An excellent floor maintenance program is also paramount in reducing the exposure (see Chapter 12). Some fastfood restaurants use the same tile in these areas as in the kitchen because their maintenance program falls short.

In the dining room, fixed seating is the norm. Here there should be no sharp edges or corners. Materials should be durable and easy to clean. Seating should be designed to sustain a lot of abuse. Aisles should be kept clear and be a minimum of 3 feet wide. Locate trash receptacles out of traffic paths in the seating areas; generally a small recessed area on the way out of the dining areas is ideal. Trash receptacles should have smooth edges and the entry flap should be lightweight and without spring hinges, to prevent finger injuries.

Most fastfood restaurants use high lighting levels, which aid in safety and security inside the facility; these are on the order of 20 footcandles or more.

FINAL REMARKS

Incorporating safety and security into the design of any restaurant is not costly. The return on investment is great in reduced losses and embarrassing customer problems. With the increased competition for customers' money, every opportunity to improve profits must be taken. Designing for safety and security is one of many ways of accomplishing that goal.

CHAPTER 12

Establishing a Slip and Fall Prevention Program

People will fall, and they will sue. A variety of causes influence how and when a fall will occur—foreign objects, design flaws, slippery surfaces, visual distractions, gait or walking style, physical and mental condition of the individual, or footwear condition and type of footwear.

Developing an approach to the prevention of slips, trips, and falls for guests and employees is not an easy matter. Current and past literature on slips, trips, and falls, reveals that the experts are more interested in a test method than in achieving the goals of accident reduction and litigation avoidance. Little guidance has been provided to the end user on how to set up an effective slip, trip, and fall prevention program. The preceding two chapters provided design criteria standards for stairs, ramps, platforms, and level walking surfaces. This chapter will focus on the steps to follow in establishing an effective program that incorporates both the design and management elements into a unified approach.

The subject of falls is a much underresearched area, yet it accounts for 12,000 deaths annually according to the National Safety Council. After motor vehicle injuries, falls are the second leading cause of death. Jake Pauls (1989) gave an estimated annual societal cost of falls in the United States at $37.3 billion. According to the National Safety Council, falls generally lead to twice as many fatalities as fires and about 75 percent of fall fatalities occur to people aged 65 and older.

CHANGING DEMOGRAPHICS

According to population experts, the US population is aging rapidly. Older consumers represent the fastest-growing segment in the marketplace. By the year 2000, 31 percent of the population will be aged 55 or older. These are the people with disposable income. The change is already being seen in the age of hotel and restaurant guests. The over-50's purchase 80 percent of all luxury travel. As the market age continues to increase, so to will liability risk. Observe the TV advertisements of a leading fastfood chain encouraging senior citizens to work for them. This type of aggressive advertising is being used in response to the rapidly shrinking unskilled labor market. But with the advent of this new older worker the exposure to potentially more serious work-related injuries will increase. This demographic change necessitates rethinking of design and management approaches so as to assimilate this new worker.

As people age they become more interested with what feels good and less impressed with what looks good. Feelings of security and safety are a significant issue because as people age they feel increasingly less secure and more vulnerable in unfamiliar surroundings. Not everyone over 50 is infirm, most are healthy and active, but abilities decline with age. Range of motion, flexibility, vision, and hearing are reduced and as a result injuries take longer to heal and tend to be more serious. This does not mean these people should not be hired or should not be allowed use of our facilities. But equally we cannot carry on business as usual. The risks have to be evaluated, and solutions have to be developed to the new exposure. Human factors and safety engineering principles have to be fully used in designing and managing facilities.

In the hospitality industry today, falls of all kinds account for 40 to 50 percent of the dollar losses for workers' compensation and general liability. Mindful of changing demographics, it is easy to foresee accident costs for falls becoming even higher in the next decade.

Even today, guests are requesting added safety devices in guestrooms: guest comment forms show a significant increase in the number of requests for grabbars in every bath tub and shower. With current changes in federal regulations to make commercial facilities accessible, the demand for safer facilities for all persons will be a paramount concern. Slip, trip, and fall prevention makes good business sense when in this changing environment.

It is because this subject is of such importance that a whole chapter is devoted to it. This chapter is a compilation of the latest research in slip, trip, and fall prevention, incorporating practical knowledge gained from hands-on implementation of a highly successful falls prevention program.

BASIC TENETS

Earlier chapters dealing with design indicated what comprises a safer stairway, ramp, elevated platform, and level floor. Part I discusses how to manage the total accident prevention effort. However, a slip, trip, and fall program is a major component in the total loss control effort for a hotel, motel and restaurant.

There are two basic tenets of a successful slip and fall program: prevention of falls, and effective claims management and litigation defense. The approach to setting up the program should be the same whether dealing with an employee or a guest.

The exposure from litigation can be quite devastating to the financial health and reputation of a business. But what is reasonable these days? Before answering that question, a definition of reasonable care is needed:

> Reasonable care can be defined for public use facilities as satisfying a legal duty to act as an ordinary, prudent, reasonable person not to do something that will cause injury to guests, customers, or invitees, or fail to do what will prevent such injury.

It is generally recognized that this definition can change radically depending on how a jury is instructed in its application to specific cases. A public facility has a nondelegable duty to provide reasonably safe premises and an obligation to warn of any dangers.

The key to the issue of reasonableness is foreseeability. Doing everything in good faith to mitigate the exposure does not mean 100 percent prevention. "Reasonable care" must take into account the risk of injury (which is frequency), possible severity (which is nearly unpredictable) and cost benefits. For instance, suppose a lodging establishment with 300 rooms has an average occupancy of 75 percent. That amounts to 82,125 guest stays in one year. If that is multiplied by 100 similar facilities in the chain, there are 8,212,500 guests stays in one year. Let us assume one slip and fall in the guestroom bath in which a guest stepped out of the tub on to a 100 percent cotton bathmat and slipped and fell. Considering that the hotel industry uses that type of mat virtually exclusively for sanitation reasons and cost, is it reasonable to replace all mats with rubber-backed types which disintegrate if washed every day?

A safety engineer must be concerned with all falls and their prevention. In the bathmat example, perhaps the mat was not the proximate cause of the fall. Perhaps the guest's foot caught on the tub apron and he tripped, or maybe his foot was still in the tub when he stepped out, slipped backwards, and fell. Answering the question of what is reasonable care is never easy, but embracing the concept of "good faith" will go a long way in the battle and subsequently win the war (Kohr, 1990).

The same can be said for workers' compensation, but because this is "no fault," when a fall does occur and an injury results, the claim must be paid. The costs for workers' compensation claims are rising every day and an assigned risk or the self-insured cannot afford not to control these costs.

It has been said that the National Safety Council reports the leading cause of accidental death, other than auto accidents, as falls and that nearly 12,000 deaths occur annually. Deaths from falls break down as follows: public areas, 24 percent; homes, 28 percent; and work related, 12.4 percent. However, 16.4% of all work-related disabling injuries are falls. Given that the average cost for a disabling injury is $16,800 and is $550,000 per death, the costs add up quickly (National Safety Council, 1989).

ELEMENTS OF AN EFFECTIVE PROGRAM

The basic elements of a slip, trip, and fall prevention program include:

1. Stating a strong policy and getting commitment.
2. Establishing a methodology and criteria for review and acceptance of walkway surfaces and related components.
3. Reconditioning or retrofitting walkways and related components in existing areas.
4. Maintenance standards and procedures.
5. Inspections, audits, tests, and records.
6. An employee footwear program.
7. Aggressive claims management and litigation defense methods.
8. Measuring results.

One of the greatest barriers to be overcome is getting people to realize that safety *can* fit into the marketplace as well as the workplace while keeping the aesthetics, cost, and sales appeal of the product intact. Once these different groups are brought together and shown the return on investment, interest peaks. As a result, setting up the program will not be as difficult an exercise as might be thought. The following sections discuss each element of the slip, trip, and fall prevention program.

State the Policy

Policies are very important because they state the purpose, commit management at all levels, and establish the goals to be achieved. When developing support for the program, input must come from top executives, operations management, safety professionals, architects, interior designers, specifiers, and construction professionals.

As a minimum, areas that should be highlighted in the policy are:

Management's intent
Scope of activity
Responsibilities
Accountability
Safety professionals' role
Authority
Standards to be met

An Example Statement

Slip, trip, and fall accidents affecting the public as well as employees represent unacceptable events that threaten the assets of the XYZ Company and cause needless personal suffering and inconvenience. This company places a high level of emphasis on the prevention and control of accidents. The overall responsibility for slip, trip, and fall accident prevention shall be with each manager. Specific responsibilities for each aspect of this program have been outlined for each department. The XYZ Company's Safety Department shall oversee and coordinate the administration of the policy and set the program objectives each year. In addition, the Safety Department shall have overall authority for materials selection and design approval on new and existing facilities that provide a slip, trip, and fall exposure.

This is not the only way to state a policy; however, it does set the expectations for what needs to be achieved and who is responsible.

Determining the Methodology

To set the criteria, a methodology must be established for determining safe walkways, materials, and related components. There have been numerous studies, articles, and papers written on the measurement of slip resistance on walkways. C. H. Irvine, inventor of the Horizontal Pull Slip Meter, stated:

> Although it would be highly desirable to be able to actually simulate the act of walking as a means of measuring pedestrian slip resistance, researchers have shown that this ideal would be difficult to attain. Efforts to make walking a safer activity by improving the slip resistance factor, both indoor and outdoor, led to the development of many devices for measuring the slip resistance of floor materials, dressings, and footwear. No device has yet been designed that does a satisfactory job of recognizing all the frictional aspects of footwear and floor materials. (Irvine, 1986)

Yet the measurement of slip resistance is the *single* most important factor in reducing accidents and improving the litigation posture.

Which test method should be followed? Before selecting a test method, first consider some basic principles of slips and falls. Physics defines friction as the ratio of the horizontal (resisting) force to the vertical (impressed) force, based on work more than 200 years ago by Coulomb. This means that friction is the resisting force that arises when the surface of one substance slides or tends to slide over an adjoining surface of the same or another substance. As simple as this definition may seem, duplicating the conditions in a laboratory or the field in order to record precise measurements is extremely difficult. In a paper written for ASTM by R. Braun and R. J. Brungraber, they stated:

> Pressure, standing time, temperature, humidity, time dependence of forces, and the geometry of the body, all impact the measurement of slip resistance. (Braun and Brungraber, 1977)

In addition, if account is made of pedestrian activity or gait, and mental and physical conditions of the person, the precise measurement of friction becomes extremely complicated. These statements were reaffirmed by other researchers at the 1989 ASTM

Symposium on Slips, Stumbles and Falls: Pedestrian Footwear and Surfaces held in Denver, Colorado.

Most researchers have concluded that when a slip occurs the static coefficient of friction is the relevant condition that must be evaluated for determination of safe walkway surfaces. Therefore, the static coefficient of friction is defined as the point at which two bodies in contact with each other begin to move and overcome friction.

Keeping in mind the objective and tenets of a slip, trip, and fall program, the test method you select should (1) be nationally recognized by ASTM, (2) have a historical base for comparison through the National Bureau of Standards (today called National Institute of Standards and Technology), (3) be usable in laboratories and the field, and (4) be portable. A slip tester recognized by many researchers and industries is the James machine, which is described in ASTM D2047 for floor finishes and ASTM F489 for footwear traction. However, the major disadvantage is that the James machine is not portable and cannot be used in the field. At the 1989 ASTM Falls Symposium, there was a challenge as to the James machine's reliability and whether it should be mothballed as a test method (Gray, 1990).

As an ASTM member, I have been involved first-hand in the testing controversy. Basically all coefficient of friction test methods have some form of a reliability problem, some more than others, when it comes to measuring the actual coefficient of friction. However, measurement of the relative slip-resistant characteristics of a walkway can be accomplished by setting a safe static coefficient of friction benchmark from your slip, trip, and fall claims history. This eliminates the so-called test method reliability challenge, because a slip resistance reading between two surfaces is correlated with an actual frequency of falls. Setting the benchmark in this manner will achieve a reduction in accidents—only a *reduction* because, in reality, given all of the factors affecting slip resistance, the total elimination of falls is difficult to accomplish. Slip resistance is only one piece in the puzzle.

On the basis of careful review, the Horizontal Pull Slip Meter (HPS) designed by C. H. Irvine (Figure 12-1) meets the criteria as an adequate test method for determining the relative slip resistance of floor surfaces, finishes, and footwear. This device is described in ASTM F609 and F695. A modified version is noted in ASTM C1028 (Horizontal Dynamometer Pull Meter). The

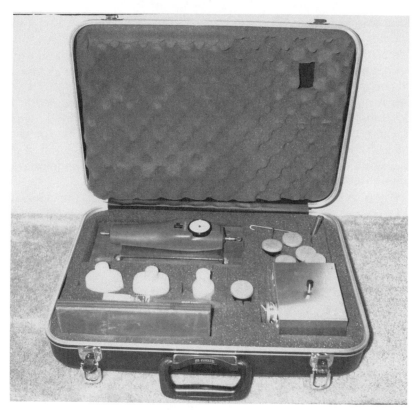

Figure 12-1. Horizontal Pull Slip Meter available from Whiteley Industries Inc., Tewksbury, Mass.

ASTM Committee C21.06, which is responsible for C1028, is currently evaluating a redraft of the standard to adopt the HPS tester. Preliminary test results show excellent reproducibility, repeatability, and correlation between the current C1028 test method and the HPS tester. The motivation for change is because the tester is portable, is not operator-dependent, is recognized by the footwear industry (ASTM F609, F695), and provides a lower standard deviation between test facilities than the current C1028 method.

Whichever test method is used, the test should be conducted under wet and dry conditions for all walkways, and under grease and water conditions for kitchens, service areas, food bars, and the like.

However, as discussed in Chapter 2, the test method of choice for bathtubs and pre-fab showers is ASTM F462, which uses the

Brungraber tester. The benchmark for this test method has already been established by the ASTM committee as a 0.04 slip resistance using a soapy water mixture; in practice a slip resistance of about 0.1 or better should be maintained.

For stair treads, NFPA Life Safety Code states that the slip resistance of a tread should meet the same requirements as for a level walking surface. This means if a tile for a lobby floor meets the slip resistance benchmark then it should be suitable for use on a stair tread. Ramps are sloped surfaces; the test method is the same as for a level floor, but the slip resistance benchmark should be higher.

There is one other test method worthy of discussion because it has passed the test of time: try it out in the real world on a controlled limited test area and see what happens. Get feedback from operations people on cleanability, maintenance, any incidents or near misses. A real world test can gain the greatest form of commitment from your operators for implementation of any product or design.

Establishing Criteria

Simply described, design criteria are parameters established by which a space can be defined and constructed. The previous section established test methods for determining safer materials and products. Criteria standards now need to be set.

Establishment of criteria standards for a safer walkway or bathing facility should be based on surfaces, materials, and designs known to reduce accidents. For instance, take a walkway surface that has represented an actual reduction in fall accidents and test it under various conditions; the results should provide an excellent slip resistance benchmark. An excellent barometer for a safe static coefficient of friction is the claims history.

From a legal point of view, a static coefficient of friction (COF) benchmark of 0.5 is considered necessary for a safe walkway, but even this may not be adequate depending on the area of use, for example, a lobby versus a pool deck.

Numerous past researchers have supported the 0.5 COF benchmark. It is in fact noted as a pass/fail requirement in ASTM D2047 for polishes and floor finishes using the James machine test. The problem with the ASTM D2047 benchmark is that it was established using leather as the sensor material under *dry* conditions. In studies conducted by C. H. Irvine and R. J.

Brungraber, various shoe sole materials were tested wet and dry. It was determined that leather on dry surfaces was the slippiest of all sensors. However, leather could not be used on smooth wet surfaces because of the adhesion between the leather and the floor, which resulted in a higher wet friction reading than dry. Bear in mind that leather is traditionally a sole material (Irvine 1976, 1986; Brungraber, 1977).

What sensor, then, should be used for measuring slip-resistant properties under wet conditions or any other condition? Currently ASTM C1028 uses neolite. Neolite has consistent manufactured qualities of hardness and low absorption rate, and similar materials are used on the heels and soles of shoes. In addition, a rubber material sensor should be used to simulate other types of heels. Finally, leather should not be excluded; tested dry, being the slippiest, it will provide more information on how the surfaces react. We cannot control what the public wear, so use should be made of leather, neolite, and rubber materials that meet material specifications addressed in current ASTM test methods as a base.

ASTM Standard Sensors

> *Leather*: KKL-165 Revision C, $\frac{1}{4}$ inch, vegetable tanned processed, Type I, typical outsole product
> *Neolite*: RMA spec. H.S.-3, Standard Neolite Cement Liner, Shore Hardness 93–96, specific gravity 1.25 ± 0.02, $\frac{1}{8}$ inch
> *Rubber*: S.B.R. Type, Durometer 70–75, $\frac{1}{4}$ inch

From the point of view of testing, neolite will give higher values dry than leather and rubber will give a higher value than neolite. Under wet conditions, leather is not a valid test because of adhesion to the surface, while neolite and rubber will provide lower slip resistance readings wet than dry. However, one of the disadvantages of the HPS method is the squeezing out of water under the feet during the wet test. When performing the test, minimize the sensor contact time and keep the test area wet throughout the test period. This will help to alleviate some of the adhesion problems. A new sensor is being developed in the United Kingdom that is under evaluation and may help to eliminate this test glitch. Also, a modified version of the HPS, which takes instantaneous readings as soon as the device is placed on the surface, was demonstrated at the Slip, Stumble and Fall Symposium. In a recent study in which I was involved, the ability of these testers to measure the slip resistance of greasy/wet floors was compared. Though the HPS reacted very favorably, the modified version holds great promise for the future. Nevertheless, if the benchmark is set on the basis of a known tested surface, this disadvantage is eliminated.

With employees it is somewhat easier because the type of footwear that can be worn in the facility can be influenced. The flooring materials should be tested with samples of the proposed footwear before final approval is given.

In testing bathing surfaces, ASTM F462 specifies a material called Silastic 382. This material is supposed to imitate the human foot. Recently it has come under fire by the tub manufacturers, but nothing has been found to replace it. Criteria for bathing facilities should be a minimum COF of 0.04 but preferably maintain 0.1 as an added safety factor.

As described before, standards should be established on the basis of walkway surfaces known to reduce accidents. However, the minimum benchmark for walkway surfaces, for litigation purposes, should be a 0.5 static coefficient of friction as measured using dry leather, wet/dry neolite, and rubber. This demonstrates reasonable care in evaluating floor surfaces with footwear material.

Other factors that impact the selection of criteria for walkway surfaces are abrasion resistance, hardness, water absorption, stain and chemical resistance, breaking strength, and cleanability. Some of these affect the coefficient of friction and need to be included in your test methodology. For instance, to determine wear and durability, use the Robinson Wheel Test, ASTM C627, and Breaking Strength Test, C486. The wear test will affect the slip resistance, so conduct the slip tests before and after the Robinson Wheel Test. This allows evaluation of slip resistance characteristics of the floor surface under heavy traffic conditions.

There is a new test under study by the ASTM Ceramic Tile Committee to determine a tile's cleanability over a period of time in order to simulate wear. The method will use a Porcelain Enamel Institute (PEI) abrasion device and a special staining media will be applied and then cleaned. The surface will then be evaluated and scored. A slip test after this process may produce good information on hard surface materials and on the safety factor over time. In any event, cleanability and stain resistance are very important considerations in selecting any product.

The Robinson Wheel Test should be done on hard surface materials, whenever high levels of traffic are anticipated, for example, in docks, kitchens service corridors and main lobby areas. COF should be measured with grease and water for kitchen and service areas. A good beginning benchmark is a slip resistance of 0.28.

A unique factor that must be considered concerning areas where grease is involved is water absorption. I have found that materials that exceed 3 percent water absorption, as measured by ASTM C373, tend to retain grease in the pores and begin to develop polymerization, a condition in which the grease literally becomes part of the walkway surface and is difficult to remove during normal cleaning processes. For kitchen tile floors, ideally use a material that absorbs only 0 to 0.5 percent water, with a maximum of 3 percent.

Each walkway may require a different benchmark, depending on the factors anticipated. To aid the design team, a chart (Figure 12-2) that communicates the various approved floor surfaces based on the area of use can be distributed and regularly updated.

Design criteria are a dynamic process that should include standards of design for level walkways, stairs, platforms, ramps, elevated areas, and bathing surfaces. It is paramount to the success of your program to involve the architects, interior designers, specifiers, contractors, and operations personnel in the total effort. This is illustrated using a specific example of setting criteria for a public lobby (see Chapters 2 and 3 for a full discussion).

Public lobby

I. **Walkway surfaces**. All hard surfaces shall meet the following criteria (if carpet is used, follow the guidelines for the selection of approved materials in the Design Guide).

1. Slip resistance: 0.6 wet and dry, before and after wear test.

2. Durability/wear:

- *Ceramic tile*
  Complete 5 cycles using the Robinson Wheel Test with steel wheels and apply 300 lb resulting in no visible chippage or breakage.
  Breaking strength 400 lb or greater.
  Mohs hardness 8 or greater.
  Abrasive resistance of 100.
  Pass stain and cleanability tests.

LOSS CONTROL APPROVED FLOOR LIST

DATE:

USERS OF THE LIST MUST VERIFY SUITABILITY OF FLOORS FOR PRICE, AVAILABILITY, COLOR, ETC.

MANUFACTURER: SERIES NAME	AREAS OF USE						
	KITCHEN (6)	SERVICE AREA (6)	BUFFET (6)	BARS (6)	POOLS	OTHER (1)	GUEST ROOMS
ABC TILE CO.:							
UNGLAZED MOSAIC						X	X
QUARRY		X(3)	X(3)	X(3)	X(3)	X	
PORCELAIN						X(4)	X(4)
XYZ FLOORING:							
VINYL NON-SLIP		X(5)				X	
RUBBER						X	
VCT						X(7)	
DEF FLOORS:							
PAVER ANTI-SLIP	X(2)	X	X	X	X	X	
DDD TILE:							
PAVER NON-SLIP	X(2)	X				X	
ABRASIVE GLAZED TILE			X	X	X	X	X
NON-SLIP MOSAIC			X	X	X	X	X
MONO FLOOR:							
VCT						X(7)	
NEW FLOORING:							
VINYL NON-SLIP		X(5)				X	
RUBBER						X	
VCT						X(7)	
ZZZ TOP COAT:							
UNGLAZED MOSAIC	X(2)	X(3)	X(3)	X(3)	X(3)	X	X
QUARRY						X	
PORCELAIN						X(4)	X(4)
NYOB TILE:							
PAVER ANTI-SLIP	X(2)						
ABRASIVE GLAZED TILE			X	X	X	X	X
NON-SLIP MOSAIC			X	X	X	X	X
PORCELAIN						X(4)	X(4)
RUBBER						X	
QUARRY		X(3)	X(3)	X(3)	X(3)	X	

- *Marble, granite, stone*
  Minimum grade C for veining (Travertine is not acceptable).
  Minimum $\frac{3}{8}$ inch thickness.

II. **Illumination:** 10–20 footcandles for general lighting.

III. **Loss prevention design considerations**

1. Limit visual distractions or confine to a specific area not in the main travel path.

2. Thresholds into adjoining areas should not exceed $\frac{1}{2}$ inch in height above the floor surface and should be beveled on both sides, 1:2 slope.

3. Revolving doors should have a mechanical governor that restricts movement to 12 rpm. Furnish decal to state "Push Slowly."

4. Provide carpet or recessed walk off mats on all entry vestibule areas.

5. All full-length windows, sidelights and glass doors should have decals or guard rails.

6. Stairs or steps should be avoided; if required, they must meet local and national codes and standards, and alternative handicap accessibility must be provided. As a minimum provide the following:

   - Minimum three risers (minimum tread width 13 inches and tread edge clearly defined).

   - Typical riser to tread relationship should be maximum 7 inches by 11 inches minimum.

   - Handrails with $1\frac{1}{2}$-inch grip cross-section and located on both sides of the stairs. Height and extension at top and bottom per code.

   - Stairs 88 inches or wider should have intermediate handrails.

   - Tread should have a minimum 0.6 slip resistance wet and dry.

Figure 12-2. Sample loss control approved floor materials listings. (1) Light traffic areas, restrooms, locker rooms. (2) Use red color for kitchen. (3) Specify with abrasive additive. (4) Available in X1, Y2, M3 colors only. (5) Use on ballroom service aisles. (6) Tiles must pass Robinson Wheel and breaking strength tests. (7) Requires Loss Control Approved nonslip finish.

- Steps should be easily seen.
- Nose should have a minimum 0.6 slip resistance wet and dry, with a contrasting edge definition by color, lighting, or some other method; also rounded to meet ANSI Z117.1 standards.

IV. **Review layouts and finishes with the Safety Department.**

More can always be added to the criteria, but the primary objective is to involve the company's key design and operations people in development and execution of the program.

Methodology for Selection, Review, and Testing

A lot of time and effort is spent in the development of criteria and the selection of appropriate test methods. How should the program be administrated?

1. Assign responsibility. The responsibility for initial screening of materials should be with the safety professionals and interior designers to ensure the materials selected will apply to the design of the facility.

2. Select an independent test laboratory to complete the ASTM test methods and other tests established to insure that the

Figure 12-3. Approval of floor finishes should be by the safety professional and designers to insure that they meet criteria.

materials meet the criteria. The reasons for using an independent laboratory are threefold: (1) consistent results from the same operator; (2) the data offer excellent defense claims support; (3) as a quality assurance measure.

3. Have the manufacturer supply copies of their laboratory tests, sales literature, and performance specifications. A remarkable number of floor surfaces are represented as suitable for a specific environment by representatives of the company, and may even pass many of the tests, but state clearly in the sales brochure "Do not use in food areas."

4. Ask the manufacturers whether the material is suitable for the proposed application. If they are unwilling to stand behind the product one-hundred percent, it is not advisable to use it.

5. Once this initial screening is complete and the material is determined as suitable for application, the final results should be published to designers, operations managers, and construction personnel so that they are aware of the approved materials. Be sure that they are included in project specifications.

6. Lastly, the architect, safety professional and interior designer need to conduct joint plan reviews to apply the design criteria to each project as well as working together in reviewing and approving proposed substitutions. This is a very important step in maintaining the quality control for the overall program. There is nothing more frustrating than visiting the project and seeing wholesale substitutions.

Reconditioning and retrofitting

Finding materials that can improve the slip resistance of a floor, shower or bathtub can be tedious and time-consuming. There are many products on the market but many manufacturers and suppliers are unaware of ASTM test methods that could demonstrate how effective their product is in enhancing slip resistance.

The criteria and test methods specified earlier should be used to review and select materials to recondition existing walkway and bathing surfaces. The following are some ways in which existing surfaces can be altered to improve the slip resistance: (1) acid etching, (2) abrasive grinding of the surface to produce a honed or grooved surface, (3) sand blasting to produce a honed finish, (4) adhesive-backed abrasive pads and strips, (5) latex or vinyl resin coatings sprayed onto a surface, (6) use of carpet, (7) ceramic tile can now be installed over existing tile with special adhesives. There are many others available—for example, deck paint with sand added can provide a slip-resistant surface, but constant repainting makes this fix less desirable than many others.

When it comes to stairs or ramps, the prudent approach is to hire an independent design firm familiar with national and local codes. Have them present a design solution for correcting any unsafe condition or defect in the stair, ramp, or elevated platform. The reason for hiring an independent professional rather than just fixing a handrail to the wall is that the responsibility for the modification now becomes the responsibility of the designer should an accident occur because of a design or construction error. It will also make life easier when seeking approval from the local building department for permits and final acceptance.

Maintenance, Inspections, and Records

Floor maintenance does not only mean cleaning the floor, but also inspections, material selection, testing, auditing and recording. Most businesses have a routine by which the floor, stair other walkway component is either swept or inspected on a regular basis (Figure 12-4). These activities are documented by

Figure 12-4. Warning barricades and employee attention to slip and fall prevention are key elements in the program.

SWEEP LOG

LOCATION: DATE:

AREAS COVERED:

TIME	CHECKED BY	CONDITIONS		COMMENTS/ACTION TAKEN
		OK	NOT OK	

Figure 12-5. Sample Sweep Log.

means of logs and check sheets, which include the date, time, personnel involved, and procedures to be followed (Figure 12-5).

The walkway maintenance program is critical to slip and fall prevention and in showing satisfaction of duty owed in the event of lawsuits. The program must be developed with the operators. The program should include:

- Selection of floor finish products, including slip-resistant polymer finishes, strippers, degreasers, and general cleaners.
- Proper application methods for products, including time schedules for each component or process.
- Documentation on products used, including independent laboratory tests, manufacturers' tests, Material Safety Data Sheets (MSDS), and especially specifications for slip resistance.
- Performance of routine slip tests to insure that surfaces are properly maintained with the HPS tester. Document these tests by date, time, and the person who conducted the tests.
- A statement in the contract of what criteria must be followed to maintain the walkways, if a maintenance company is used.
- Auditing of the maintenance program on a periodic basis and especially after any reported claim.

An excellent way to involve operations people is to have them assist in the performance of slip testing. An adequate slip meter for their use can be constructed for less than $140. For the overall design and construction of this meter see Figure 12-6. In contrast, the HPS tester costs approximately $1,700. The HPS can be obtained from Whitley Industries Inc., Tewksbury, Mass. However, this cost is more than justified for a medium to large operation when the average cost of a hip fracture from a fall is considered.

Documentation of these tests and inspections is critical in demonstrating "reasonable care" in the event of a lawsuit (Figure 12-7). Also, having a slip meter on site allows testing of the surface in question soon after the accident has occurred. This will assist the claims people in properly managing the case. If possible, use an independent laboratory to conduct additional tests, if warranted.

A cautionary note: If waxes, polishes, or polymer finishes are used, remember that the test results reported by the manufacturer are for dry leather only using the James machine, D2047 test method. In addition, do not be misled by the statement that they

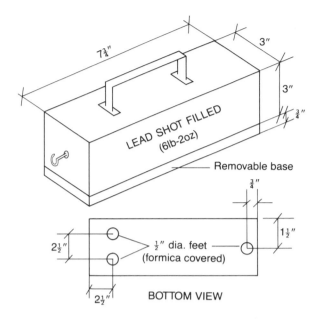

Figure 12-6. How to build a homemade slip meter. (1) The meter is constructed of plywood with removable base for different feet. (2) The feet can be leather, neolite, or rubber. Neolite or rubber will yield high values and it is necessary to adjust the benchmark. (3) A good-quality spring scale that measures in pounds is needed. (4) It is necessary to sand the feet with 400-grit sandpaper after each test. (5) Each spot should be tested four times at 90° and the results should be averaged. The answer is expressed as 0.1 times the average value.

are UL (Underwriters Laboratories) rated for slip resistance; again this is only tested using dry leather. Have finishes tested by an independent laboratory under both dry and wet conditions.

Footwear for Employees

Most companies have a footwear policy. The classic specification involves steel toes and shanks that protect the foot from sharp objects penetrating the shoe. Recently, shoe companies have been marketing footwear that reduces slips and falls. The program should include specific types of shoes that are allowed to be worn in various areas of the operation. Obviously, there is no control over what the public wears. Accordingly, test walkway surfaces with various sole and heel materials like leather, neolite, and rubber.

QUALITY SAFETY COMMITTEE
SLIP TEST RESULTS

LOCATION:

AREA TESTED	DATE	TESTER	SLIP TEST RESULTS					COMMENTS
			1	2	3	4	AVG.	

Most large restaurant chain operators have a footwear program for both appearance and safety. They require waiters/waitresses and bus personnel to wear shoes with low or no heels. A walking type of shoe is usually very good. They offer good stability and the sole is of a type of neoprene or rubber that provides good slip-resistant qualities. The no-heel versions are excellent for kitchen personnel. An additional advantage of the Horizontal Pull Slip Meter is the ability to test the shoe sole and heel materials on various walkway surfaces that employees will be using to determine that the approved shoe types are indeed compatible and slip-resistant.

Another type of shoe has recently come onto the market. It has a unisole and heel. The bottom has a specially designed tread to enhance slip-resistant factors. Also, the shoe combines the slip-resistant qualities of rubber with urethane, to provide a very lightweight shoe, which reduces worker fatigue.

However, keep in mind that labor laws require the employer to buy the employees' shoes if only one kind is specified. To work around the laws and yet be able to effect some control, offer a selection and provide a payroll deduction program that takes a little money out each week while providing a shoe at a significant saving to the employee. As an added incentive, the employer may buy the shoes or contribute a portion of the cost as a benefit. In any event, setting up a footwear program will significantly enhance the slip and fall prevention effort.

Claims Management

The final phase of the program deals with "Murphy's Law" which is alive and well. Someone, sometime will fall, and they will sue.

When establishing a slip, trip, and fall policy, include a section on the company's posture towards managing slip, trip, and fall claims. Businesses are not insurers of the public; however, they are required to provide reasonable management of the property

---

Figure 12-7. A sample Slip Test Results form to be used by the Quality Safety Committee to regularly check the facility's floor maintenance program. (1) More than one location must be tested. (2) Four readings at 90° should be taken at each location; the results are averaged and multiplied by 0.1. (3) If any reading falls below 0.5, the management should be contacted immediately.

and to foresee the possibility of injury to others and prevent any unreasonable risk of harm.

A good slip and fall claim management program begins with writing the slip, trip, and fall policy. There must be active review and dialogue between operations, legal, claims, and safety representatives. The critical time in any claim is the first 15 minutes after the accident. A task force should be set up so that after an injury report is filed, evaluation of all factors of the case can be put together immediately, including ordering of independent tests, auditing of the floor care program, obtaining inspection logs, interviewing of witnesses, and gathering of other accident data. If litigation results, this same group of professionals should develop the defense strategy to: (1) answer the complaint and interrogatories; (2) review the plaintiff's testimony, expert witness reports, and statements; (3) employ a defense expert and finally prepare for trial. But if you have established an effective policy and executed all of its elements, it is more than likely that you will not go to trial.

In today's litigious environment, as Frank MacHovec has said, "Suing for some is like buying a ticket to a lottery—but with better odds." Why is this the case? Basically, today many people file a lawsuit, even though it is frivolous, knowing all too well that insurance companies will probably settle out of court rather than pay high legal costs. Another reason is that most damage suits are filed charging several defendants, even those indirectly involved, so that if the plaintiff is successful, they will receive an award from those who can best pay the bill, the so-called *deep pocket approach.*

What can the operator do? The name of the game is having every possible defense tool at his disposal. The "tool box" should include policies and programs, laboratory test reports, manufacturers' reports and specifications, field test reports, inspection reports and sweep logs, subrogation to a third party (in case of product failure or defect), shared defense with the architect/engineer or designer of record, for comparative negligence purposes, and even the homemade slip meter test program.

The burden of proof rests with the plaintiff in having to establish the proximate cause that the fall was based on the operator's negligence in not meeting the ordinary duty of care for providing a safe environment. They must show both actual notice and constructive notice for there to be liability on the operator's part (Kohr, 1989, 1990).

Measuring Results

Any program must be able to show a return on investment if it is to remain important to top management. The simplest way to measure the results of a slip and fall program is through accident statistics, audits, and personal observations. Watch how people walk; you will see missed and near-missed steps. Evaluate them, run tests, and solve the problem before a claim occurs. Remember that the two basic tenets are (1) prevention of falls, and (2) effective claims management and litigation defense. Do not get caught up in the controversy; set your own standards and criteria; stick by them, and you will get results.

CHAPTER 13

A Systems Approach to Loss Control

With changing demographics, labor shortages, litigation threats, and consumer demand for increased security and competition, maximizing technology to help solve these concerns is an ever increasing activity in today's business world. Previous chapters have discussed safety and security design criteria and briefly discussed systems. The focus of this chapter is to provide some guidance in selection of systems that can (1) enhance operating efficiency, (2) cut operating costs, and (3) significantly improve the overall loss-prevention picture. The chapter will be broken down by system type and includes a discussion on function, applications, benefits, and potential for integration with other systems.

ACCESS CONTROL

As the name implies, the primary function of this type of system is to control entry to and exit from a room, area, or building. Traditionally this has been accomplished in the hotel and restaurant industries by using a mechanical lock and metal key. In many ways this is adequate control, so long as there is a good key control program, for most areas. However, there are certain back-of-house areas, guestrooms, remote entries, and other public areas that need more security control than can be offered by a conventional lockset.

There are many different types of electronic access control devices on the market today. They range from hardwired to battery-operated, on-line and off-line in both cases. Before implementing them of course it is necessary to match the security objectives and threat to the costs of implementing any system as well as any anticipated return on investment (ROI). As this covers such a large area and expenditure, the analysis begins with guestroom access control.

Guestroom Access Control—Litigation or Security Threat

In reality, both reasons apply. Hotels and motels are facing an explosion in litigation and there is an increasing security threat. But there is another reason—reduced operating costs in materials and labor.

The most frequently asked question is which system is the best. To answer this it is necessary first to state what the security objective is. The electronic locking systems on the market at present for all intents and purposes meet the security objective, which is

> To provide a high level of controlled access to a guestroom by (1) using a grade I, ANSI mortise lock case with 1 inch throw deadbolt, $\frac{3}{4}$ inch latchset with single-action panic retract of both assemblies; (2) being reprogrammable after every guest stay and on all master levels; and (3) preferably providing an audit trail of access to the room and all keys issued.

Consideration of this objective reveals that it could be achieved manually with a conventional lock except for part (3) and this would cost a huge amount annually in maintenance. However, reprogrammable mechanical locking systems are used in many facilities, and for a small motel of less than 150 rooms the conversion to an electronic lock system might not show the ROI from reduced maintenance as quickly. It could take several years because there is an active program of rekeying the rooms and soliciting for return of every room keycard. But with an eye on the future, I would still advise that hoteliers go electronic.

A key advantage of electronic locking systems today, is the capability of "interrogating" the lock—being able to know who gained access, when and where. Some earlier versions did not have the capability of showing specifically who entered or exact times; this important information alone can justify changing to electronic locks.

Some of the general benefits of electronic locking systems include:

- Interrogation and audit trail of all functions.

- Interfaces to PMS and POS systems, which reduces up-front cost and speeds check-in.

- Remote entry control.

- Elevator access control.

- Reduced labor by eliminating the need to go to a door to reprogram after a guest leaves.

- Reduced labor and material cost in key issuance, sorting, administration, and so on.

- Greater security for the guest.

And one very important advantage is a projected return on investment of less than 3 years. Use of electronic lock systems thus makes good business sense. But their use can be maximized and broadened further. Consider placing them on the liquor room, silver storage, health club, AV room, dry storage, service bars, and engineering tool storage room. There are losses from theft in these areas; consider the advantage of, on doing a surprise inventory and discovering a loss, being immediately aware who gained access and when.

The next natural question relates to cost. If it is only to be used on a couple of doors, and the computer support equipment already exists, the cost will be about $100 dollars greater than for a commercial mechanical lockset. This is a modest investment considering the return through reduced theft losses. This will be covered later in the section.

The range of equipment covers everything from on-line hard-wired locking systems to off-line smart battery-operated locking systems. A recently introduced product professes to provide all the advantages of on-line systems without requiring a wire to every door. No attempt will be made to review an exhaustive list of the various types of electronic locks because it would be out of date by the time this book is published. There is no point attempting to wait until the technology settles down in order eventually to buy the definitive system, the rate of development is too great and is constant.

Becoming an "Educated Consumer"

Step 1. Establish the relevant criteria by answering these basic questions:

1. What is the internal and external risk exposure?
2. What are the security objectives?
3. What are the current maintenance expenditures on the current lock system annually?
4. What are competitors doing next door and along the street?
5. Is there any planned property renovation that might feasibly be combined with lock installation?
6. What is expected of the system?
7. What is expected of the supplier and manufacturer?
8. If new construction, what kind of coordination issues will exist, hidden costs, design costs, impact on various trades?
9. If a retrofit, what type of doors, frames, and locksets exist?
10. Is there a desire or need to interface to other systems, and which ones?
11. Are there any special applications, such as liquor room, remote corridor entries, elevator control?
12. How much can the business afford to spend? Perhaps it should be how much can it afford *not* to spend?

Having answered these questions, it is time to set criteria for system review and selection. Before that step, let us examine the rationale of a couple of the questions.

Question 5 seems straightforward, but combined with question 9 it can save money or cause the spending of more. In an older property, there are probably frame, door, or even lock problems that must be addessed first. Many older hotels used knockdown frames. This type of frame, unless it is equipped with a special type of security anchor, can easily be spread, allowing rapid entry to the room.

Question 10 asks whether there is a need to interface to other systems, which is important because it can improve operating efficiency and reduce costs on many of the systems currently on the market.

Considering integration, probably the single most cost-saving interface is to the PMS system. This allows use of that equipment without the need for separate computers at the front desk; and the types that read credit cards or other coded magnetic cards can eliminate the need for separate readers and reduce keycard costs. Others will interface for data entry only, but card key encoding or punch equipment is then needed at the front desk. Another possible interface provides access control on storage rooms, employee entry, dock, count room, health club, elevators, remote grade entries, and even the main lobby entry in small hotels.

One of the advantages of on-line systems is the capability of secondary smoke alarm monitoring, security alarm monitoring, and passive energy management.

There are systems that allow for remote check-in terminals in the lobby. The guest enters the data into the terminal and passes a credit card through a reader; in one case the guest receives a coded keycard and in another case their credit card becomes the key. For budget hotels this may be a future way of meeting manpower shortages by eliminating the desk clerk at night and using that person instead to monitor the hotel's activities rather than be behind a desk.

Step 2. Invite the salesperson in. Have them do a complete survey of the facility for a retrofit or show them the construction documents for a new facility. Then request a proposal that includes:

- All costs including cabling and installation.
- Projected annual maintenance costs and assumptions used to determine costs for replacement of keycards, batteries, and electronic and mechanical components.
- Service plans available after the warranty has lapsed and their costs.
- Independent test data on projected failure rates of electronic and mechanical components.
- Training and associated costs including follow-up sessions.
- References, and number and location of installations.
- Company annual report and a Dun & Bradstreet report.

Step 3. Narrow the field by:

1. Verifying references, visiting some installations, and making phone calls.

2. Checking out all sales claims, including interfaces and applications beyond guestroom access control.
3. Comparing the data with the criteria established in steps 1 and 2.

Step 4. Have a demonstration. Get feedback from the staff on which of the systems that made it past steps 1, 2, and 3 will fit into the operation the best.

Step 5. Test the remaining selections; more than one type may be selected. If the system is to be used as a retrofit, obtain a couple of locksets and place them on offices and store rooms. If there are exterior guestroom doors, definitely place some outside. Check them over the course of 3 to 4 months. On new construction, it may be desirable to test a floor or a hotel to see whether the system meets expectations.

Step 6. Critique: pull the staff together, survey the guests ask them what they think. Check the numbers and compare operating costs to the claims made by the salesperson.

Step 7. Commit: now is the time to decide on replacing or upgrading. It may be worth considering leasing the system; this allows implementation without having to put up a great deal of cash. Leasing is also attractive because it can allow future upgrades as technology changes.

Back-of-House Access Control—Proactive Theft Prevention

As with hotel guestrooms, the advantages of electronic access control on selected back-of-house areas can provide a significant return on investment in reduced internal pilferage. It has already been pointed out that the lock used on the guestroom can be used effectively on storage rooms and employee entries. Free-standing restaurants can also benefit from similar technology. There are stand-alone door systems that allow control of who can enter, when, and where. They are also able to provide an audit trail of all activities and still provide a high-security mechanical key override in case of a problem. One of these systems uses a PIN set-up in which personnel are assigned a five-digit number that they must enter on a touch pad at the door. If it is valid, the employee is allowed access. The system also allows retrieval of all the stored access data from the lock. Another does the same thing using a person's voice and another uses a magnetic card reader or wiegand card reader. Costs vary and can range from several hundred dollars to about two thousand dollars installed.

Use of these systems is only recommended on employee entries and high value storage rooms. Other areas can use a commercial grade $\frac{3}{4}$-inch latchset, in some cases a deadbolt, with a removable core and a secure keyway dedicated to specific facilities. This will prevent duplication and possible compromising of the lock through picking of the cylinder. It will also facilitate key inventory and replacement, as all the keys must be purchased ready-made from an authorized dealer.

One rather new application is to combine electronic access control on the employee entry with the time and attendance payroll system, thus accomplishing two objectives.

On major facilities, using the electronic guestroom locks on back-of-house areas may not be as cost-effective as on smaller facilities. One reason is volume of access. Other reasons include the capability of performing other system functions, including alarm monitoring, inspection tour recording, and fire alarm annunciation. These functions can be performed separately and each will be covered later, but an advantage in combining these elements on larger facilities is to facilitate better response and monitoring by hotel security staff.

There are many electronic access control systems on the market. Most use some form of distributive data-gathering system that is processed by a personal computer. The primary components are (1) access control via card or key readers, (2) inspection tour recording via card or key readers, and (3) security alarm monitoring of perimeter areas, storage areas, hold-up and duress alarms, and motion sensors. Since it is a centrally processed system, time schedules can be set up to control access and shunting of alarms, provide productivity reports via tour recording, maintain an audit trail of all activities, and process employee data. In essence the security of the facility is run out of a centrally monitored area. Additionally, the system can be interfaced to CCTV camera monitoring equipment to activate cameras and video recording equipment and to verify employee status.

Some of these systems are also capable of monitoring fire alarm systems, either as a primary monitor or for secondary annunciation. The secondary system is probably preferred for eliminating conflicts regarding priority of calls and possible tying up of either system. "Secondary" means that there is a typical fire alarm system contained in the fire control room, and that system provides an output relay to the security system so that fire or security alarm data is posted on the computer monitor. Many systems will also display a floorplan in order to pinpoint the exact location of the alarm.

The decision on the best approach goes back to determining the risks, operating efficiencies, and investment costs versus proforma savings or vice versa. A good independent consultant along with the operations managers and loss control personnel can help with the analysis.

ALARM MONITORING—A MUST

Alarm monitoring is what the name implies and the importance of this function cannot be overstated. Every commercial facility needs a burglary and hold-up alarm system; the type varies according to the location. Typically all perimeter access points and cash-holding areas should be alarmed, and all cashier points with direct public contact should have hold-up protection.

The purpose of the perimeter alarms is to indicate when someone has gained unauthorized access say by a stairway to the guest tower, or to detect employees using exits to bypass the control point. Alarms on perimeter doors will also alert to their being propped open.

The need for hold-up alarms can be debated for a small facility for which dialing 911 might be an adequate response. The advantage of a hold-up alarm system is that it is tied to a UL (Underwriters Laboratories) approved central station. If a hold-up occurs, an employee should not go for the hold-up alarm as the first response—or they could end up dead. However, the alarm does provide security in the sense that after the perpetrator has left the employee only has to push a button to summon help. It will also provide an audit trail at the central station for response times, which could be important if a guest is injured and a lawsuit results.

One other critical alarm point is the general cashier's office or wherever a money safe is located. Motion sensors within a room or a surface-mounted safe alarm can serve two functions: When staff are forced to open a room up during a hold-up a motion sensor will pick up that activity and send a signal to the central station, or an alarm mounted on the safe will transmit if the safe is opened. All hold-up alarms, cash traps, and safe alarms should be of the silent annunciation type. The other function involves afterhours burglary attempts on the safe, which will again send an alarm to the central station. For free-standing restaurants the burglary and hold-up protection should be centrally monitored in all cases. For large hotels central-station monitoring may not be needed owing to the presence of a large security staff and a dedicated monitoring area.

Another feature to be included in an alarm monitoring system design is an audit trail. This can be accomplished easily, either integrated to an access control system or as a stand-alone system. Many of the new microprocessor alarm panels allow alarms to be turned on or off automatically, and include the telephone connection for central-station monitoring and provide an RS232 port for a small printer. The printer records all alarms and reset conditions in what is termed *real time*, which means as it is happening. This documentation provides management with another tool for checking whether employees are using unauthorized exits or whether someone is gaining access to areas that are protected. The report gives the date, time, and location of the alarm.

INSPECTION TOUR RECORDING

Hotel security has not changed radically. The single most important aspect is walking around the facility keeping an eye out for anything unusual—90 percent of hotel security is patrol. As discussed in covering management, MBWA (managing by walking around) is the way to keep on top of the situation. The difficulty is that not everyone does their job as well as management would like. Therein lies the importance of inspection tour recording. It is very similar to the traditional concept of the watchman punch clocks; the difference lies in automating it so that it becomes a productivity tool and a means of documenting conditions around the property.

With the advent of barcode scanning and hand-held computer technology, a revolution took place in the retail and utility industries. Inventories could be taken by reading the barcodes directly from the products and input data could be read from household utility meters, and the data could then be transferred to a host computer directly or via a modem. The same technology is now being used to check in rental cars and even hotel guests on airport vans.

The same technology can be used for documenting security patrols or even engineering activities such as meter readings or fire extinguisher inspections. There has been a proliferation of systems that record security patrol activities. My own preference is barcode technology, which is not only inexpensive but allows capabilities to be added to the hand-held computer such as fixed-asset inventory and other types of inspections.

The best system is one that tells you who, when, where, and—most important—what. The "what" is important because it allows the person making the patrol to document what they have seen and what corrective action they took. I call this the electronic clip board. A preferred form is one that allows typing in sentences of information along with the usual activity codes. It also allows various reports to be generated as well as processing office information, thus eliminating the log book typically used in a security office.

One very significant difference between these systems and a regular clip board and checklist lies in eliminating the honesty factor. It is impossible to know whether the manager on evening shift who is supposed to do an MOD tour or the graveyard security person who is supposed to walk the whole property actually does what is expected and does it as often as they are supposed to. Electronic systems provide the documentation needed to demonstrate fulfillment of "duty of care". They also provide reports to help determine trends and the productivity of manpower.

An advantage to these systems is their ease of retrofitting—no wires, no power, and in many cases they can use one of the office PCs. They are generally very inexpensive, starting at around $3,500 including tour stations, reading devices, software, and transmission cable or devices.

At large hotels with on-line security systems, the inspection tour recording function can be an adjunct of that system. The advantage is that the same key or card used to gain access back of house can be used in readers strategically placed throughout the facility. Even a housekeeper could clock in and indicate everything is all right in their area. Security is everybody's job.

Other uses for an inspection tour recording system include tracking preventative maintenance on guestrooms. The engineer simply clocks-in on arrival at a floor and clocks out once finished, at the same time documenting the activities completed. The system can also take the place of the manager on duty report.

Use of these types of systems is limited only by the user's

capability to maximize its effectiveness. Their importance as a management tool cannot be overemphasized. Even small hotels and motels can take advantage of the benefits of this technology. The systems are inexpensive, whether using barcodes or integrating with the access control and alarm system, compared with the return on their cost.

CCTV CAMERAS AND MONITORING

The tendency of some security professionals, operators, and designers is to correct a physical security problem simply by putting a CCTV camera up on the wall. This is a big mistake.

In a major resort acquisition survey some years ago I reviewed the general safety and security of the facility. I could scarcely believe the security office, for within it must have been two full walls of television monitors. Asked how many cameras were tied to the system, the security manager replied that there were about 100, considering that there were 1000-plus guestrooms and about four cameras per guestroom floor. When he was asked how he managed to watch them all, his answer was "We don't."

Cameras *are* beneficial if (1) they are properly located, (2) someone is able to monitor them 24 hours a day, and (3) they are interfaced with a video recorder that is activated by various alarm conditions.

Another idea is to tie the new electronic delay restraint door hardware to the alarms and the CCTV system. As an example, consider a set of fire doors leading off a banquet aisle area. The area is sufficiently secluded and distant that if an employee walks out with 20 steaks, even with a security alarm annunciating at security, the officer cannot get to the scene before the employee disappears. From a systems standpoint, the first thing is to specify a maglock to hold the door secure with a special panic-exiting device that requires 15 seconds continuous pressure before the maglocks will disengage. A relay is also provided so that in the event of a fire alarm the door will automatically open. Next provide a recessed magnetic door-sensing switch. This will indicate whether someone has propped the door open. Over the door, to one side, locate a CCTV camera positioned so that it will view the face of someone approaching the door. All of this is now tied together in the security office. If someones tries to exit at that door, a motion sensor will pick them up and activate the VCR. The maglock will delay the individual for 15 seconds while the video recorder records the event. If the tapes are reviewed regularly they will provide the documentation needed for taking action.

This same type of an approach to automatic video recording can be used with any alarm, such as a hold-up alarm at a cashier station. The recorder can also be set to manually monitor other areas for later viewing. An example is monitoring cash drops in the drop safe.

Chip or CCD cameras should be used. These eliminate problems of tube burn and prolong the life of the system at least threefold. The monitoring area should be comfortable for the person monitoring; neck strain results from placing the monitors high up. Incorporate a video recorder, even if it is not tied to the alarm system. Finally, only provide cameras in public places if 24 hour monitoring of the system is possible. An exception would be a camera at the front desk or gift shop; here there are sufficient employees in the area to implement guest security as well as the purpose of the camera in assets protection, so there will be little risk in not monitoring these cameras continuously. An alternative is to put a redundant (backup) monitoring system in with the PBX operators, but be careful in a high-crime area: operators have enough to do without monitoring cameras.

EMERGENCY AND STAFF COMMUNICATIONS SYSTEMS—A NEED NOT A WISH

Emergency and staff communications systems covers those wireless communications systems that allow various hotel staff members to communicate with each other. Every hotel and motel should have an emergency communications system. However, not all need a staff communications system.

Traditionally, staff communications has been a proprietary pocket page system, sometimes referred to as a "beeper" system. Housekeeping, engineering, and management staff wear pagers so that at any time during the day the individual can be reached via the pager. This is one-way communication only. Systems can be arranged to have a feature called "group call," which allows for the paging of a number of people at the same time with the same message. This feature transforms a routine staff system into an emergency system.

During a fire alarm or other similar event an individual can summon a group of people to assemble in an area and then dispatch them to various duties. The clear drawback again is that communication is only one-way, so that a second system is needed to allow for two-way communication.

The two-way communication system performs a dual role. Traditionally these systems have been used by security and engineering staffs, but in an emergency they can communicate back and forth, which is a significant advantage during any emergency condition.

Facilities are increasingly using two-way radio systems instead of pagers for the staff system for the whole hotel. In large convention hotels it is not uncommon to have four of five different radio systems with different frequencies, but from an emergency point of view someone should be able to access all channels. This can be accomplished easily with a master console with scanning capability and located in security, so that all channels are monitored and in the event of an emergency a large group can be summoned to assist in protecting people and property. It is even possible to convert some radios into portable telephones so that a telephone call can be made from the walkie-talkie, an excellent feature for the MOD or security manager.

With state-of-the-art technology it is now even possible to interface a two-way radio system with a voice synthesizer and a special alarm-transmitting device. This allows hook-up of boiler alarms, security alarms, and even fire alarms so that during any alarm emergency a computer voice broadcasts over the radio that, for example, there is a fire in the ballroom.

All hotels and motels need an emergency communications system. The small 100-room motel might need three radios with a shared frequency. This will cost you less than $1,800 including FCC (Federal Communications Commission) licensing. (CB radios should not be used, for reasons of lack of privacy.) One of the radios forms the base station and will be located at the front desk. The other two would probably be with the property manager and with the maintenance person. At night, when there are usually only a few people on duty, radios can save a lot of walking and solve guests' problems quickly while affording roving employees some ability to communicate if they encounter a difficulty or an emergency situation.

Cellular phones are already making inroads into management communications. Cellular technology will be the future for many forms of communication.

SUMMARY—SYSTEMS CAN BE OF VALUE

Systems can play a significant role in improving operating efficiency and reducing loss exposure. But it is necessary to be an educated consumer and not to buy for the sake of the technology. Evaluate the emphasis that needs to be placed on technology and do not forget the most important resource—people. Train people how to handle situations and then give them the tools of technology.

References

Anderson, Carl and Senne, John (eds) (1978). "Walkway Surfaces: Measurement of Slip-Resistance," *ASTM STP 649*. American Society for Testing and Materials: Philadelphia.

Archer, John, Collins, Belinda and Stahl, Fred (1979). *Guidelines for Stair Safety*. U.S. Department of Commerce and National Bureau of Standards: Washington, D.C.

ASTM (1983). "Static Coefficient of Friction of Shoe Sole and Heel Materials as Measured by the James Machine," F489-77. American Society for Testing and Materials: Philadelphia.

ASTM (1983). "Static Coefficient of Friction of Polish-Coated Floor Surfaces as Measured by the James Machine," D2047-82. American Society for Testing and Materials: Philadelphia.

ASTM (1984). "Static Slip Resistance of Footwear Sole, Heel or Related Materials by Horizontal Pull Slip Meter (HPS)," F609-79. American Society for Testing and Materials: Philadelphia.

ASTM (1987). "Evaluation of Test Data Obtained by Using the Horizontal Pull Slip Meter (HPS) or the James Machine for Measurement of Static Slip Resistance of Footwear, Sole, Heel or Related Materials," F695-81. American Society for Testing and Materials: Philadelphia.

ASTM (1989). "Evaluating the Static Coefficient of Friction of Ceramic Tile and Other Like Surfaces by the Horizontal Dynamometer Pull Meter Method," C1028-84. American Society for Testing and Materials: Philadelphia.

Braun, R. and Brungraber, R.J. (1977). "A Comparison of Two Slip-Resistance Testers." *ASTM STP 649*, pp. 49–59. American Society for Testing and Materials: Philadelphia.

Brungraber, R.J. (1977). "A New Portable Tester for the Evaluation Of the Slip-Resistance of Walkway Surfaces." *National Bureau of Standards Technical Note 953* 1–50.

Chrest, Anthony, Smith, Mary, and Bhuyan, Sam (1989). *Parking Structures, Planning, Design, Construction, Maintenance and Repair*. Van Nostrand Reinhold: New York.

Crosby, Philip (1984). *Quality Without Tears*. McGraw-Hill: New York.

Culbertson, Charles (1981). *Managing Your Safety Manager*. Risk and Insurance Management Society Inc.: New York.

Davies, Thomas and Beasley, Kim (1988). *Design For Hospitality, Planning for Accessible Hotels and Motels*. Nichols: New York.

De Reamer, Russell (1958). *Modern Safety Practices*. Wiley: New York.

Drucker, Peter (1988). "The Coming of the New Organization." *Harvard Business Review*, (Jan.–Feb.): 45–53.

Ellis, J.R. and Raymond, C. (1986). *Security and Loss Prevention Management.* Educational Institute fof the American Hotel and Motel Association: East Lansing, Mich.

English, William (1984). "What Floor Tile is Safest?" *National Safety News*, December, 63–66.

English, William (1988). *Strategies For Effective Workers Compensation Cost Control.* American Society of Safety Engineers: Des Plaines, Ill.

English, William (1989). *Slip, Trips and Falls: Safety Engineering Guidelines for the Prevention of Slip, Trip and Fall Occurences.* Hanrow Press: Del Mar, CA.

Fruin, John (1988). "Escalator Safety, an Overview." *Elevator World*, 42–48.

Geller, E. Scott, Lehman, Galen, and Kalsher, Michael (1989). *Behavior Analysis Training For Occupational Safety.* Make-A-Difference, Inc.: Newport, Va.

Gray, B. Everett (ed.) (1990). "Slips, Stumbles, and Falls, Pedestrian Footwear and Surfaces," *ASTM STP 1103.* American Society for Testing and Materials: Philadelphia.

Gross, Vernon (1987). *Managing Risk.* Van Nostrand Reinhold: New York.

Irvine, C.H. (1976). "Evaluation of Some Factors Affecting Measurements of Slip Resistance of Shoe Sole Materials on Floor Surface." *Journal of Testing and Evaluation*, 4, No. 2: 133–138.

Irvine, C.H. (1986). "Evaluation of the Effect of Contact-Tile when Measuring Floor Slip Resistance." *Journal of Testing and Evaluation*, 14, No. 1: 19–22.

Jefferies, Jack P. (1983). *Understanding Hotel/Motel Law.* Education Institute of the American Hotel and Motel Association: East Lansing, Mich.

Kaufman, John R. (ed.) (1987). *IES Lighting Handbook.* Illuminating Engineering Society of North America: New York.

Kira, Alexander (1976). *The Bathroom.* Viking Press: New York.

Kira, Alexander (1987). "Comment." *Kitchen and Bath Concepts*, November, 8–11.

Kohr, Robert (1989a). "Washroom Safety Things to Consider." *Safety and Health*, November, 57–60.

Kohr, Robert (1989b). "Safety Factor in Bathroom Design." *Lodging*, May, 27–30.

Kohr, Robert (1989c). "Slip, Slidin' Away." *Safety and Health*, November, 52–56.

Kohr, Robert (1990a). "Recognizing and Preventing Slip and Fall Accidents." *Lodging*, February, 53–56.

Kohr, Robert (1990b). "Security by Design." *Security Management*, August, 100–103.

Lathrop, James (1988). *NFPA Life Safety Code Handbook.* National Fire Protection Association: Quincey, Mass.

MacHovec, F.J. (1987). *The Expert Witness Survival Manual.* Charles C. Thompson: Springfield, Ill.

National Safety Council (1988). *Accident Prevention Manual For Industrial Operations.* National Safety Council: Chicago.

National Safety Council (1989). *Accident Facts.* National Safety Council: Chicago.

Occupational Safety and Health Administration (1985). *All About OSHA,* OSHA 2056. Department of Labor: Washington D.C.

Pauls, Jake (1989). "Safety Standards, Requirements and litigation in Relation to Building Use and Safety Especially Safety From Falls Involving Stairs." Paper presented at First World Conference On Accident and Injury Prevention, Sept. 1989, Stockholm, Sweden.

Peters, Tom and Waterman, Robert (1982). *In Search of Excellence.* Harper and Row: New York.

Peterson, Daniel (1971). *Techniques of Safety Management.* McGraw-Hill: New York.

Ratliff, John and Grogan, Terry (1989). "Early Return to Work Profitability." *Professional Safety,* **34**, No. 3: 11–17.

Rutes, Walter and Penner, Richard (1985). *Hotel Planning and Design.* Watson-Guptill: New York.

Sinnott, Ralph (1985). *Safety and Security in Building Design.* Van Nostrand Reinhold: New York.

U.S. Chamber of Commerce (1987). *Analysis of Workers' Compensation Laws.* Washington, D.C.

Index